New Photography of the

Dog.

Written by

JILKE GOLBACH

HOXTON MINI PRESS

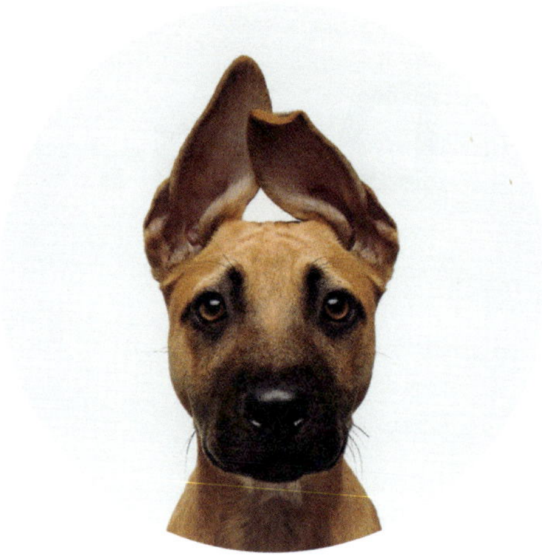

CONTENTS

Opposite: *Kona,* German Shepherd American Pit Bull Terrier, 2020, Randal Ford

A MODERN DOG'S LIFE

'We don't find our dogs, our dogs find us,' a wise friend once told me – a few weeks after my partner and I had adopted Rosie and were seriously questioning our decision. At three years old, this sweet but troubled wirehaired Podengo mix had had a rough start to life, and it showed. Rescued from the streets of Portugal – pregnant, deeply malnourished and in poor condition when a shelter took her in – by the time we first encountered her picture, she was ready for adoption, but her sad eyes and curled-up body spoke more than a thousand words. Rosie came home with us as a scrap of a dog: anxious, scared, unable to settle and desperate for love. Those first weeks and months were probably among the most challenging of my life, in both good and bad ways. As we navigated her fears and anxieties, we slowly gained her trust, watching her grow into a cheeky, strong-willed and extremely affectionate creature with the best floppy ears in the world.

Rosie sat on my lap throughout the writing of this book, most likely because I dared sit in the chair she considers her own. Post-rescue life looks very different for our dear furry friend, whose early abandonment reflects a wider mistreatment of hunting dogs like her. The Podengo, an ancient and intelligent breed once considered among the noblest of hounds, now often endures terrible living conditions, with thousands ending up on the streets of Southern Europe – left behind, or worse, once the hunting season is over. With luck on her side, Rosie now has four comfy beds to choose from (not counting mine), snubs her actual food to hold out for 'fish sushi' and 'duck jerky' treats and wears an elegant turtlenecked fleece when the weather is cold. She's a good-looking girl (and she knows it), stubborn beyond all reasonable limits and has a fan club wherever she goes. Partial to Parmesan and sourdough croissants, she seems pretty far removed from her ancestral roots, precious to the point of refusing to get her paws wet. But when there's a waterbird or rabbit in sight, the fearless stalker in her comes to the surface: the only sign that a hunting instinct might still be running through her veins.

It's a strange and wondrous thing to share a life with a different species. No other animal, not even cats, gets as close to us humans as dogs do. Over thousands of years, they have evolved to keep us company, learning ever-more complex behaviours and developing increasingly refined ways of interpreting – and influencing – human expressions and emotions. There are hundreds of variations across breeds, from Chihuahuas to Great Danes, and while most modern breeds are only a few hundred years old, others, like the Africanis, date back centuries, if not millennia.

Dogs read us better than most other animals, detecting subtle shifts in mood, tone and body language before we are consciously aware of them ourselves. Beyond companionship, they support human life across an extraordinary range of roles, from therapy, guide and medical alert dogs to search-and-rescue and sled dogs. We have even sent dogs into space – spare a thought for Laika, for example, the Russian street dog launched on a one-way trip aboard Sputnik 2 in 1957. A dog's affection is pure and unconditional: they couldn't care less about status or success, they don't hold grudges and their reservoirs of love are practically unlimited.

Given this bond, it is no wonder dogs have captured our hearts and attention for millennia. Growing up in the 1990s, my childhood was marked by *Lassie*, *Beethoven*, *Scooby-Doo* and *101 Dalmatians*, while kids today are hooked on *Paw Patrol* and *Bluey*. Numerous phrases in the English language cement the age-old connection with our canine friends (think 'hair of the dog', 'let sleeping dogs lie', 'dog-eared' or 'gone to the dogs'), and dogs have long been a beloved subject for writers, artists and performers. John Steinbeck wrote about travelling America with his French Poodle, Charley; Virginia Woolf authored a biography of a Cocker Spaniel named Flush. Lucian Freud painted his Whippet, Pluto, many times, as did David Hockney with his Dachshunds Stanley and Boodgie. The Australian comedian Hannah Gadsby has woven her dogs, Douglas and Jasper, into her shows, while the British comedian Adam Buxton records his rambling podcasts on walks with his Poodle–Whippet cross, also called Rosie.

But if dogs have been at the centre of any medium, it is, of course, photography. Iconic 20th-century photographers such as Elliott Erwitt and William Wegman pictured them in strange and familiar settings – on the streets of New York and Rome, or dressed up like people in a studio. In the age of social media, 'petfluencers' like Doug the Pug, Jiffpom and Tucker Budzyn steal the show, with the account @dogsofinstagram accruing more than 5 million followers, offering a slice of what it's like to live a modern dog's life.

The photographs in this book present the best new photography of dogs out there today, capturing both a new generation of image-makers and a new generation of dogs – one that has graduated from the field and the yard into the house and onto the sofa. Making the most of contemporary camera techniques and new approaches to animal behaviour, the photographers here document the world of our canine companions and cherished 'fur babies' in surprising, humorous and heartfelt ways. Their pictures run the full gamut of emotions – from the tragic to the comic, the sweet to the absurd – while spanning the diverse worlds dogs inhabit, from the plains of South Africa to the pavements of metropolitan cities, and from the Art Deco landscape of Miami to award-winning architect-designed homes.

There are some real characters populating these pages. In striking portraits by Elke Vogelsang (p.122), Tim Flach (p.28), Randal Ford (p.174), Winnie Au (p.80) and others, we get a full display of personalities in soulful images that reveal the dogs' identities as if they were human. Others catch dogs mid-motion: dashing across a beach (p.184), doing a full-body shake (p.138), or (yes, indeed) levitating above the ground (p.88). Daniel Naudé (p.160) captures ancient breeds in their natural habitat; others shoot contemporary canines in the most unnatural settings: Dougie Wallace's (p.46) 'designer' dogs spotted on the streets of New York, Cait Oppermann's (p.38) prized specimens at the Westminster Dog Show, Sophie Gamand's (p.130) wet dogs in grooming salons and Marcel Heijnen's (p.56) dogs standing on duty in the garages of Hong Kong. I have a personal soft spot for the shelter and senior dogs in this collection. Traer Scott's (p.64) and Martin Usborne's (p.70) images of abandoned dogs pull at the heartstrings and make you want to run to the nearest shelter, while Nancy LeVine's (p.198) aged dogs and Charlotte Dumas' (p.166) retired search-and-rescue dogs teach us a lesson or two about life.

If there's one thing to take away from these pictures, it's that our bond with these lovable, noble, ridiculous and fiercely loyal companions is one of the great wonders of the world. Rosie, currently asleep by my feet, would agree – but she'd also like me to mention that her next treat is well overdue.

Jilke Golbach, 2026

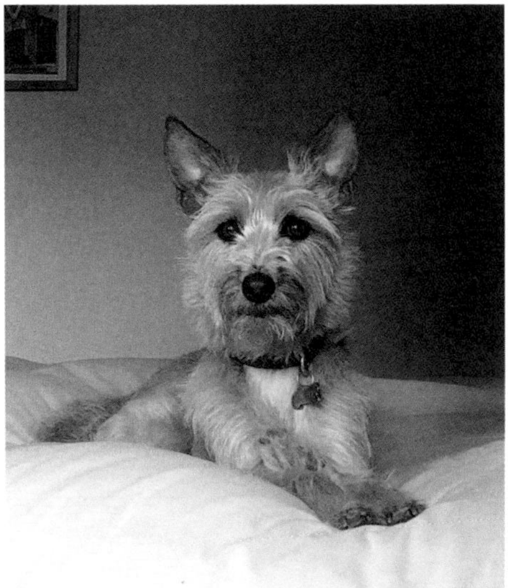

For Rosie, and all rescues waiting to be found

Jilke Golbach is a photography curator, writer and researcher. She is Head of Artistic Programming at Foam Photography Museum in Amsterdam, and previously held curatorial positions at London Museum and Barbican Art Gallery. She has published widely on art and photography and lives in Amsterdam with her partner, Colin and their dog, Rosie.

RESIDENT DOG
Nicole England

Is a home really a home without a four-legged friend to walk mud into the carpet? While many owners like to think a property is theirs, dog lovers know the truth: it's the dog who truly commands the residence.

In these top-tier homes found across the globe, acclaimed architecture and interiors photographer Nicole England captures how our canine family members inhabit some of the world's most exceptional spaces. From mid-century modern to concrete chic, her subjects bring an irresistible energy to these architect-designed houses – and often steal the show entirely.

Some of these furry residents add to the feng shui with their elegance and effortless composure; others gleefully disrupt their owners' pursuit of harmony by goofing around or causing havoc. England is at her happiest when a pup comes bounding down a staircase, a sleepy old-timer drapes himself across a designer sofa or a boisterous pedigree injects some much-needed chaos into an otherwise pristine interior. The unplanned moments, she'll tell you, are always the best ones.

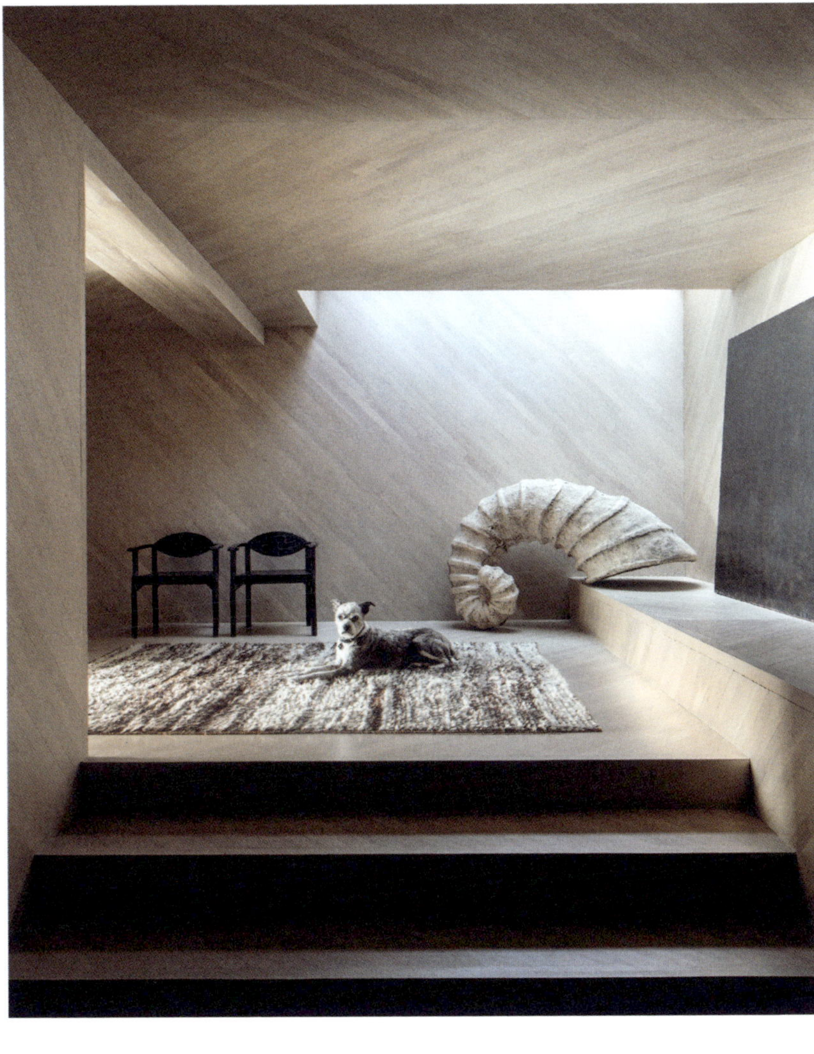

The Residence of Willie Wearstler by Kelly Wearstler, 2019

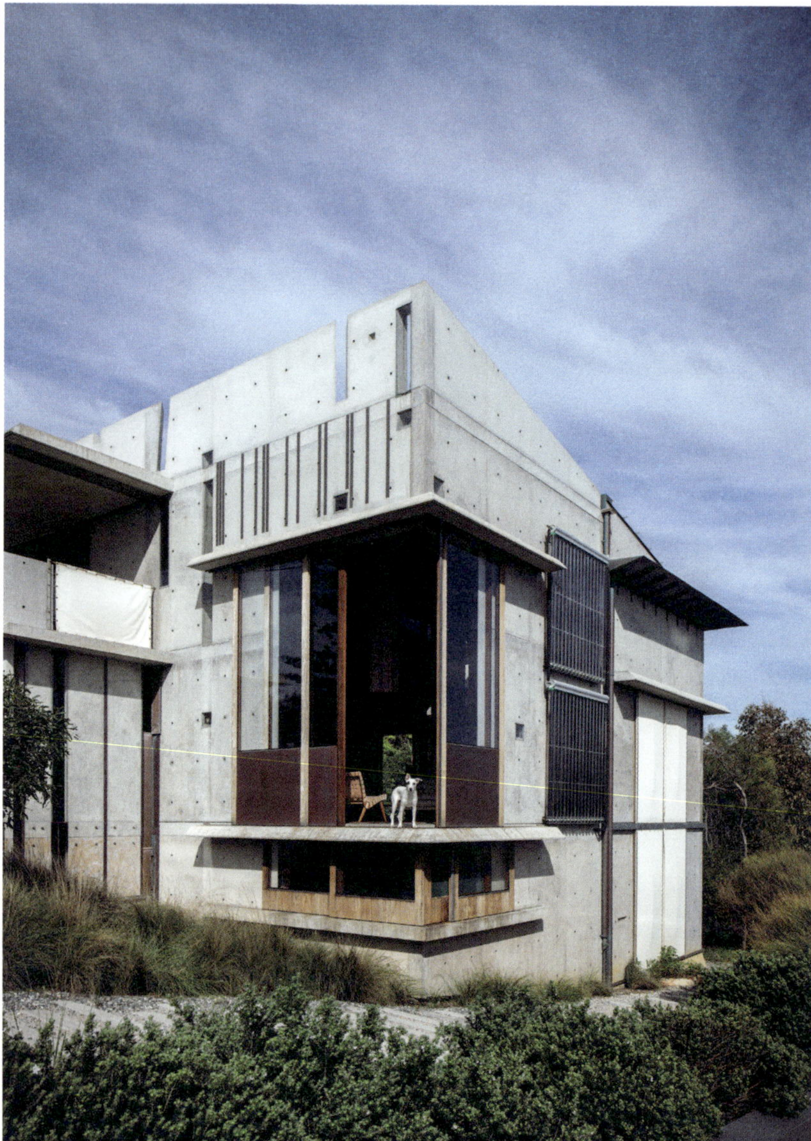

The Residence of Maybe by Peter Stutchbury, 2019

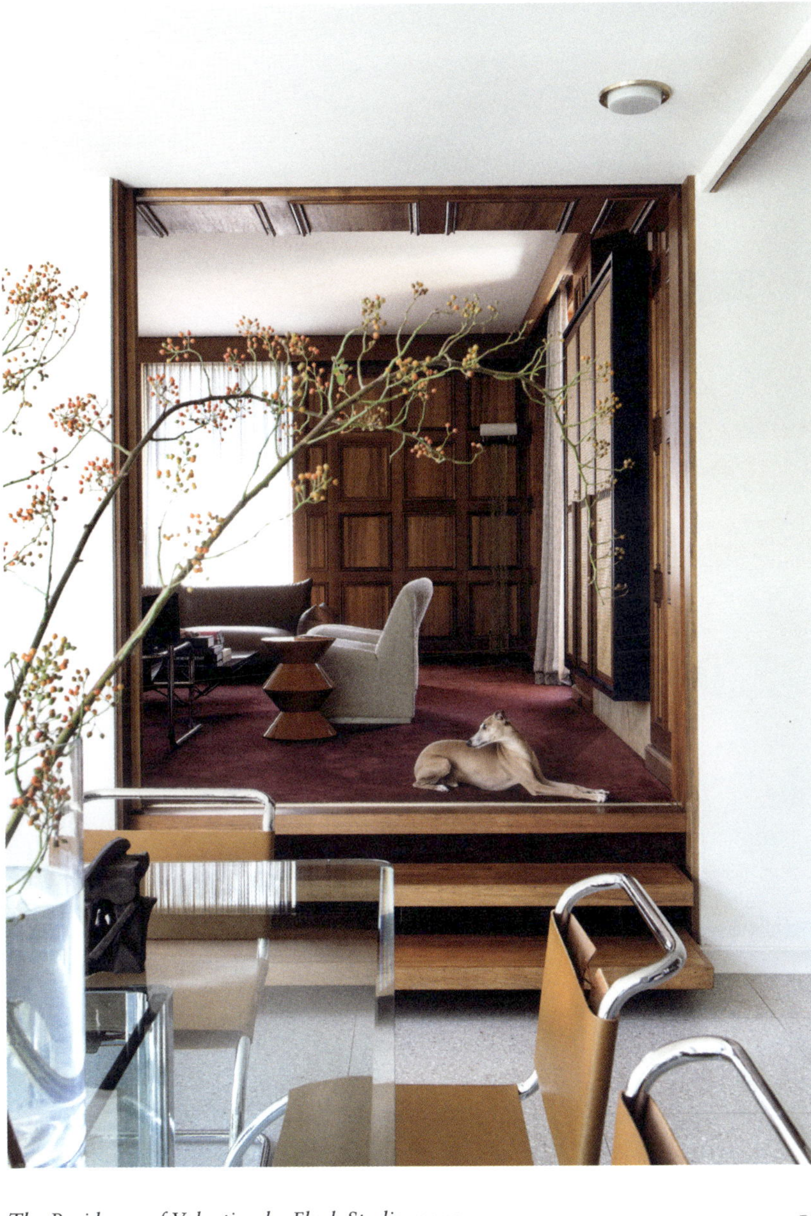

The Residence of Valentino by Flack Studio, 2019

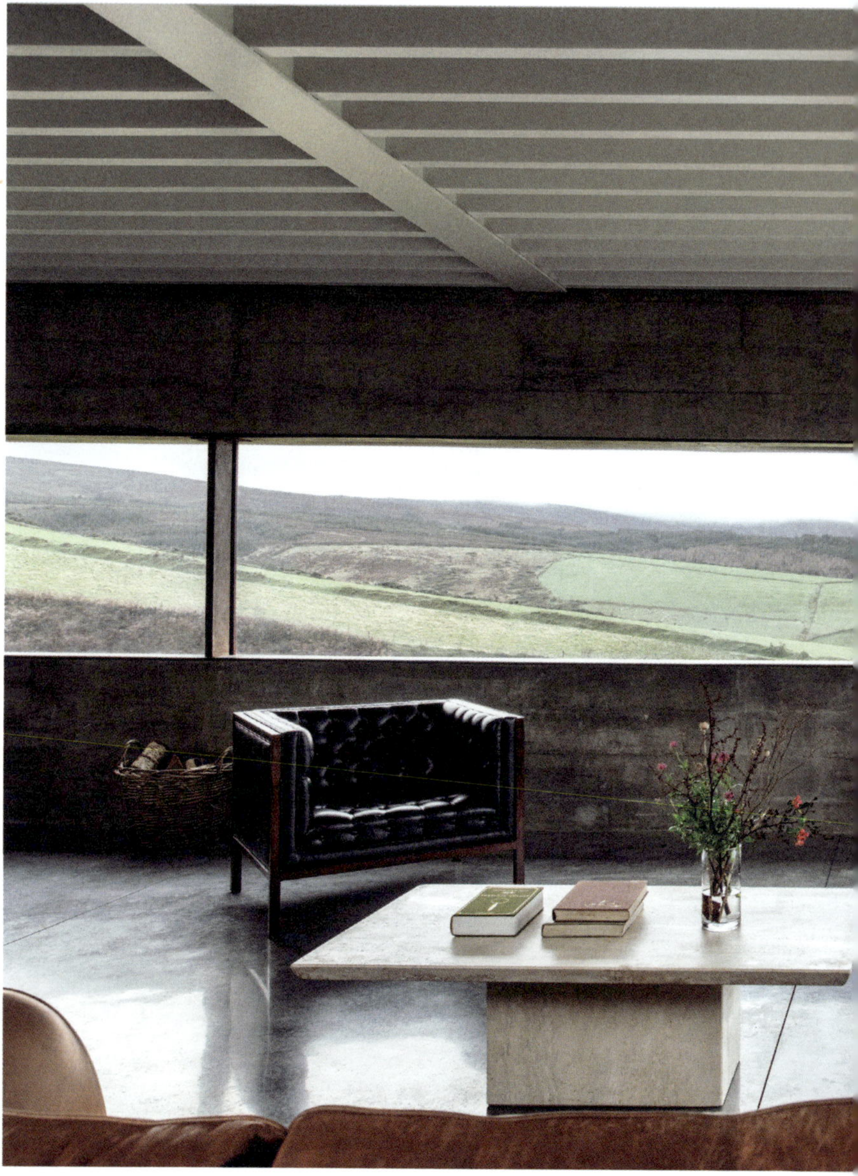

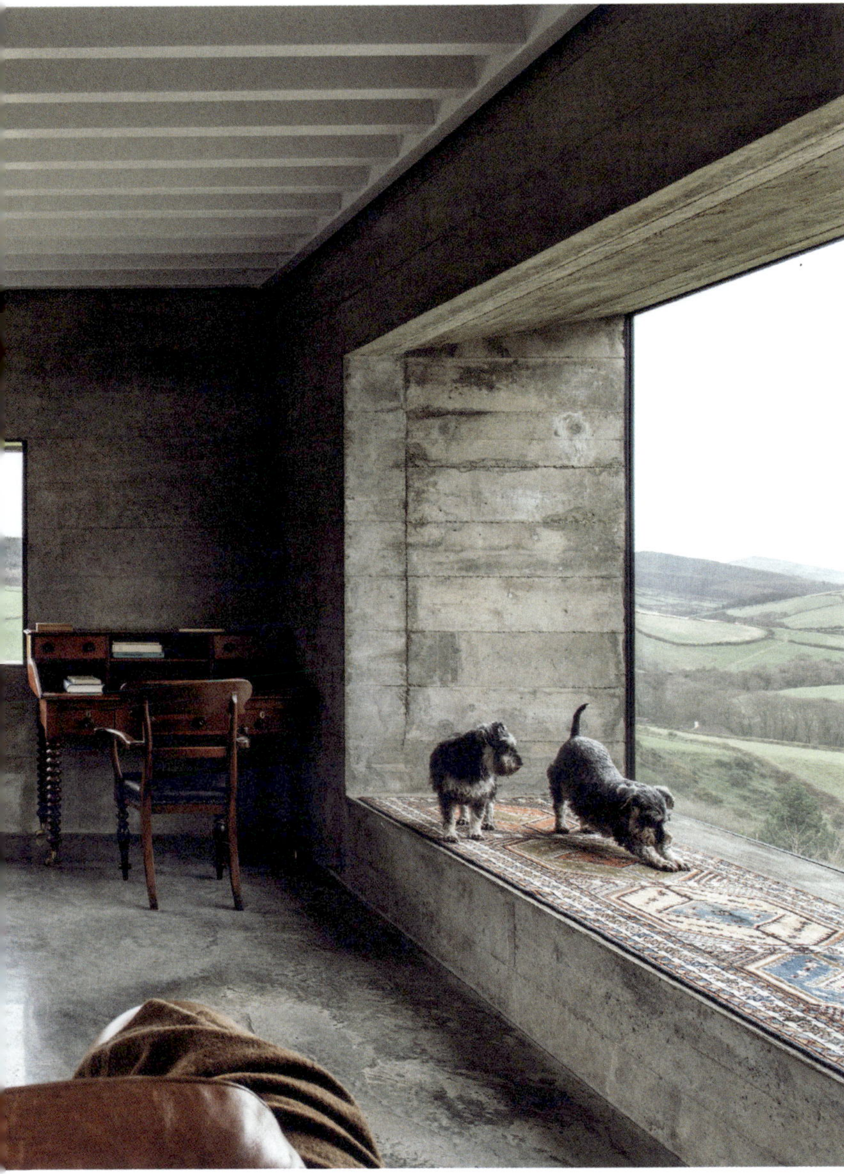

The Residence of Noodle and Poppy by Foster Lomas, 2019

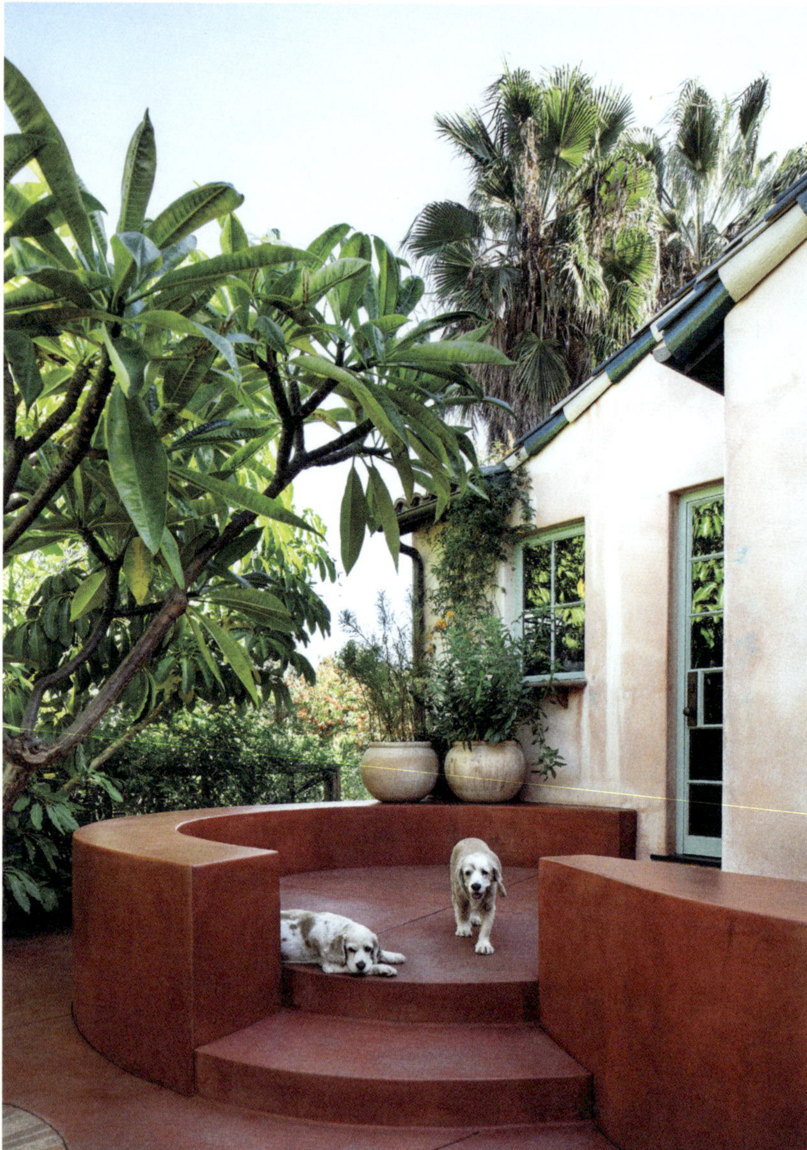

The Residence of Daylesford and Freeway by Studio KO, 2019

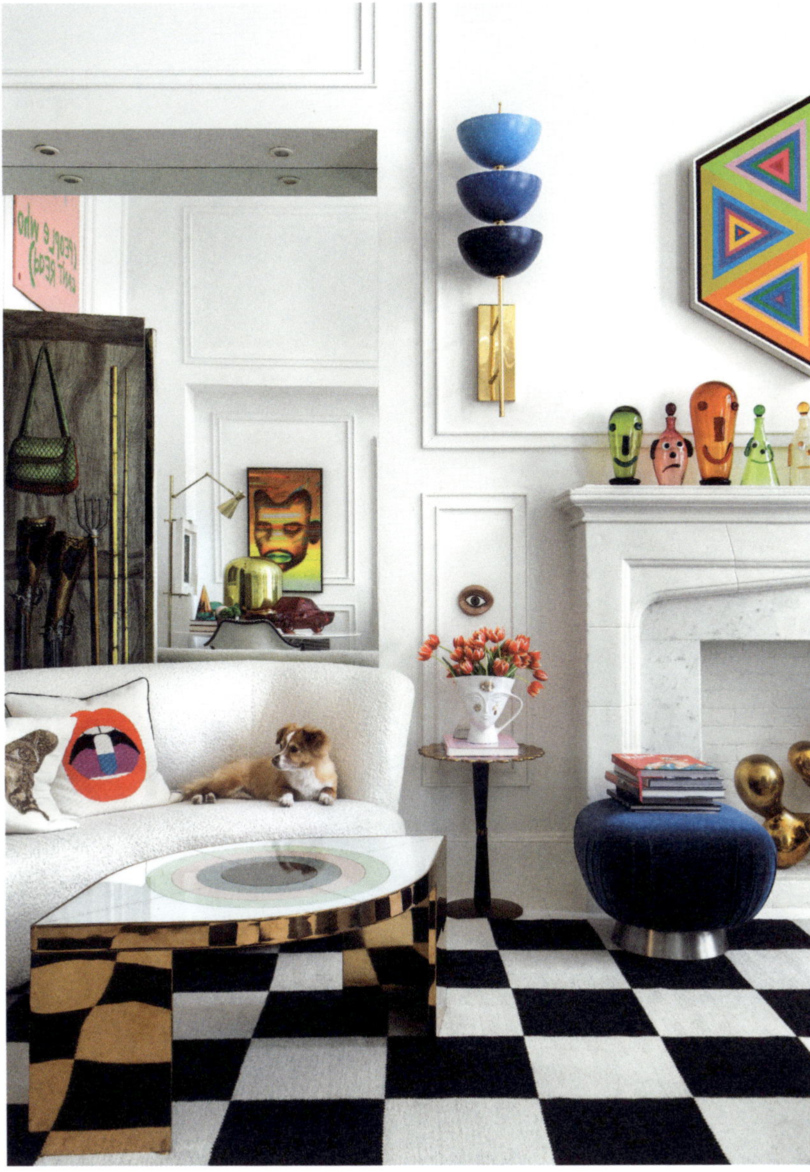

The Residence of Foxylady by Jonathan Adler, 2019

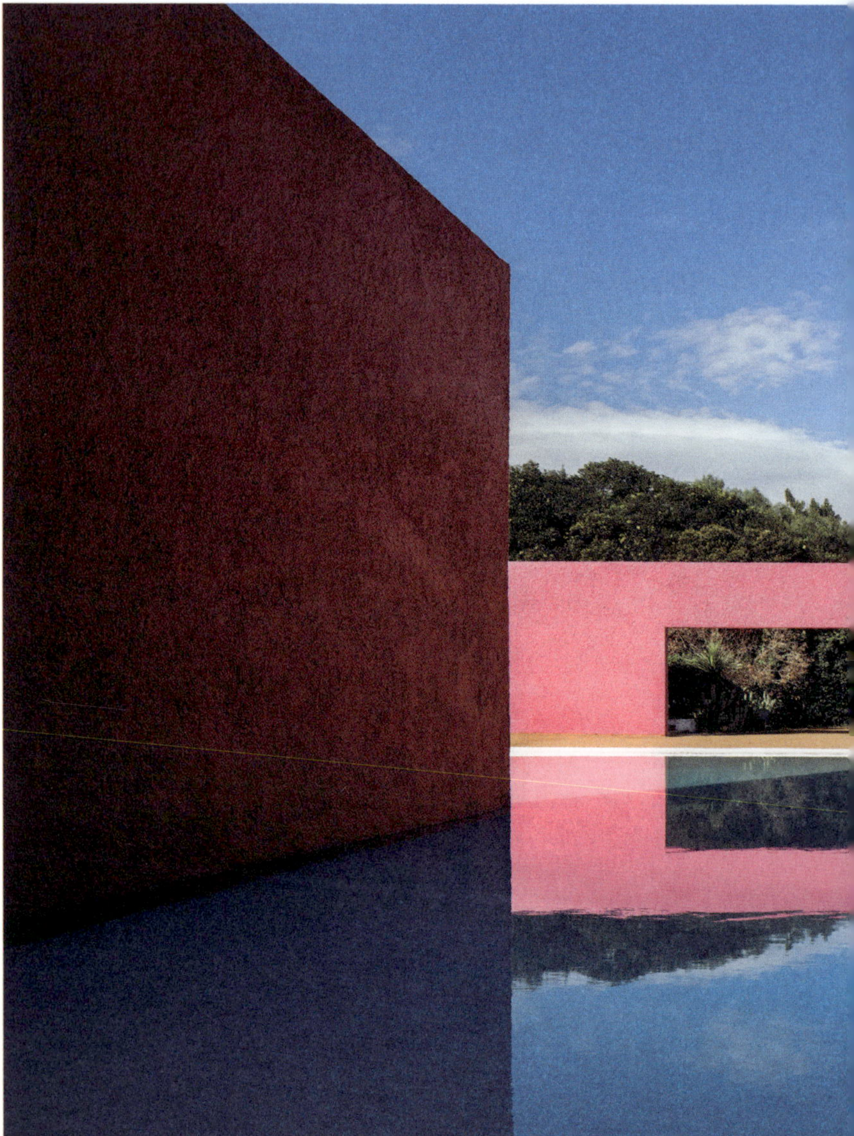

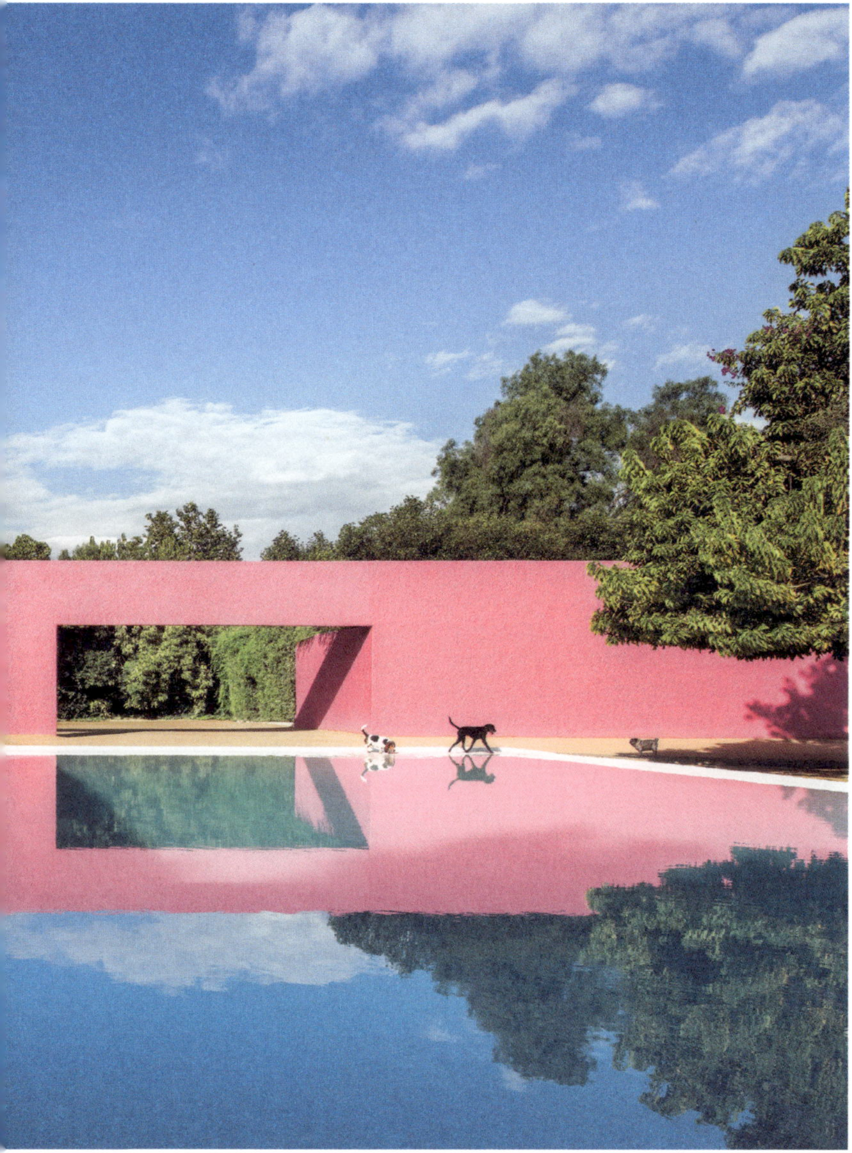

The Residence of Frida, Boris, Chich, Kuma, Carlots, Solovino, Chuleta and Yrrol by Luis Barragán, 2019

THE SILENCE OF DOGS IN CARS
Martin Usborne

It's the sad eyes that get you. Haven't we all seen them? A dog tied up outside the shop, tail tucked between its legs, waiting patiently for its owner to re-emerge. A return in five or fifteen minutes means nothing to a dog. So, the fear of abandonment kicks in, heart racing.

In his cinematic series of dogs left alone in cars, Martin Usborne summons this deep-seated fear of disconnection – a sentiment not only experienced by our canine companions, of course. At dawn or dusk, or in the middle of a deep, dark night, dogs stare out of car windows in dramatically lit pictures. Isolated and silent, their eyes tug at our hearts: only a human can release them from their predicament.

As much as the photos evoke a sense of painful longing, the series toes the line between tragedy and comedy. The scenes are staged. The dogs are carefully matched to their cars. Some are so big they barely fit in. While some appear glum, despondent or soulful, others seem rather more at ease, quite content to curl up and avoid the rain. And so it is with our own experience of loneliness – at times we may feel it lightly, at other times it can be too much to bear.

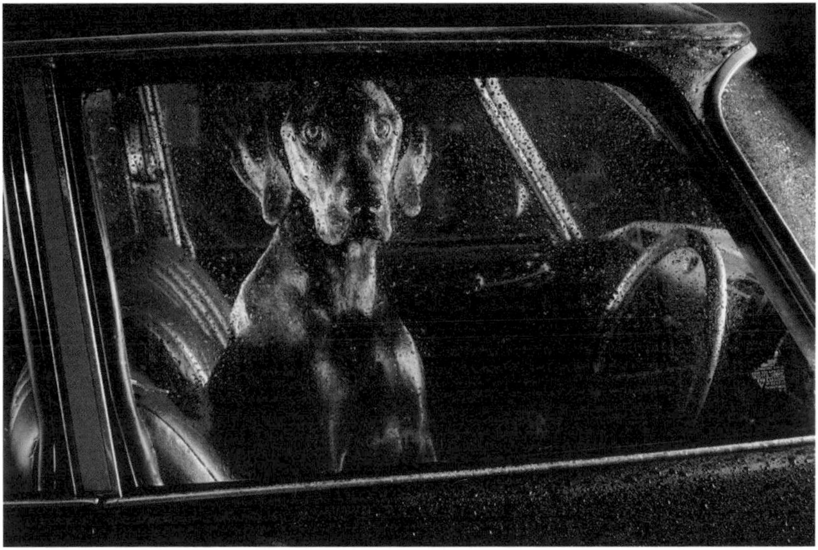

Above: *Prospero*, 2012
Overleaf: *Shep*, 2012

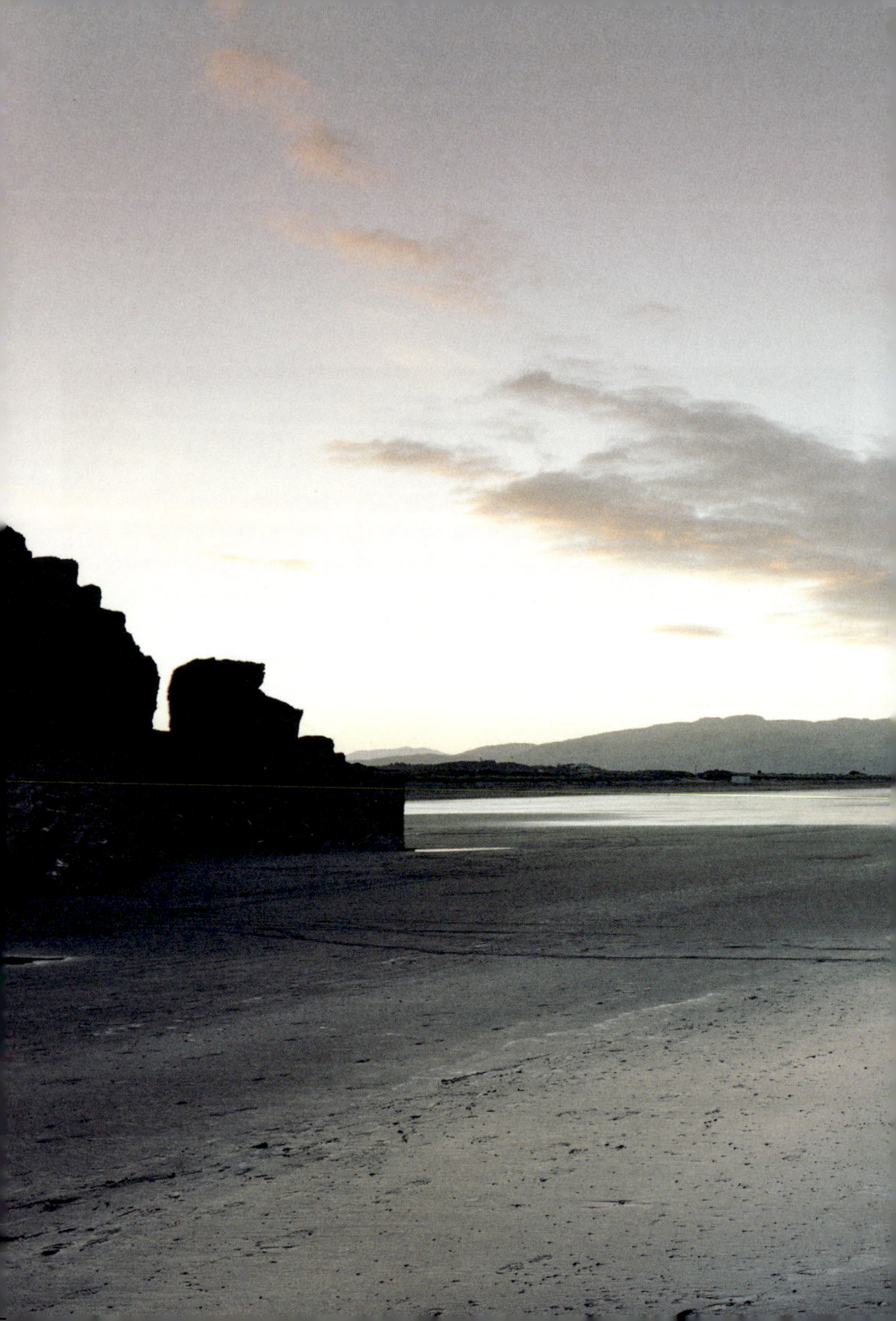

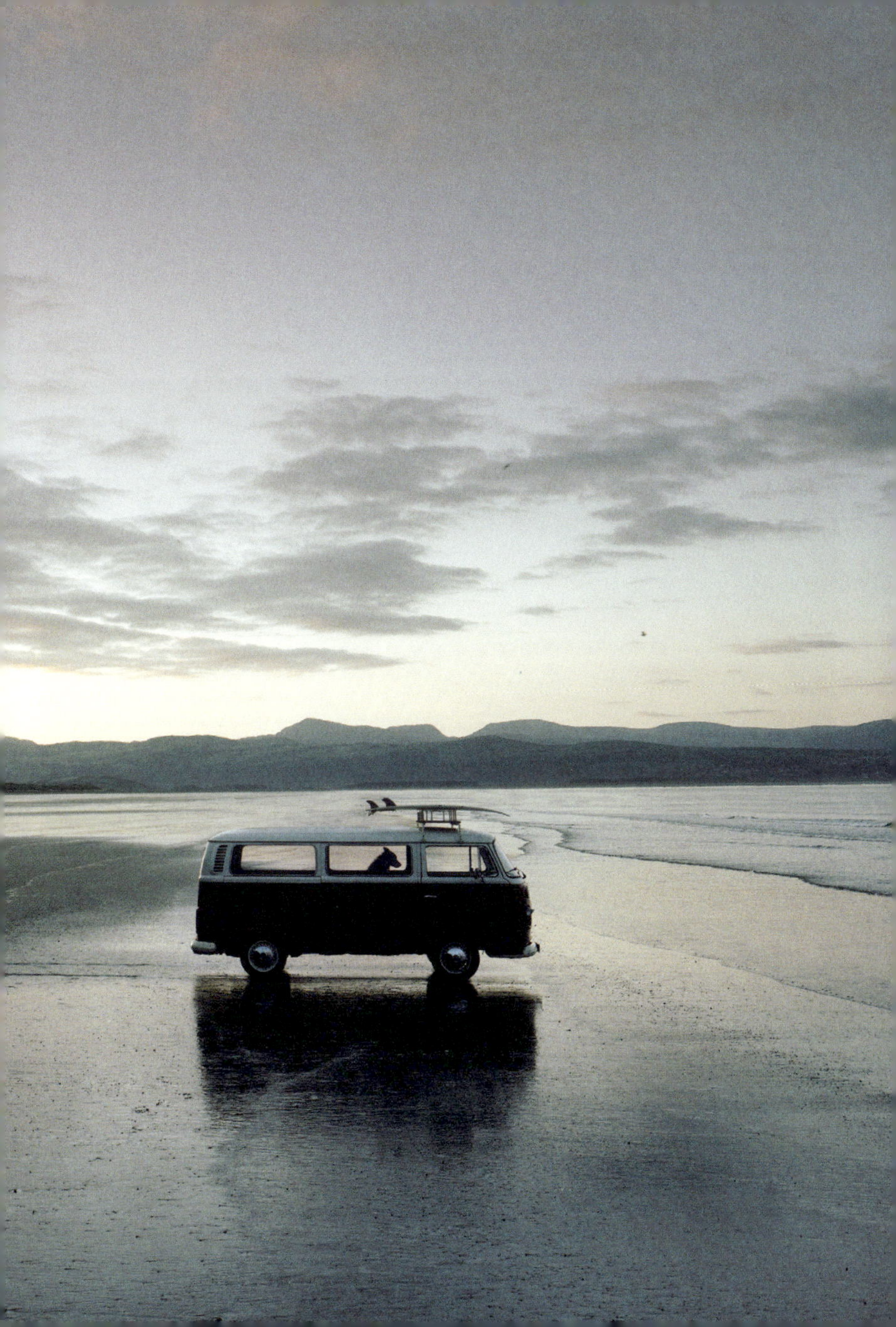

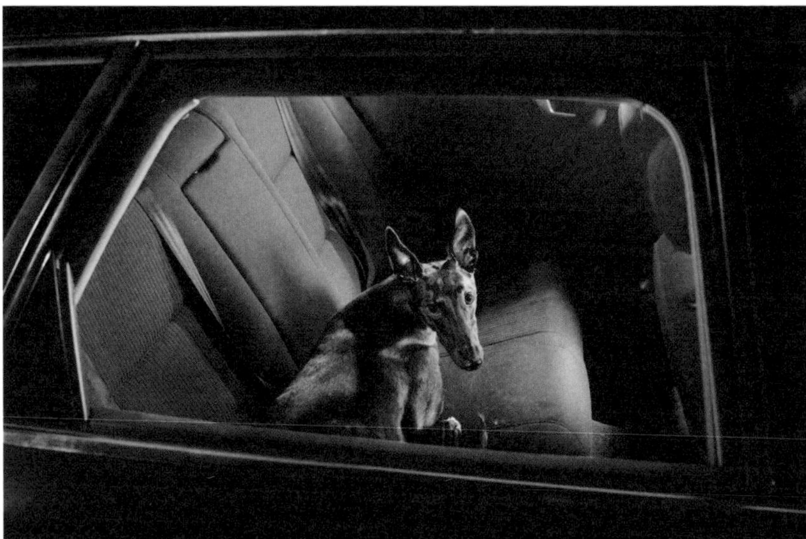

Peggy, 2012

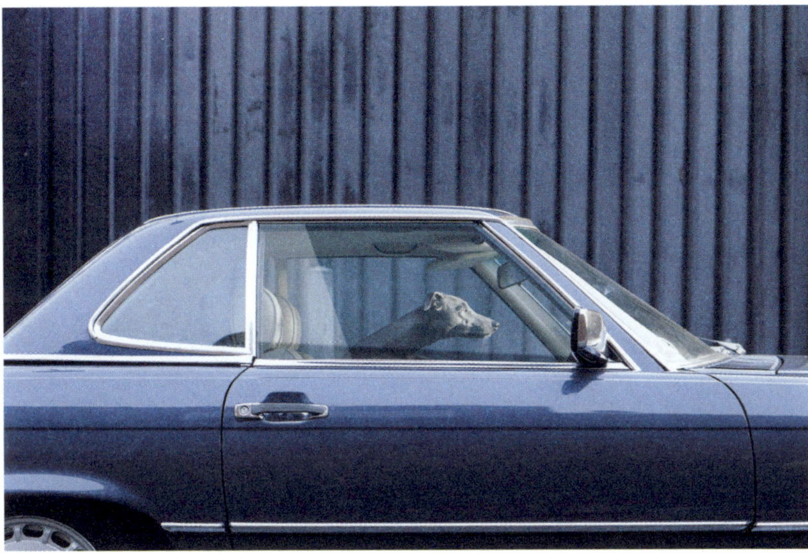

Above: *Maus*, 2012
Overleaf: *Hector*, 2012

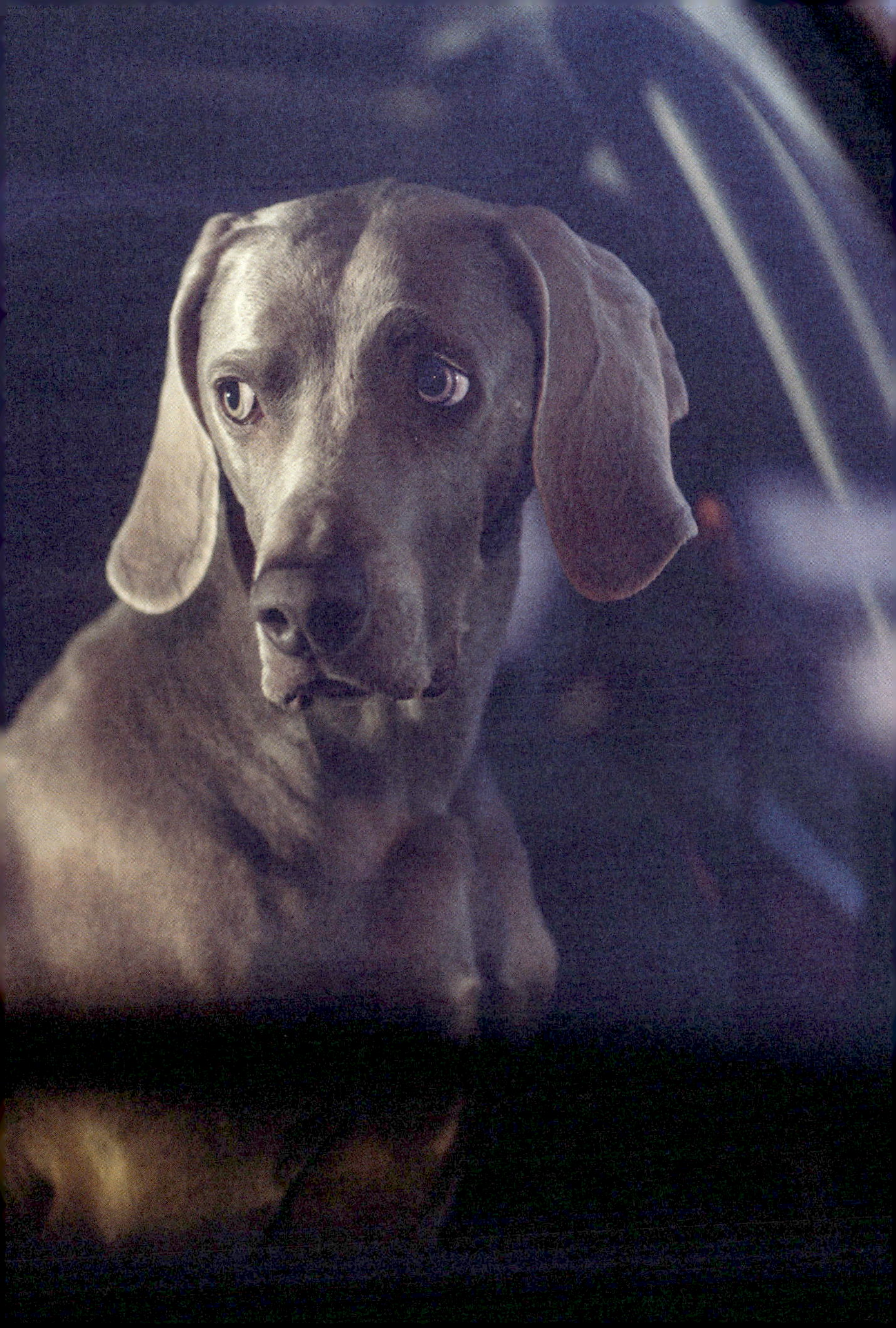

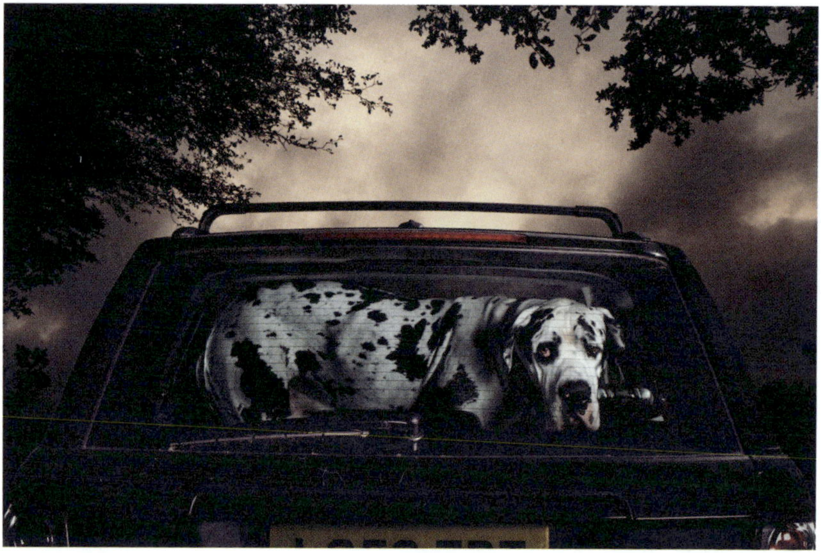

Alfie, 2012

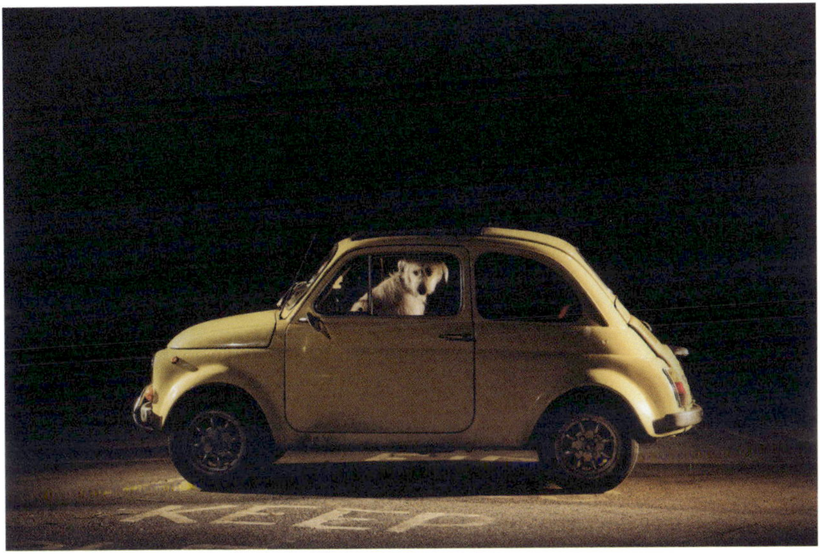

Milo, 2012

DOGS GODS
Tim Flach

Dogs are magnificent creatures – there's no denying it. They might steal your food, chew the furniture or leave drool all over the walls, but they are also (sometimes) noble, gracious and dignified beings. In Tim Flach's meticulously stylised photographs, they are shown from their most divine angle – every snout, tail and strand of fur rendered with precision, not a whisker or wrinkle out of place.

Flach is fascinated by the long-standing relationship between humans and domesticated dogs – a bond that we now know stretches back more than 15,000 years. He pairs his striking images with scientific research into different breeds and with reflections on how people have shaped dogs in our own image, both in form and character. Some of the titles – such as 'Afterglow Sugar Daddy' and 'Flying Mop' – are nearly as entertaining as the photographs themselves.

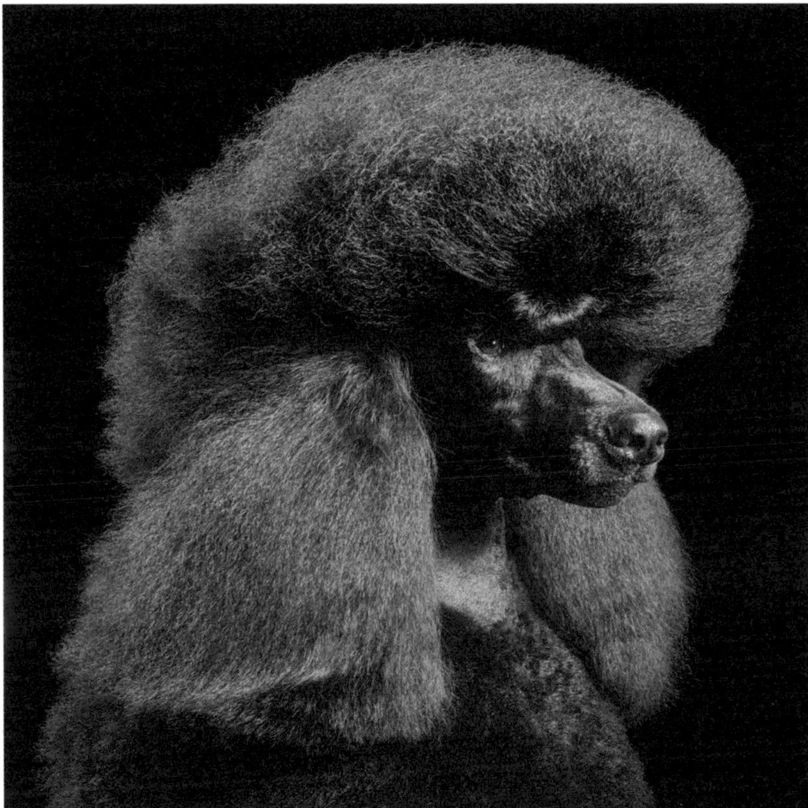

Afterglow Sugar Daddy (Standard Poodle), 2010

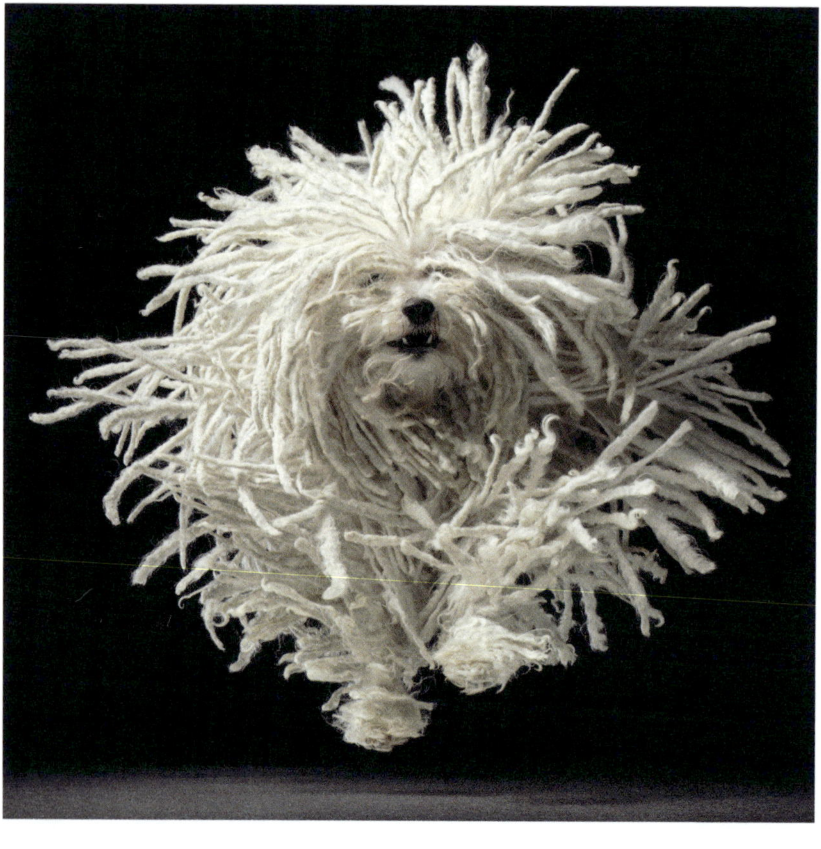

Flying Mop (Hungarian Puli), 2010

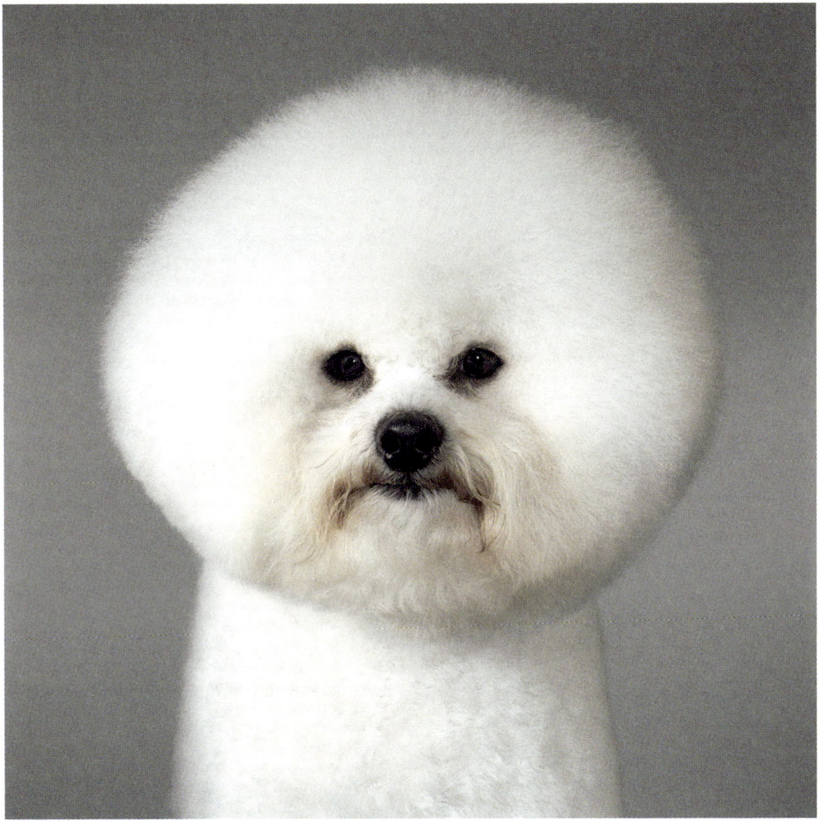

Above: *Eric (Bichon Frisé)*, 2010
Overleaf: *Labrador Retriever Shaking*, 2010

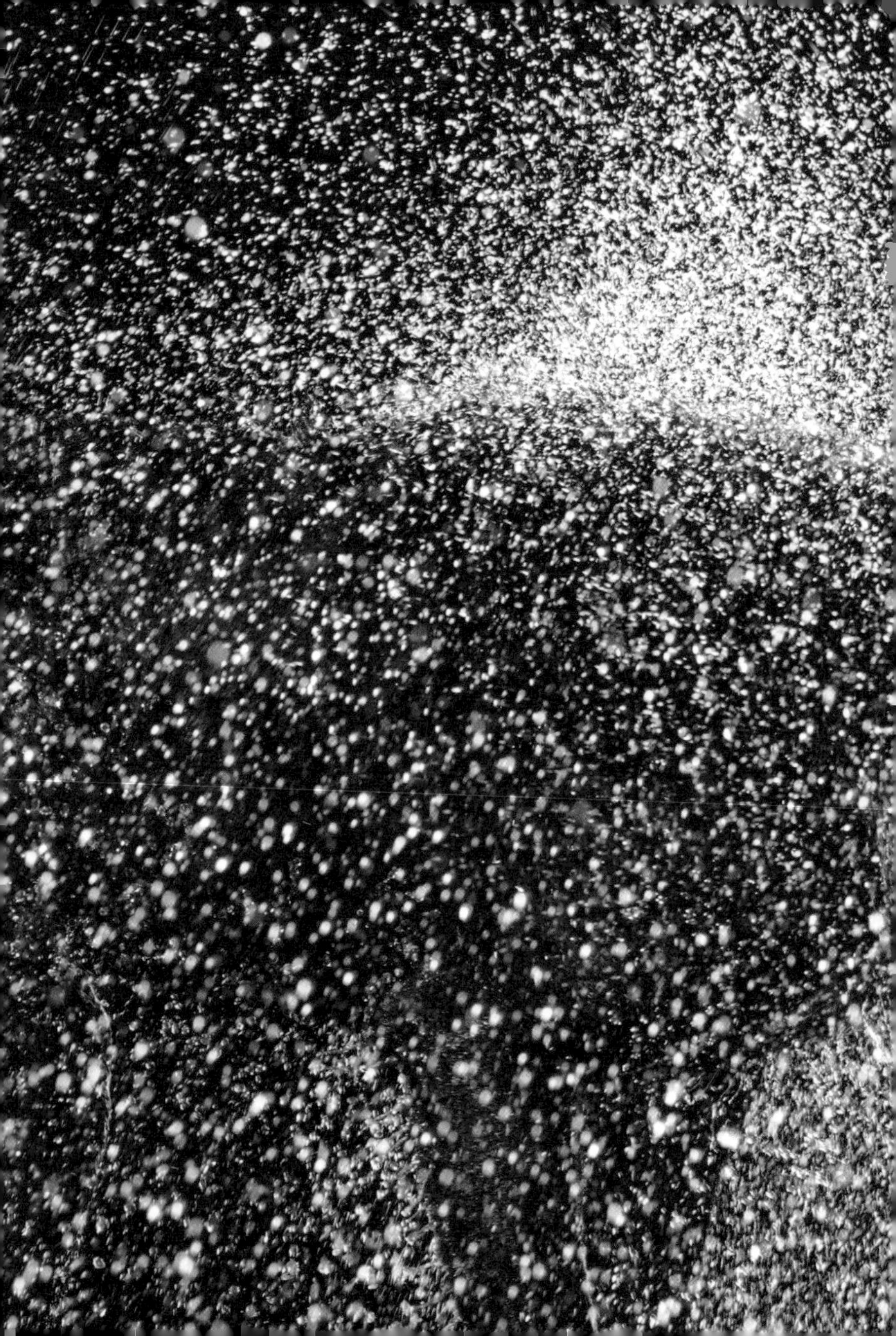

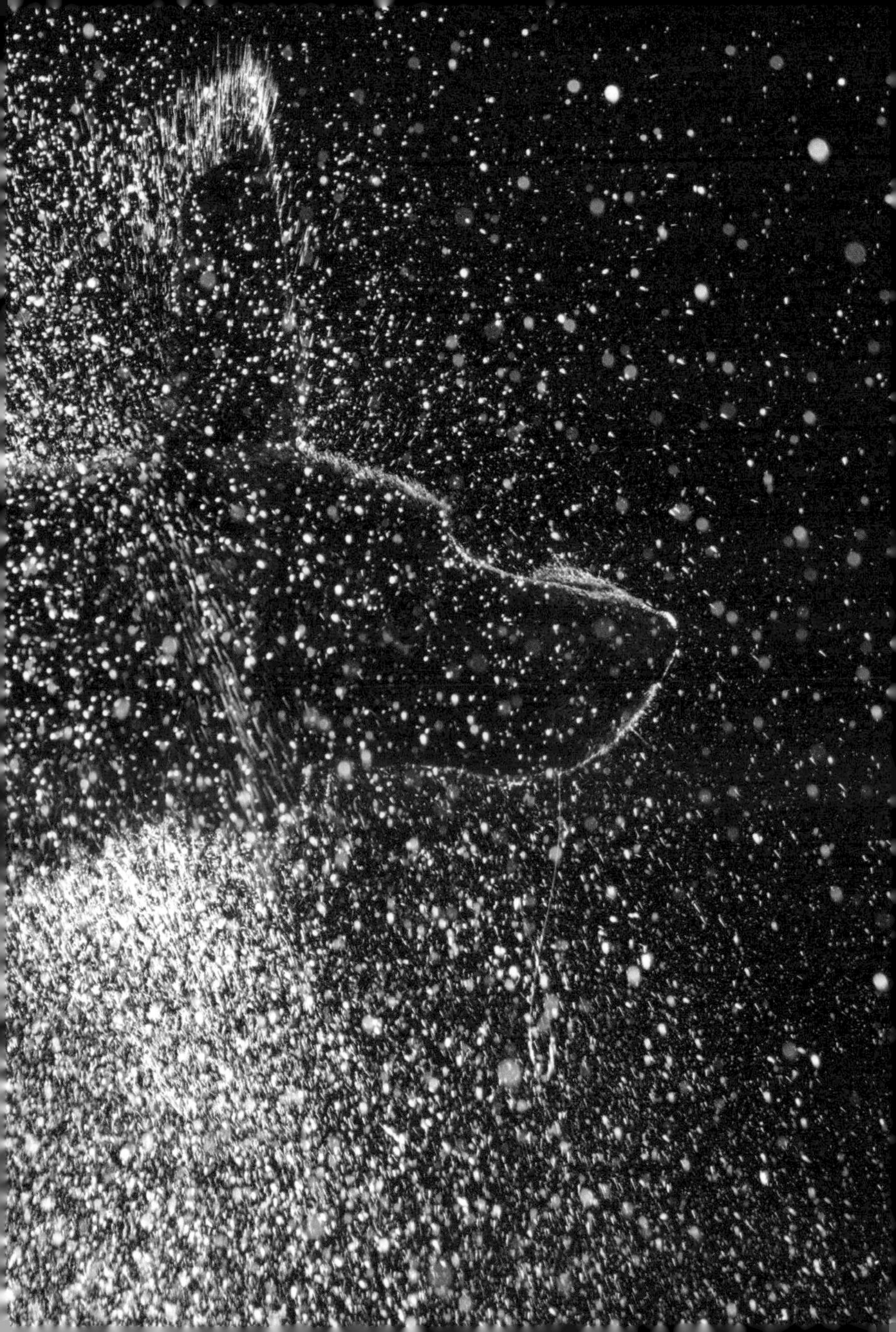

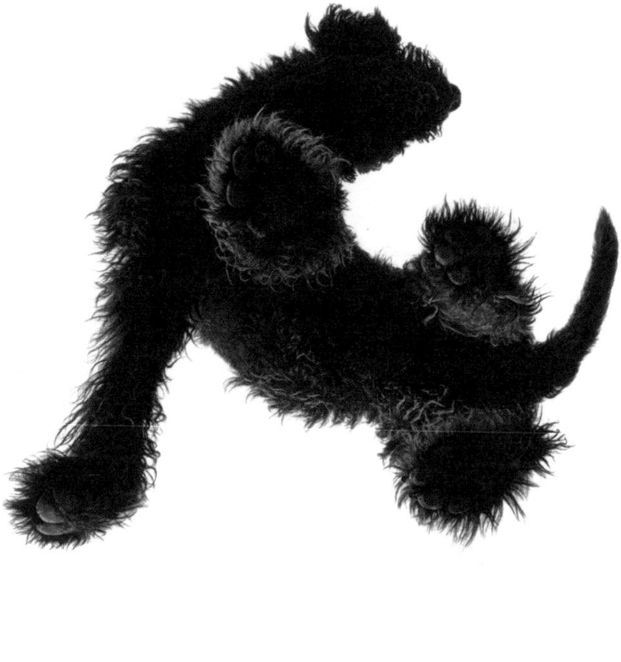

Labradoodle, 2010

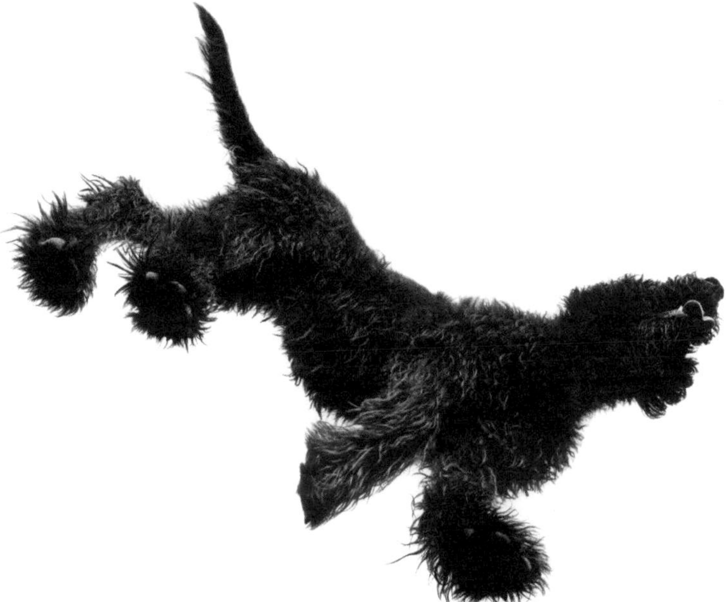

Labradoodle, 2010

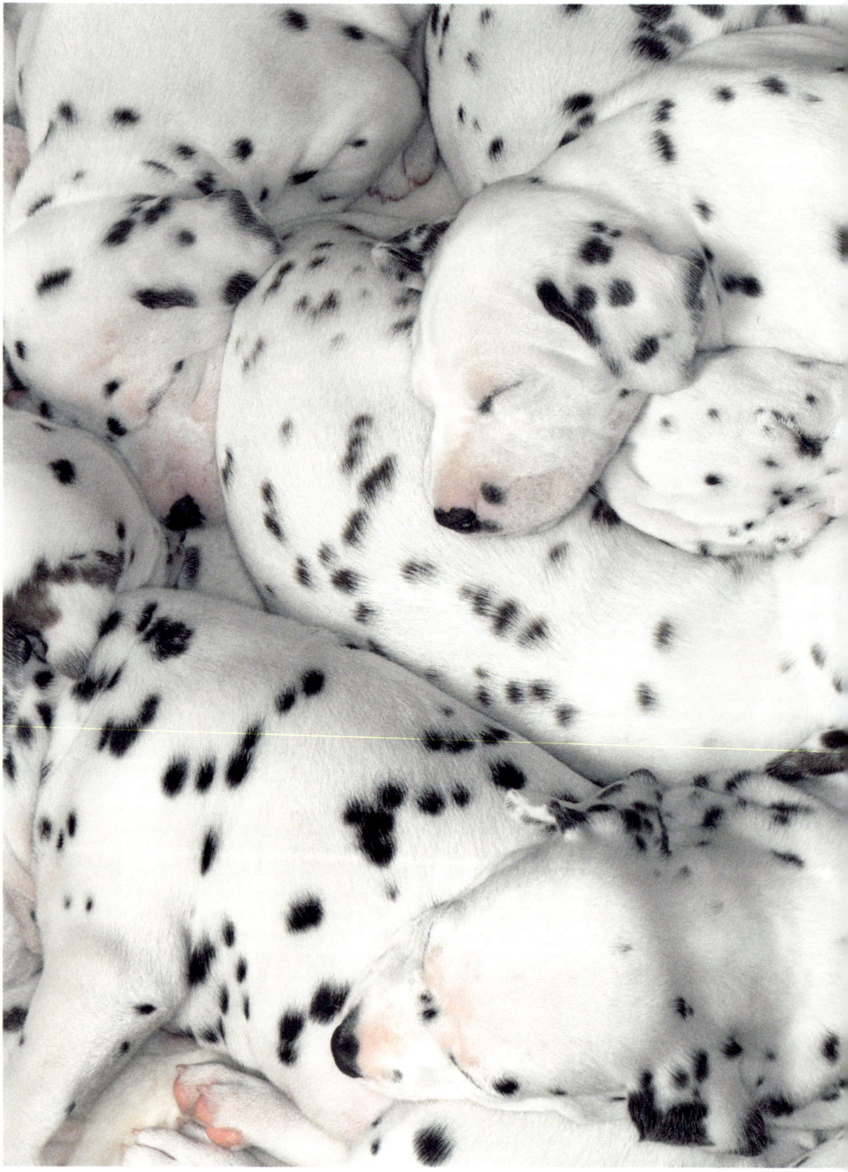

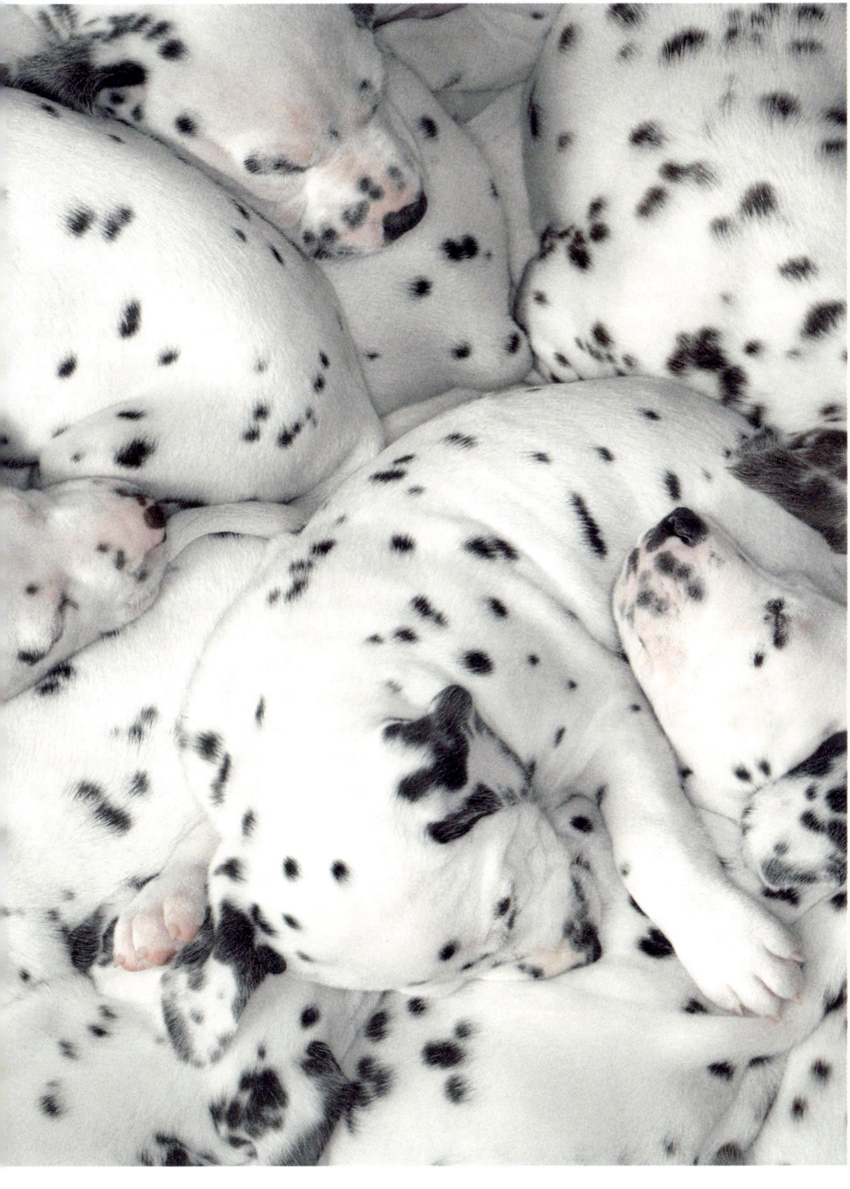

Dalmatian Puppies, 2010

WESTMINSTER DOG SHOW

Cait Oppermann

The Westminster Kennel Club Dog Show in New York City isn't your neighbourhood 'everyone gets a ribbon' kind of affair. As the United States' second-oldest sporting event (the first show was held in 1877), it pits thousands of dogs across 200 breeds against each other in categories such as agility, obedience and showmanship.

For photographer and creative director Cait Oppermann, shooting the prestigious dog show was a dream commission. Backstage at Madison Square Garden, she caught a peek at dogs getting coiffed, fluffed and preened – many of them giving her a knowing side-eye. She was as intrigued by the dogs' eccentricities as by their owners' desire for the spotlight and attention lavished on their fur-coated stars.

With some tickets selling for more than $125 and plenty of cash poured into grooming and exhibitor attendance, the dog show means serious business. Tensions run high as judges decide which top dog will earn the ultimate bragging rights of Best in Show, strutting home with a silver trophy and a hand-engraved crystal bowl.

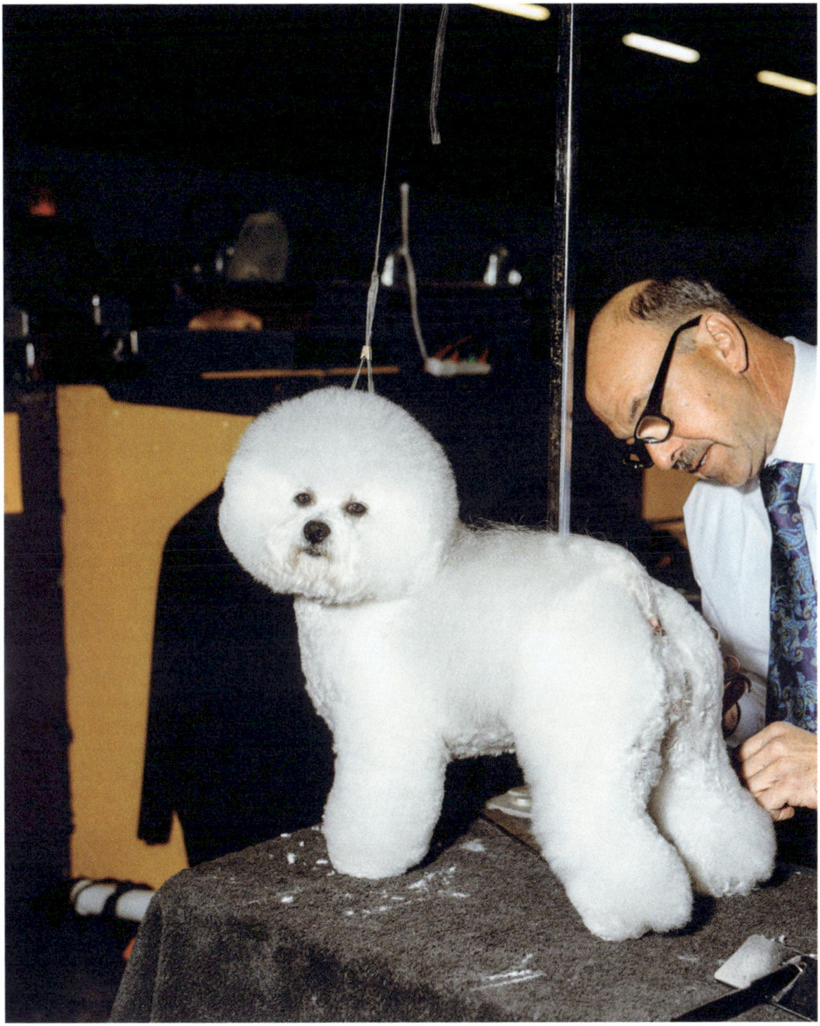

Westminster Dog Show, 2016

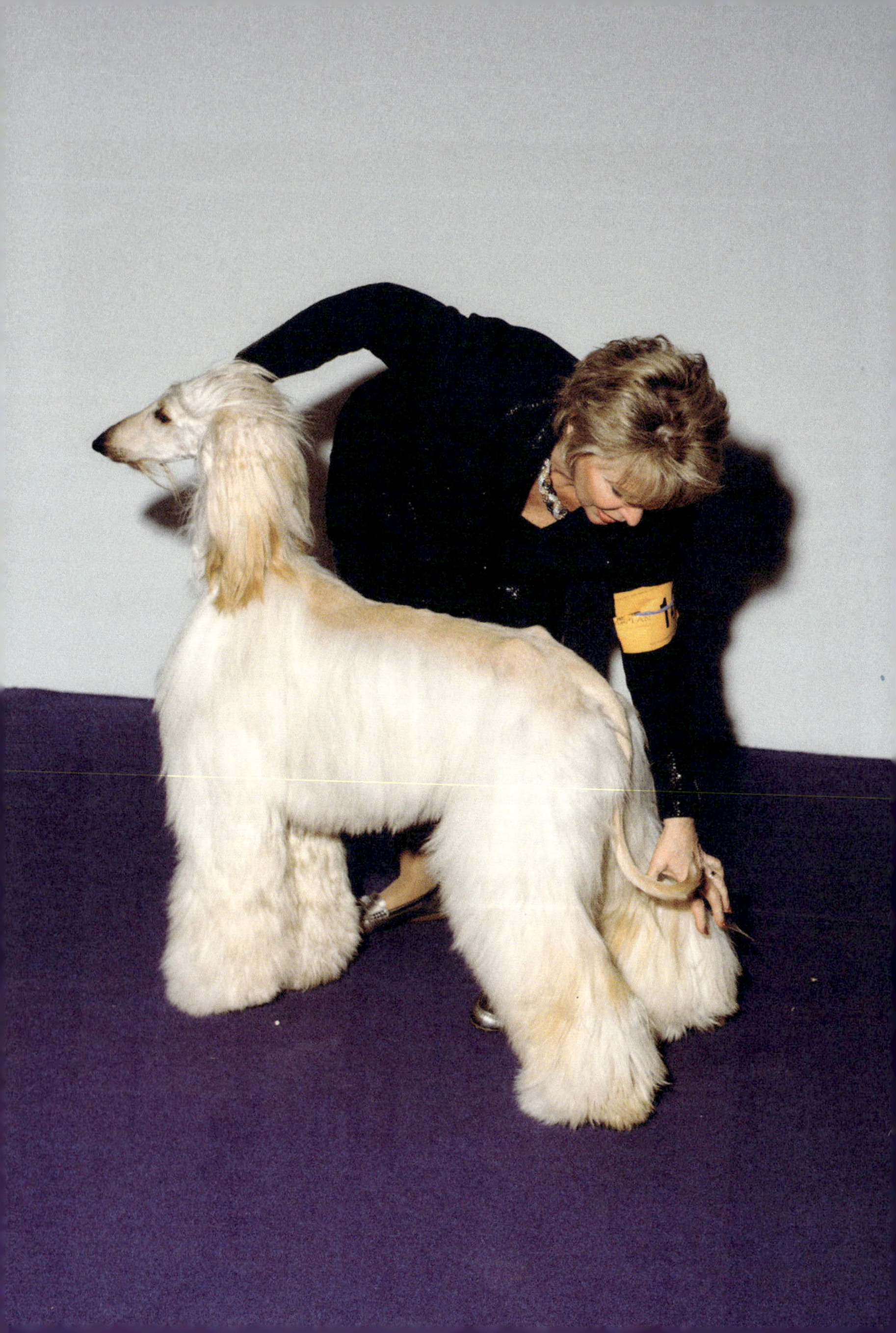

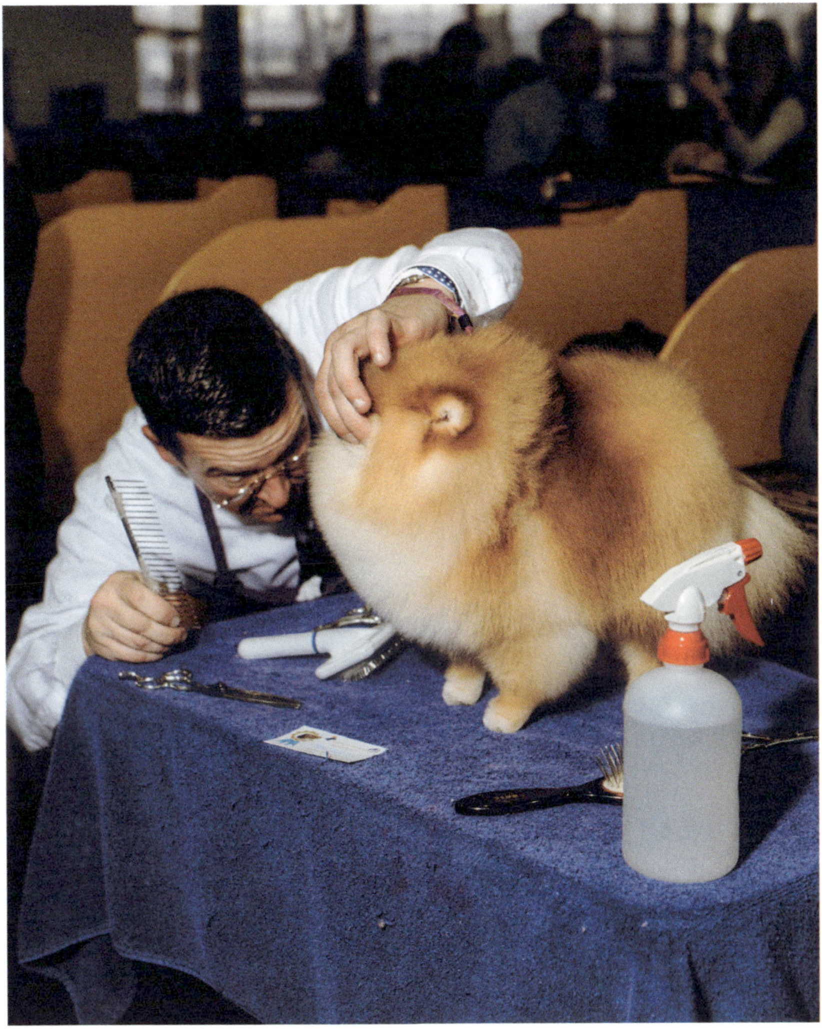

Above and opposite: *Westminster Dog Show*, 2016

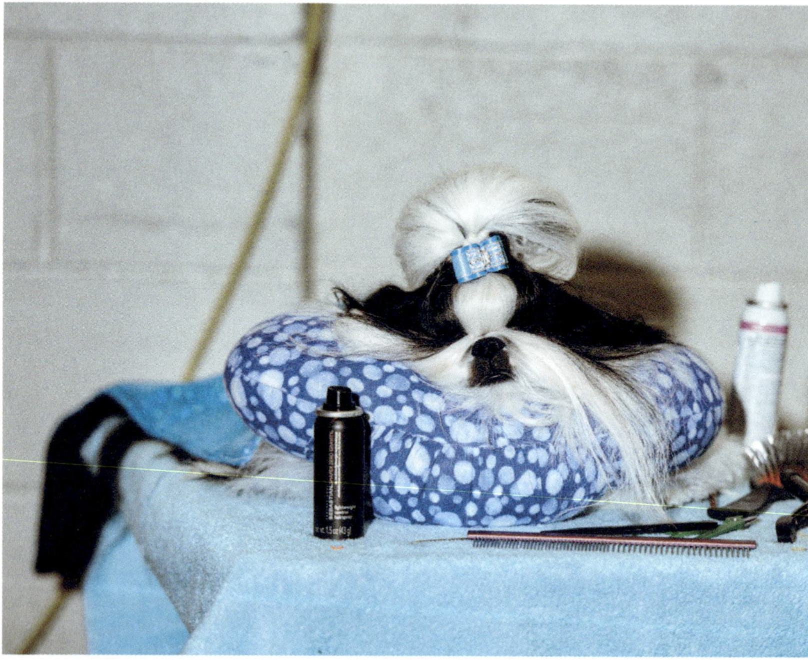

Westminster Dog Show, 2016

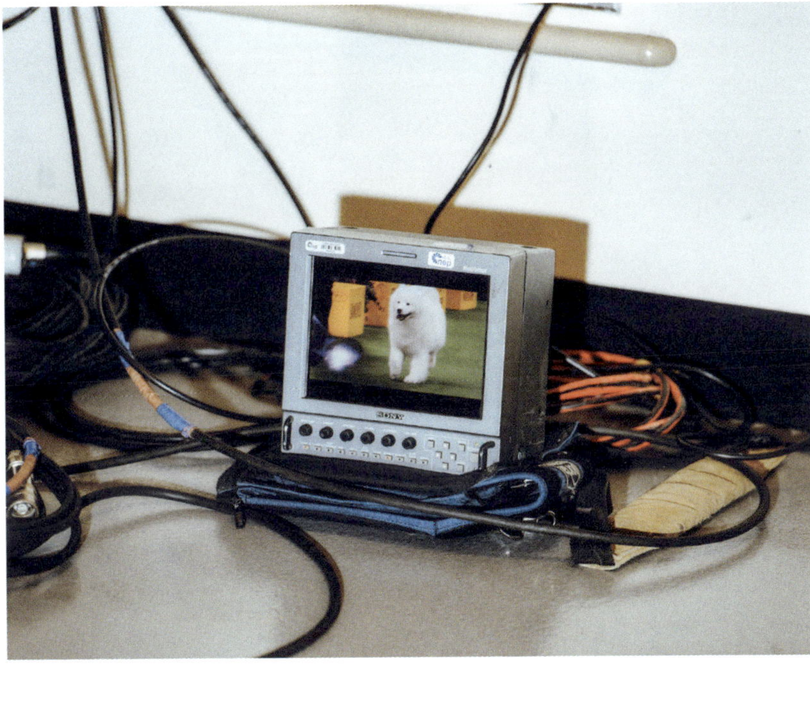

Westminster Dog Show, 2016

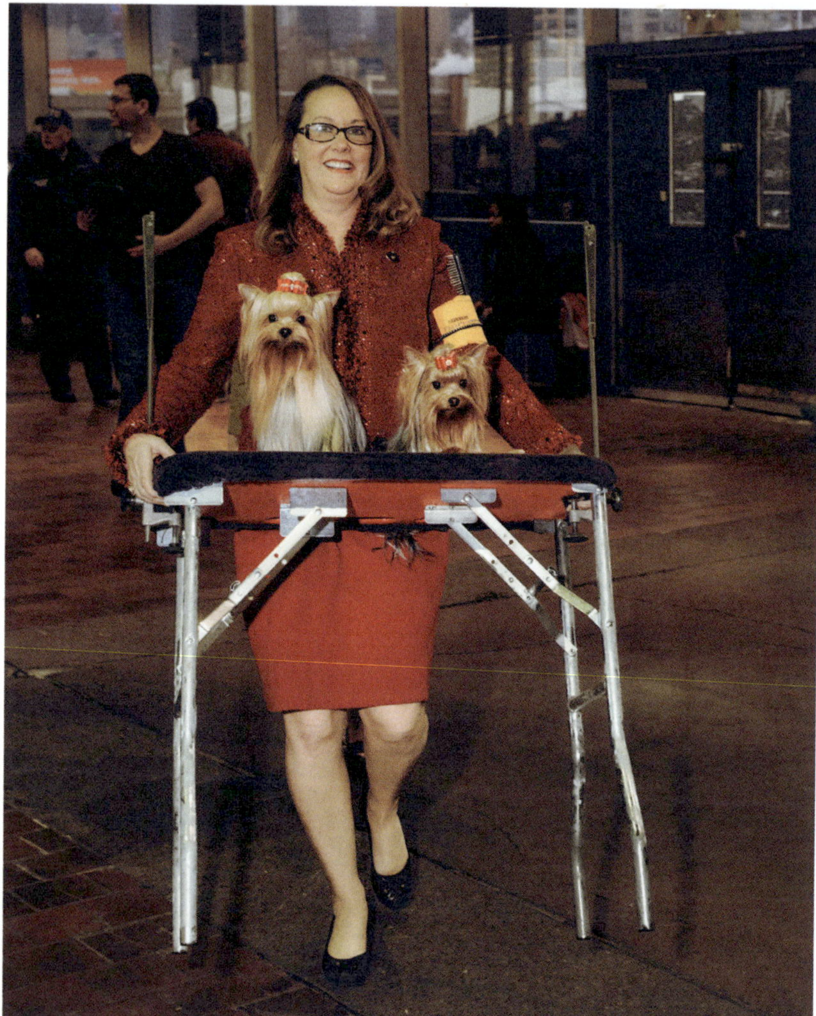

Above and opposite: *Westminster Dog Show*, 2016

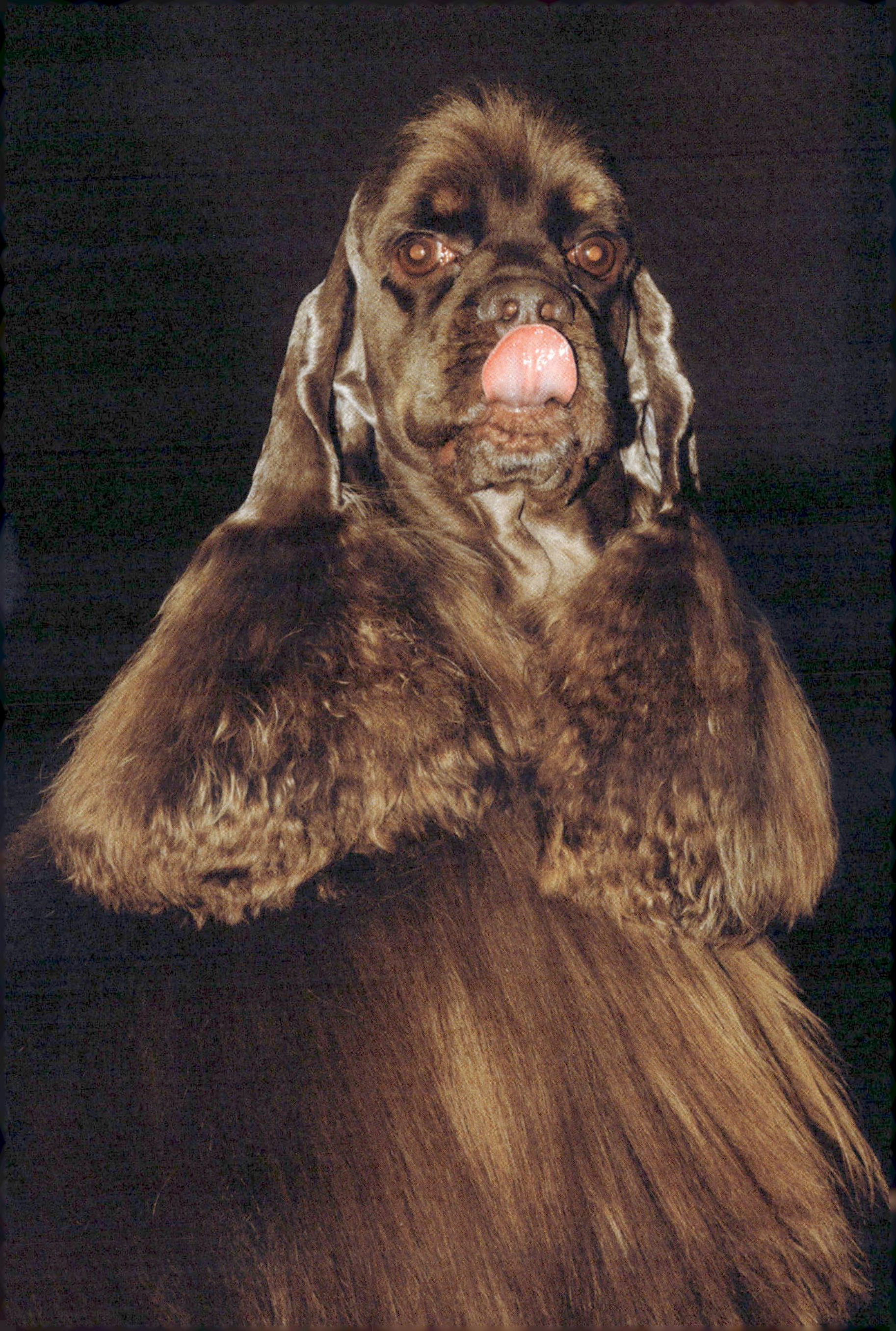

WELL HEELED
Dougie Wallace

Cosmopolitan, streetwise and strategically cute, these four-legged urban dwellers own the streets just as much as their humans do. They are a busy lot. There's barely a moment to relax between the park and the beauty parlour, office and shopping mall… as the motto goes: 'You snooze, you lose'.

Using street photography techniques such as unexpected camera angles, in-your-face close-ups and dramatic use of flash, Dougie Wallace turns the lens away from people and onto their canine companions. Pounding the pavements of London, Milan and New York, these pups dish out street cred as if they have nothing better to do – and really, who's going to argue?

The dogs show no hint of being camera-shy, looking straight into the lens and putting their best paw forward. Wallace captures their personalities with wit and observational humour. But beneath their polished exteriors and manicured paws, one can't help wondering: what feral instincts lie hidden? Did someone say… squirrel?

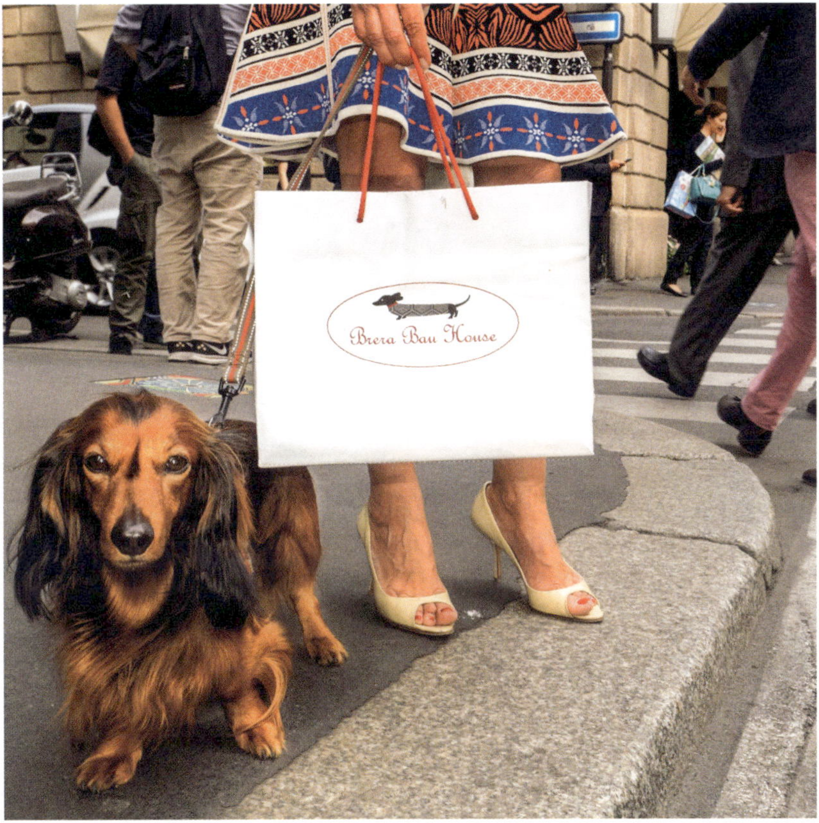

Well Heeled, 2018

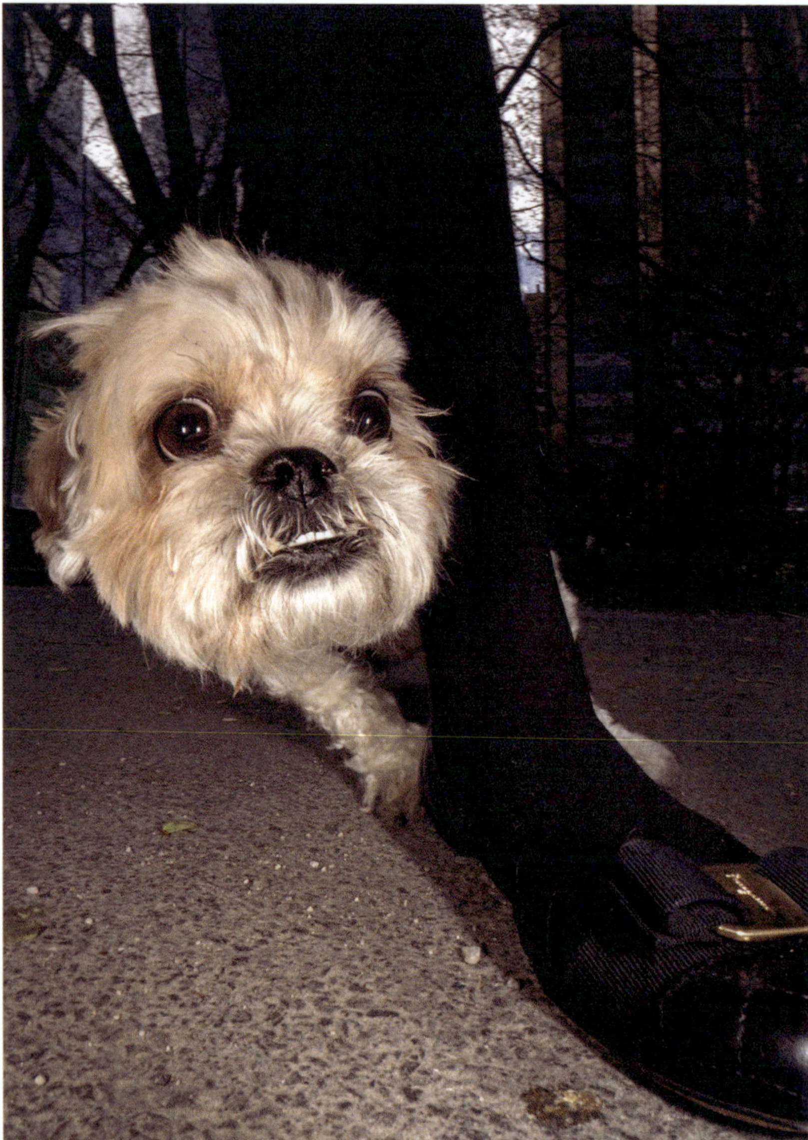

Well Heeled, 2017

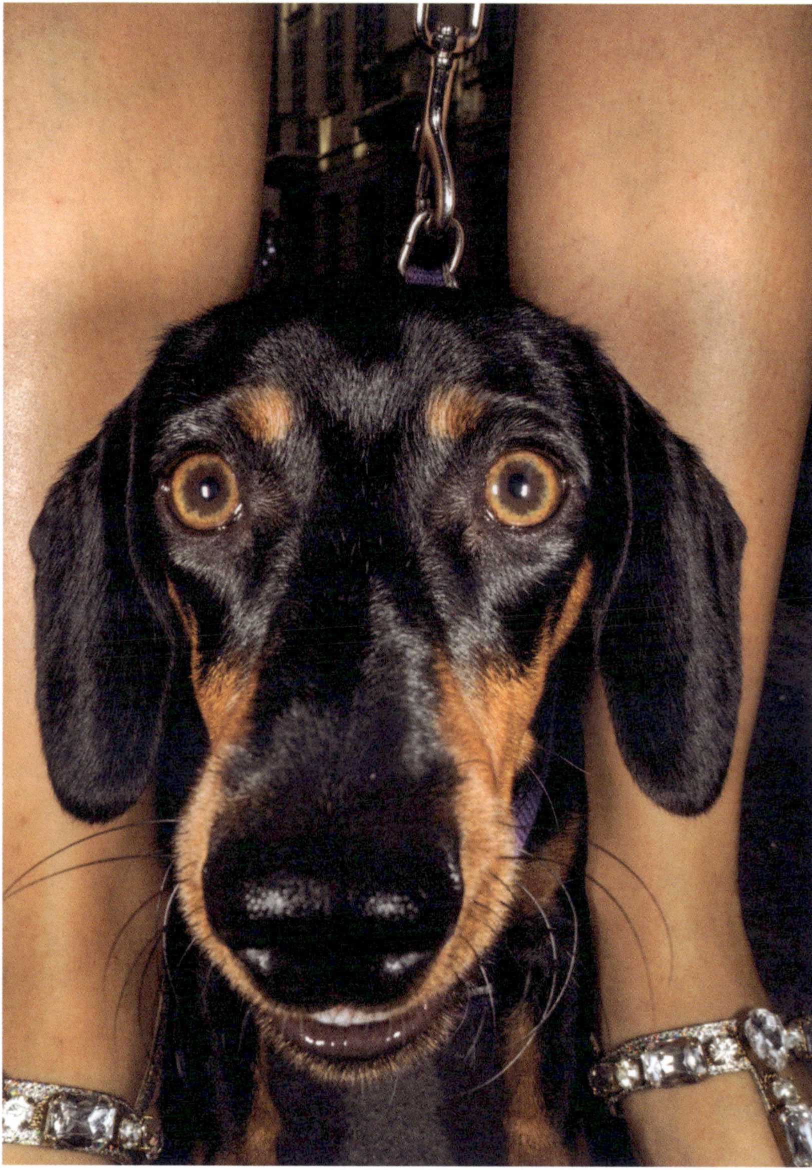

Well Heeled, 2018

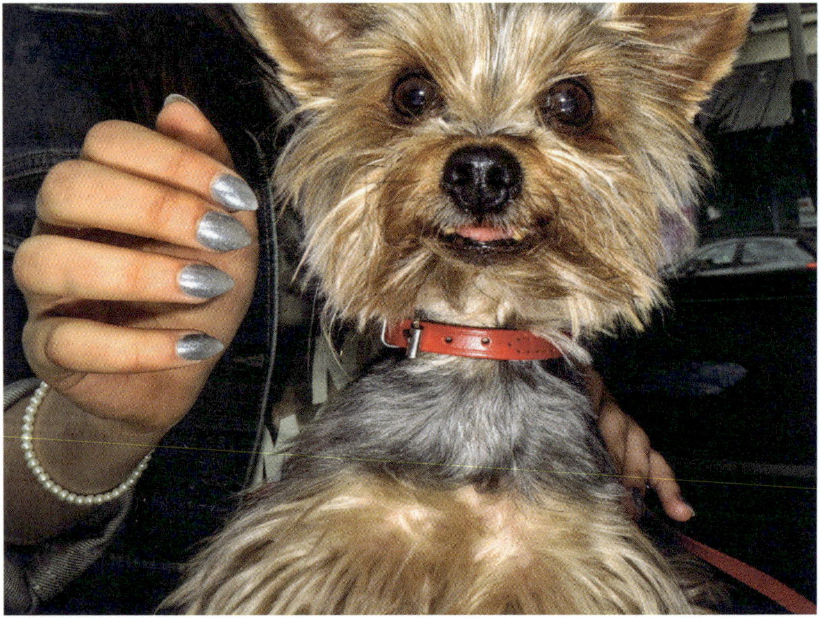

Well Heeled, 2017

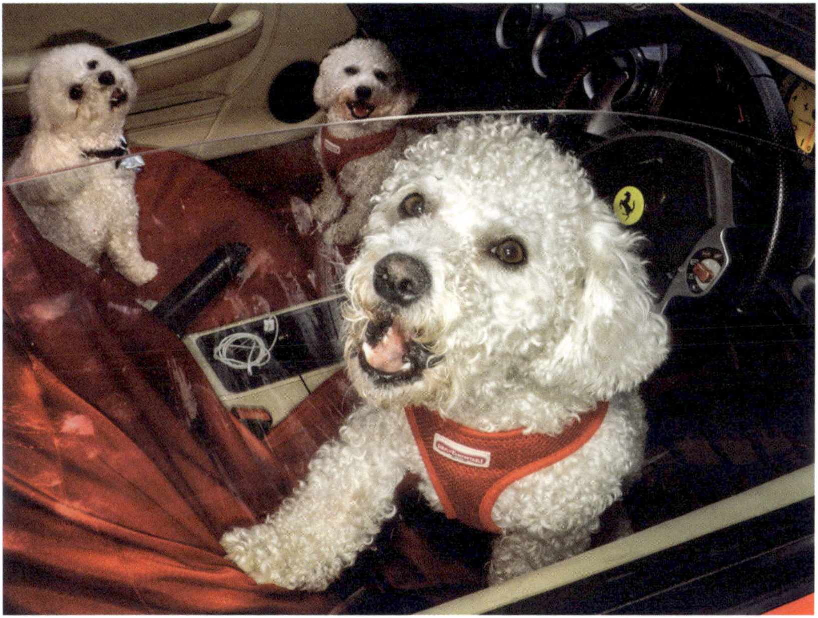

Well Heeled, 2018

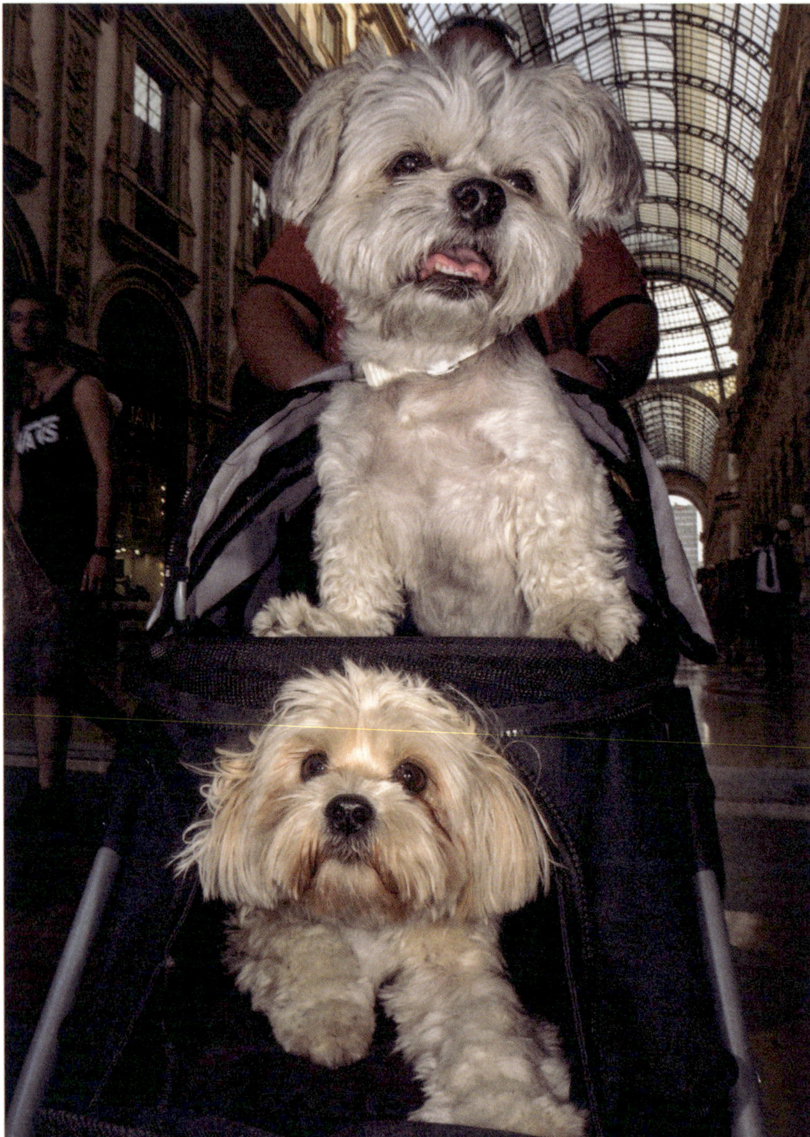

Well Heeled, 2017

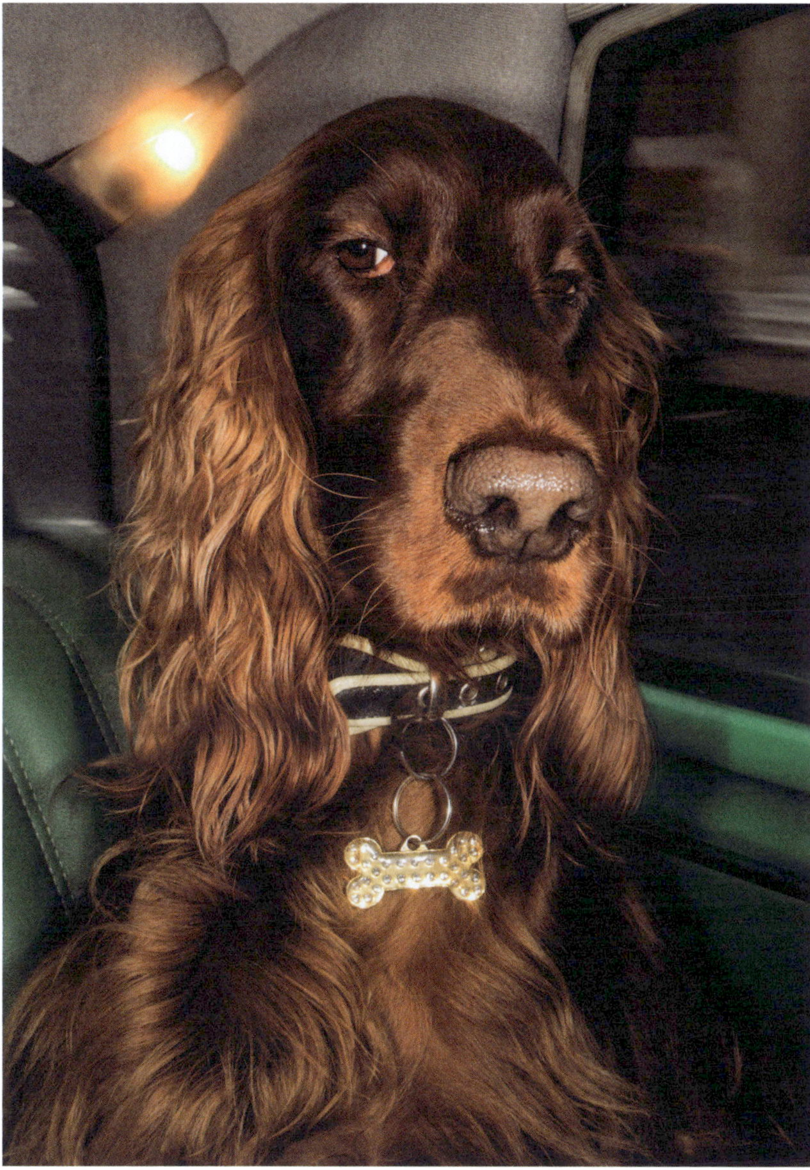

Well Heeled, 2018

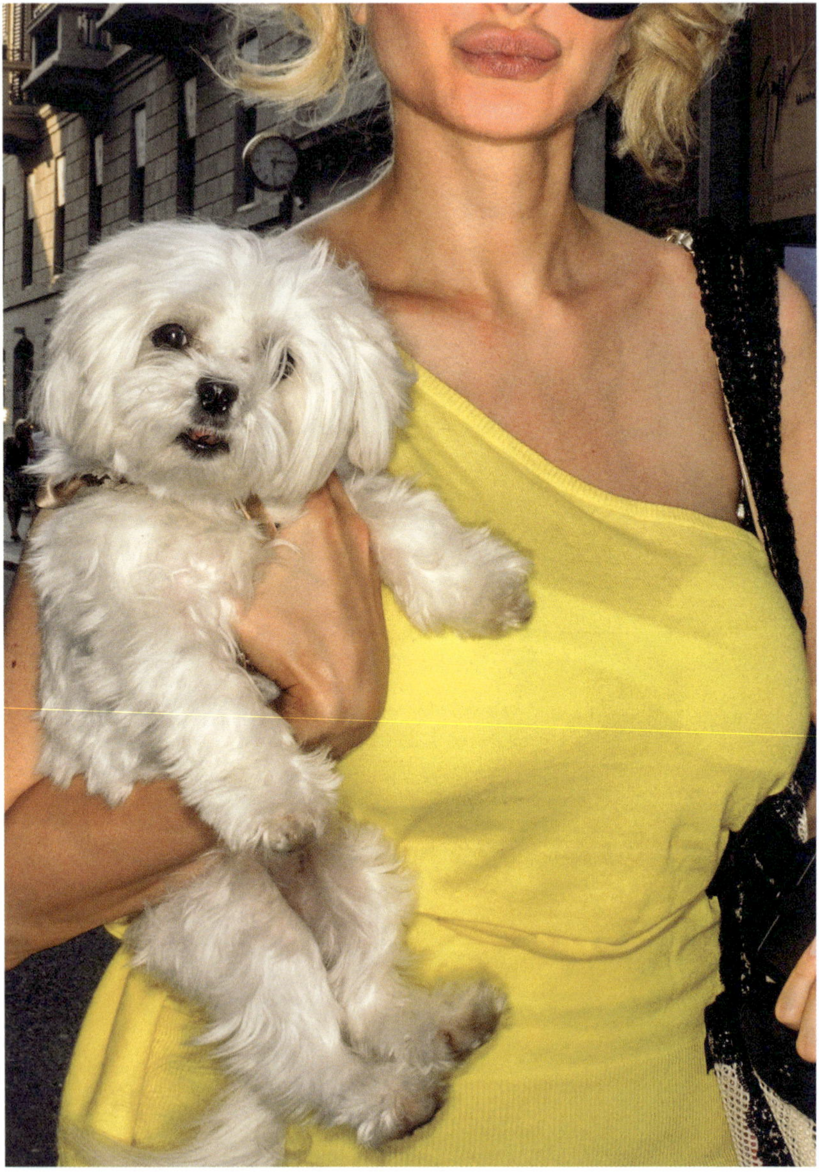

Well Heeled, 2018

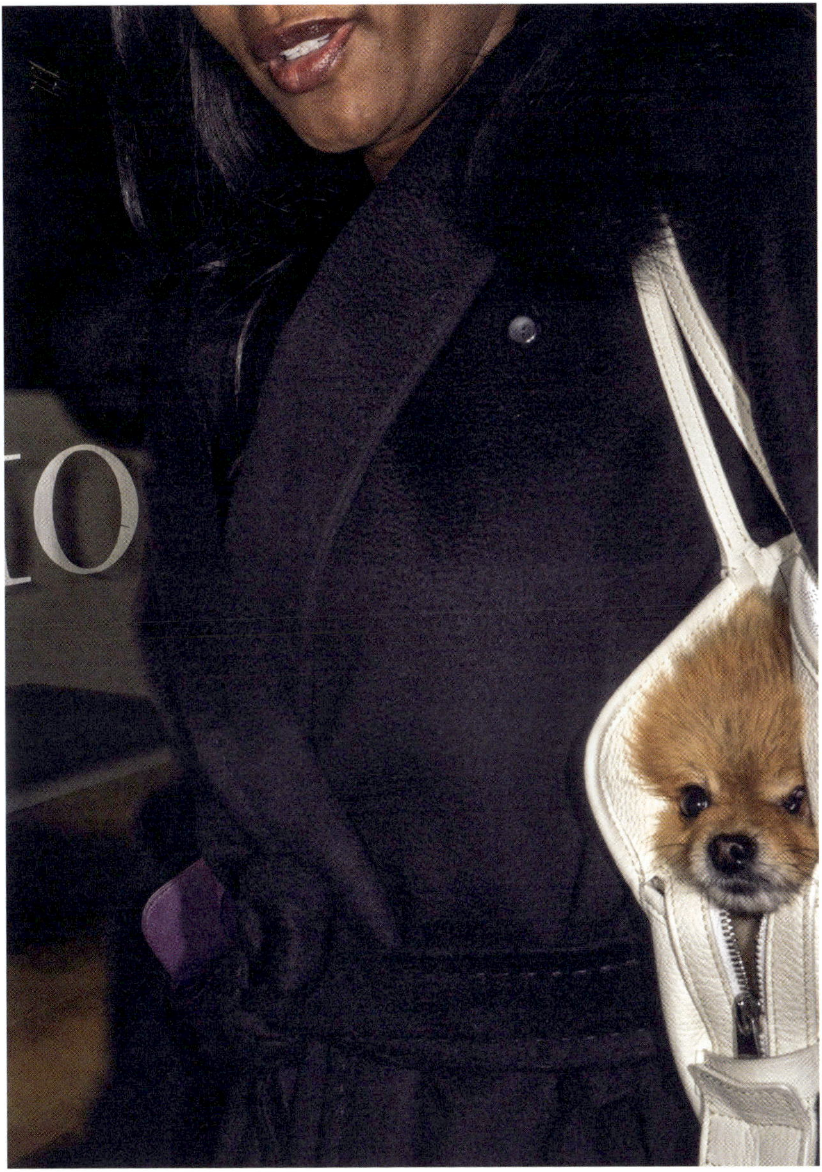

Well Heeled, 2017

HONG KONG GARAGE DOGS

Marcel Heijnen

Dutch photographer Marcel Heijnen stumbled into Garage Dogs shortly after photographing Hong Kong's shop and market cats. Only slightly worried about being pigeon-holed as a cat photographer, he swapped hunting for felines in the alleys and back streets of the city for tracking down dogs doing the 9-to-5 at garages.

'Like the cats,' he told his Hong Kong gallery, Blue Lotus, 'these dogs are functional animals, rather than pets. While the cats protect the goods in the stores against mice, the dogs guard the car workshops against thieves.'

These dogs are on duty. While some look the part and act as if they know a thing or two about a *ruff* workday, others seem too sweet or sensitive to live up to the job. The comical pug perched atop a motorbike? Let's just say he might have bitten off more than he can chew.

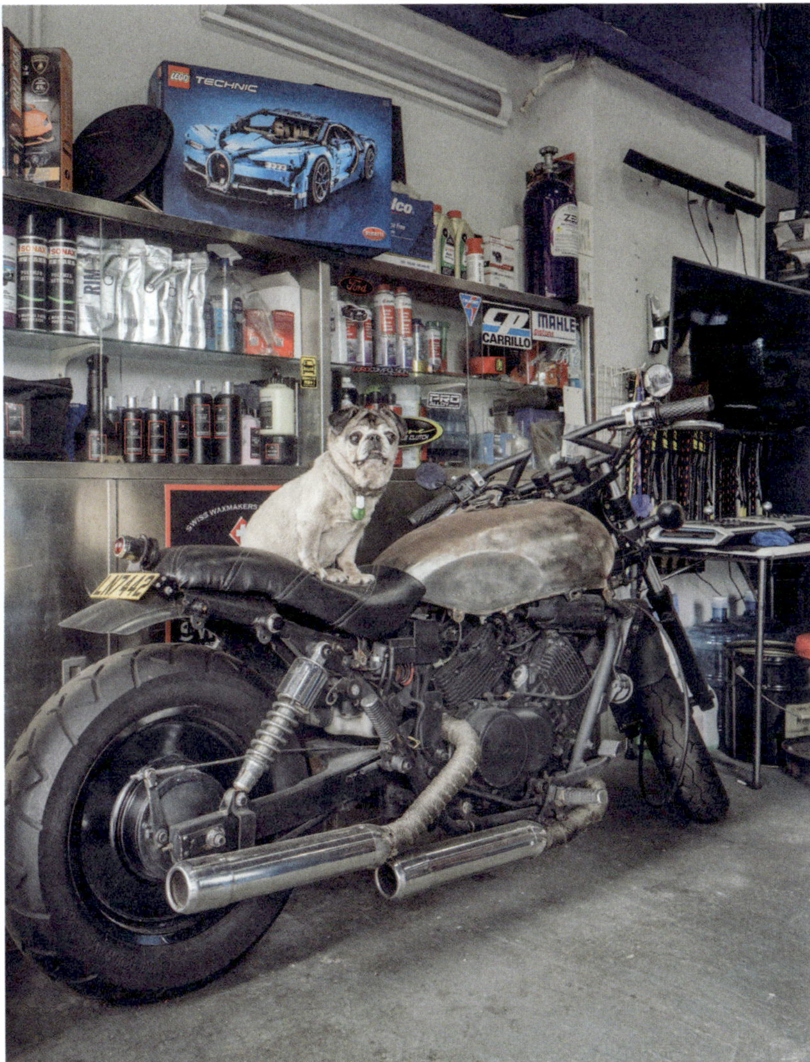

Pugatti, 2017

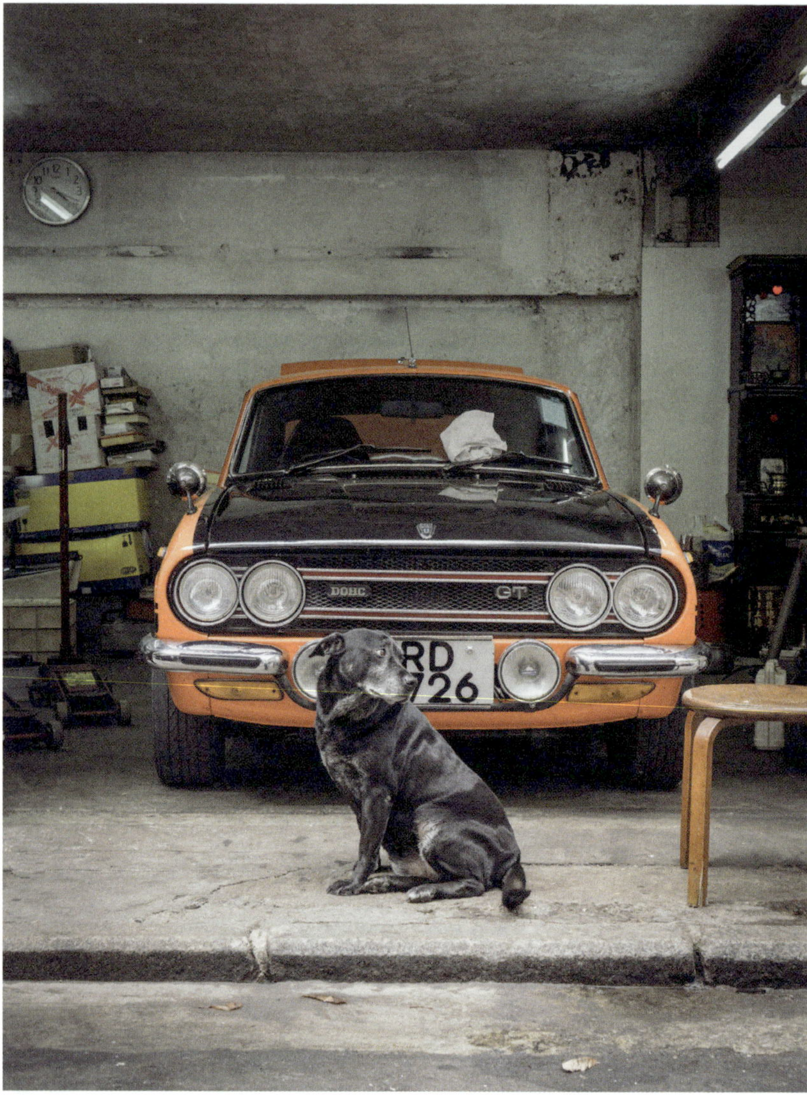

Above: *Black is the New Orange*, 2017
Opposite: *Puppy Love*, 2017

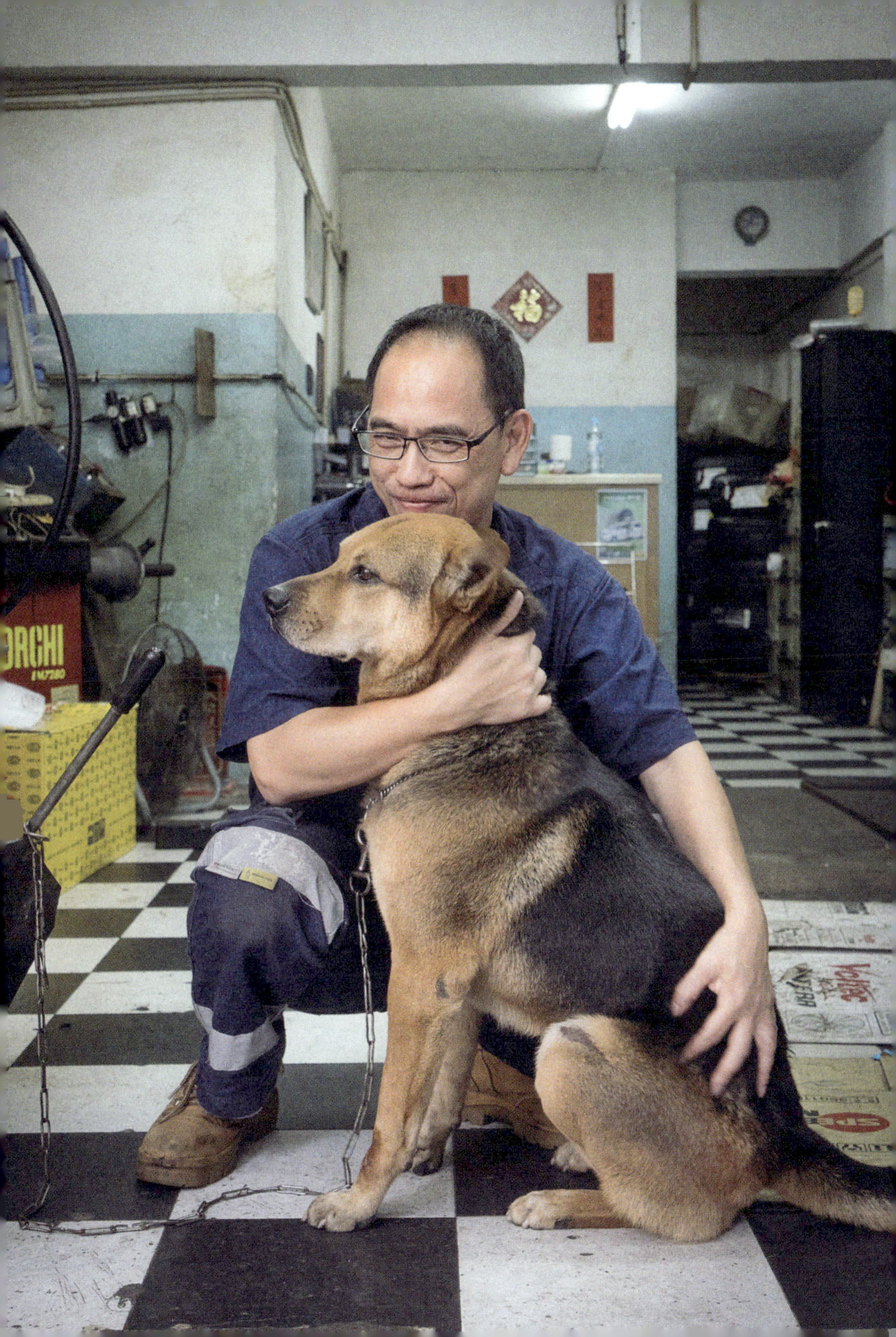

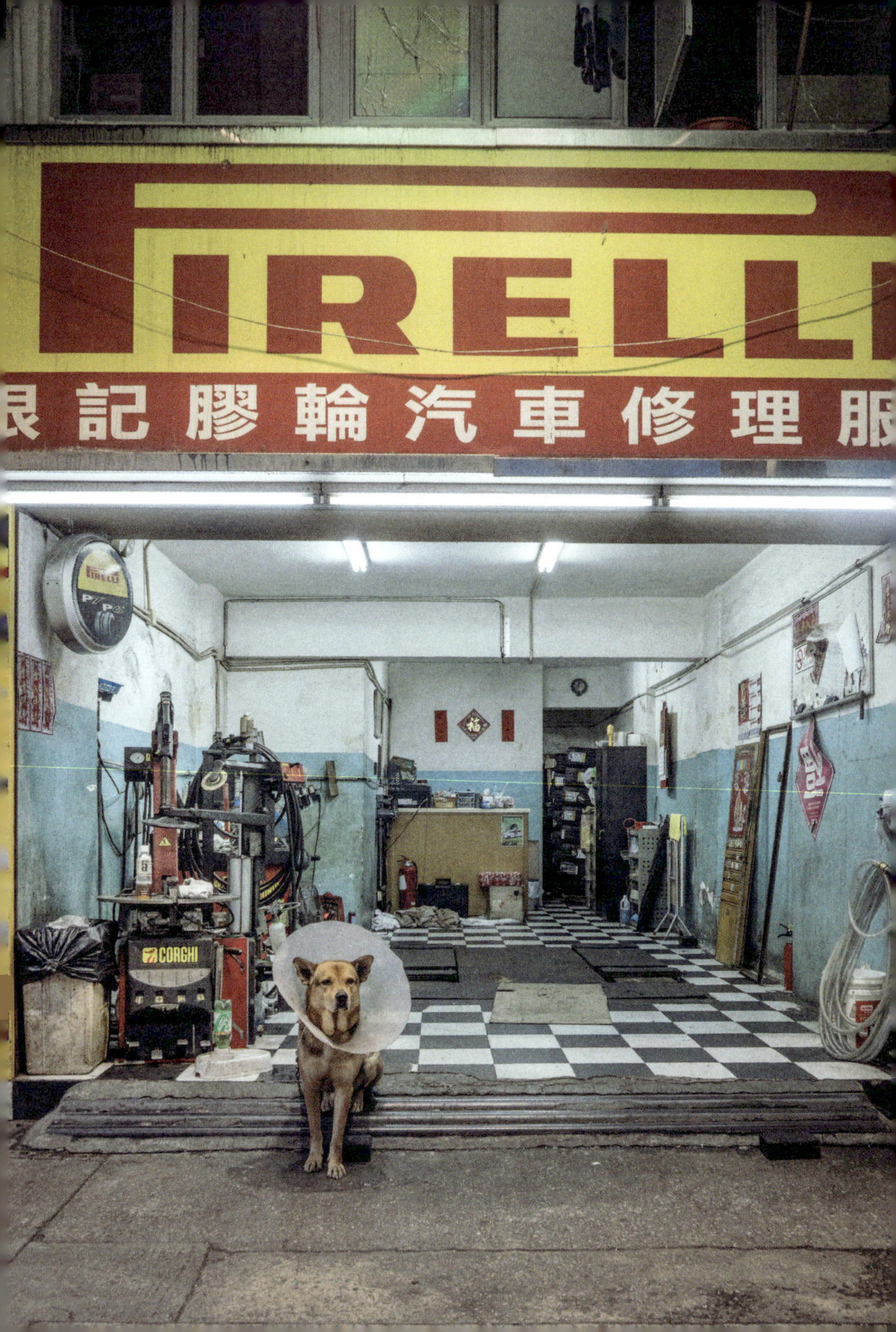
PIRELLI
記膠輪汽車修理
CORGHI

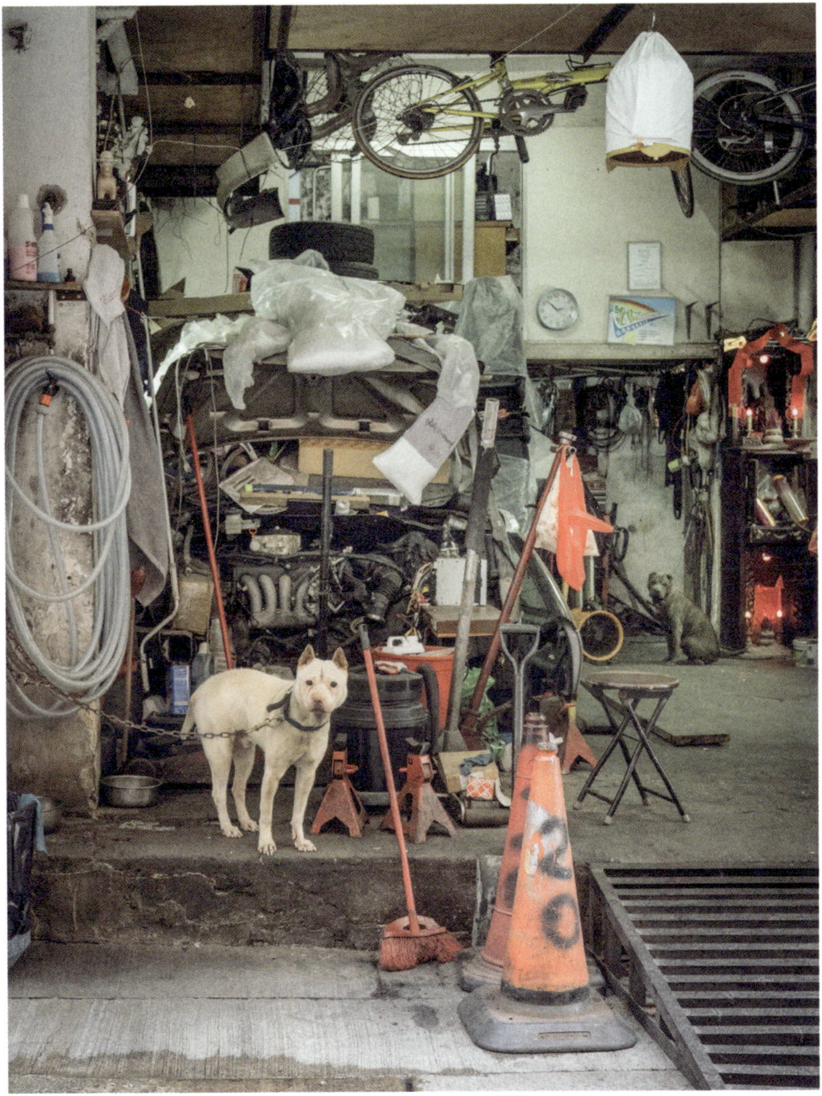

Above: *Chain Gang*, 2017
Opposite: *Cone of Shame*, 2017

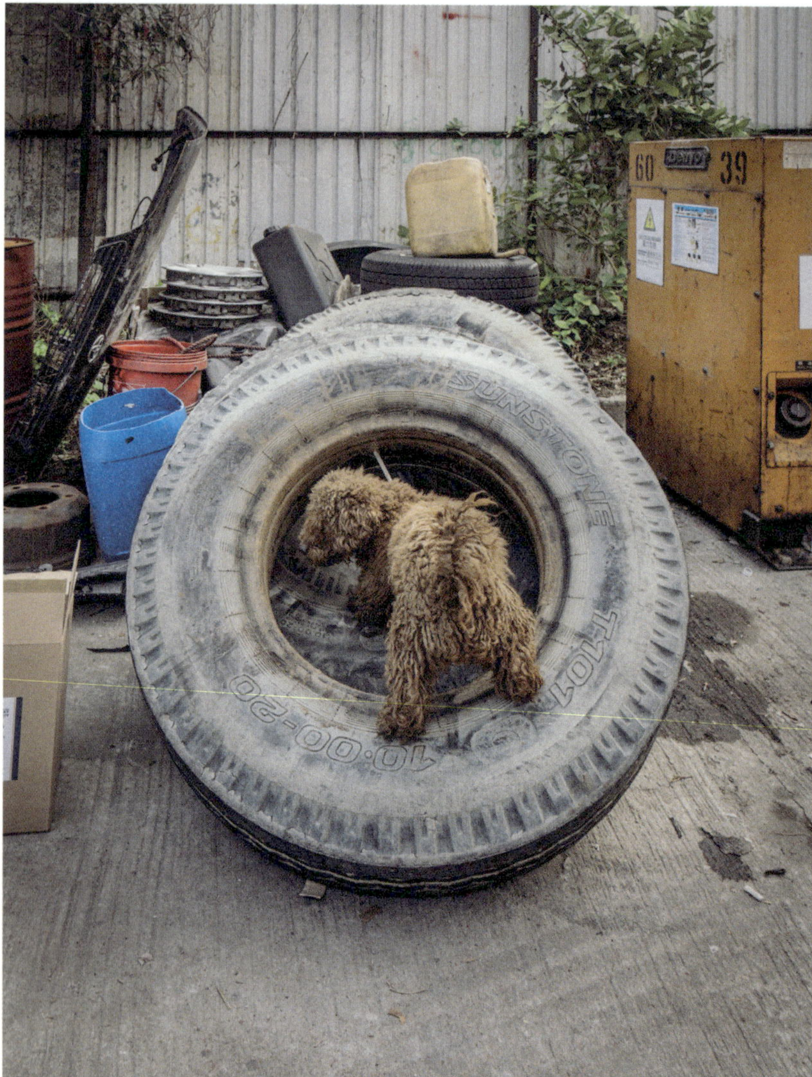

Above: *Kick the Tyres*, 2017
Opposite: *Puppy Yoda*, 2017

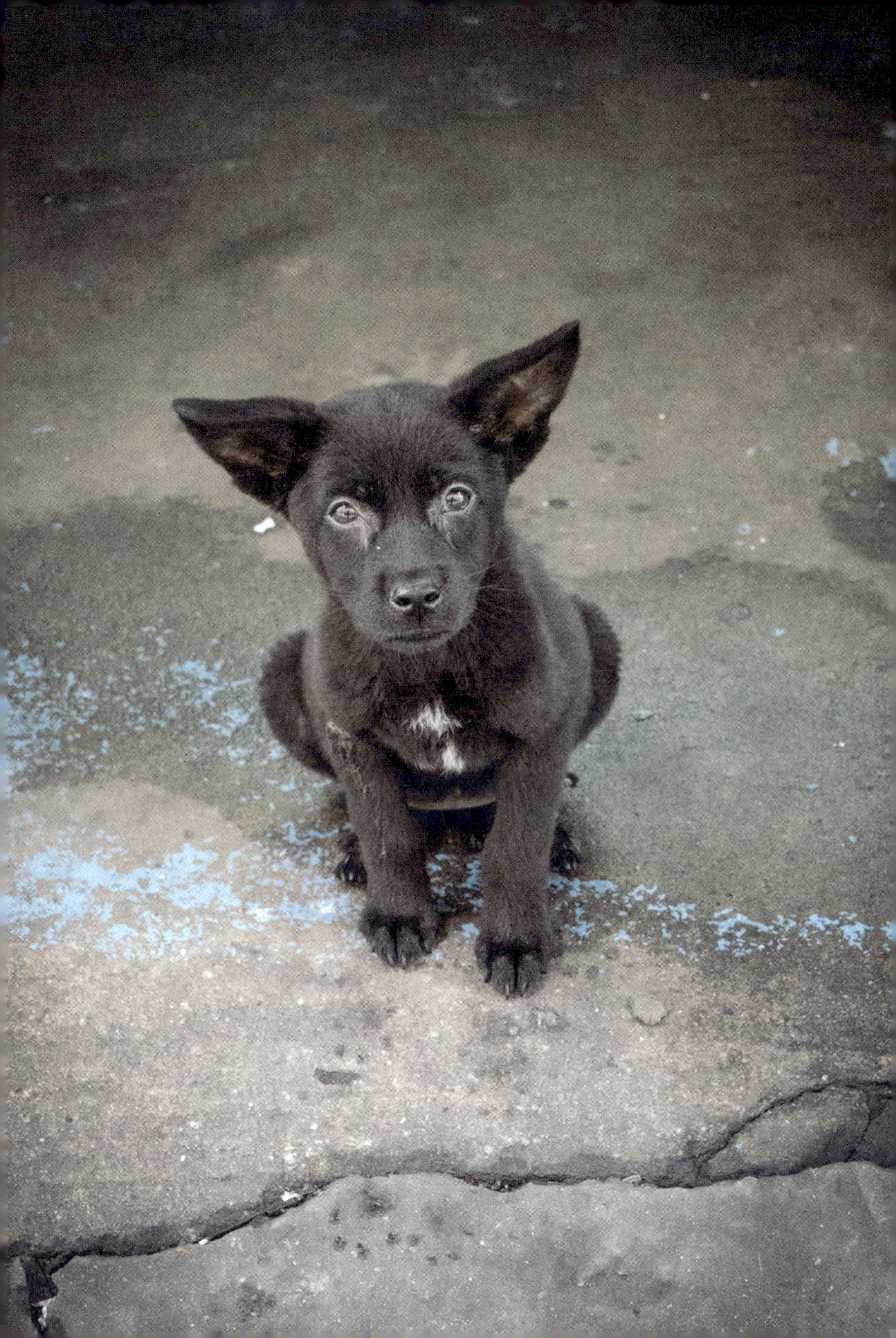

SHELTER DOGS
Traer Scott

As a volunteer at a local shelter in Rhode Island, Traer Scott watched dozens of dogs pass through the doors. Many eventually found new homes; others, more tragically, did not and were euthanised. Each arrived with a story of its own: abandonment, financial hardship, owners moving into care homes, uncooperative landlords or simply becoming lost.

As her sense of responsibility for the dogs in her care deepened, Scott decided to put her camera to good use. While photographing them for kennel records and adoption websites, she created a series of portraits so affecting that they make you want to rush to the nearest shelter and bring every last unlucky pup home.

'I wanted to strip away every environmental element and create dignified, individual portraits that presented each dog's unique personality,' Scott writes in her 2006 book *Shelter Dogs*. 'When people view these images, they are often locking eyes with a captivating being who has been cast aside, abused or left behind.' Her portraits knowingly tug at the heartstrings: she hopes to raise awareness of their plight and inspire action, helping more shelter dogs find their forever homes.

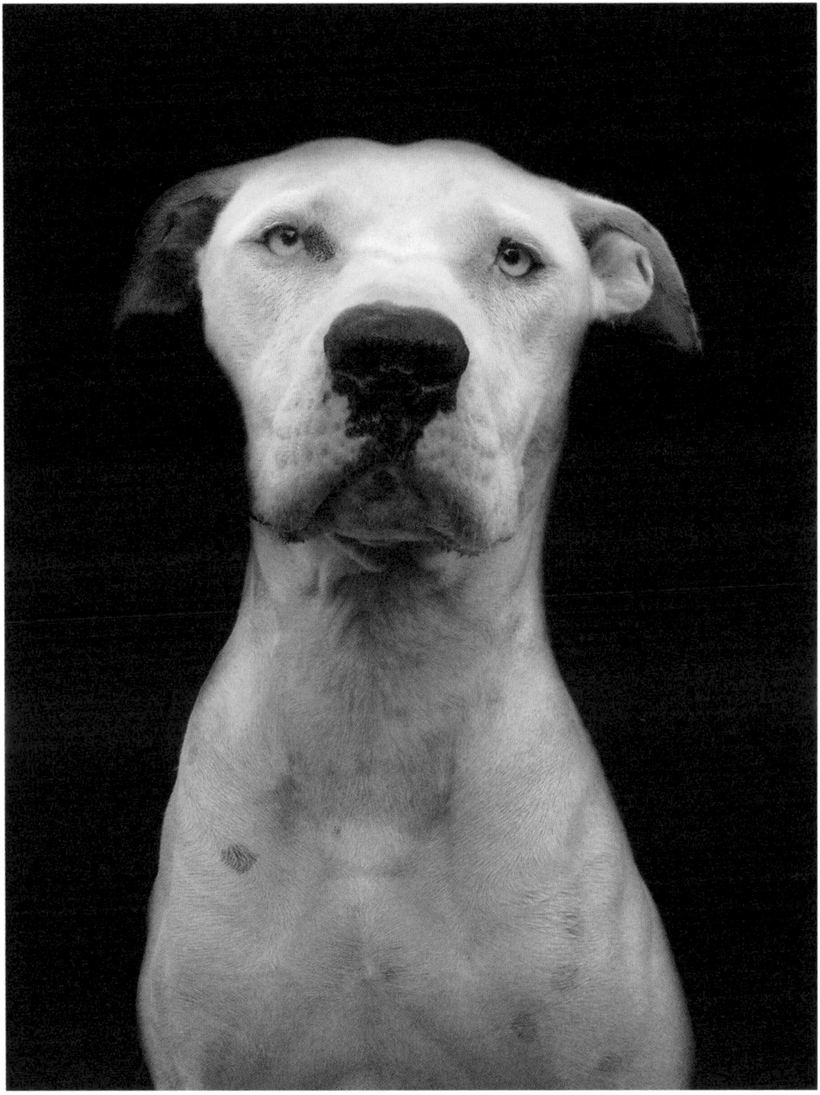

Bailee, Euthanised, 2006

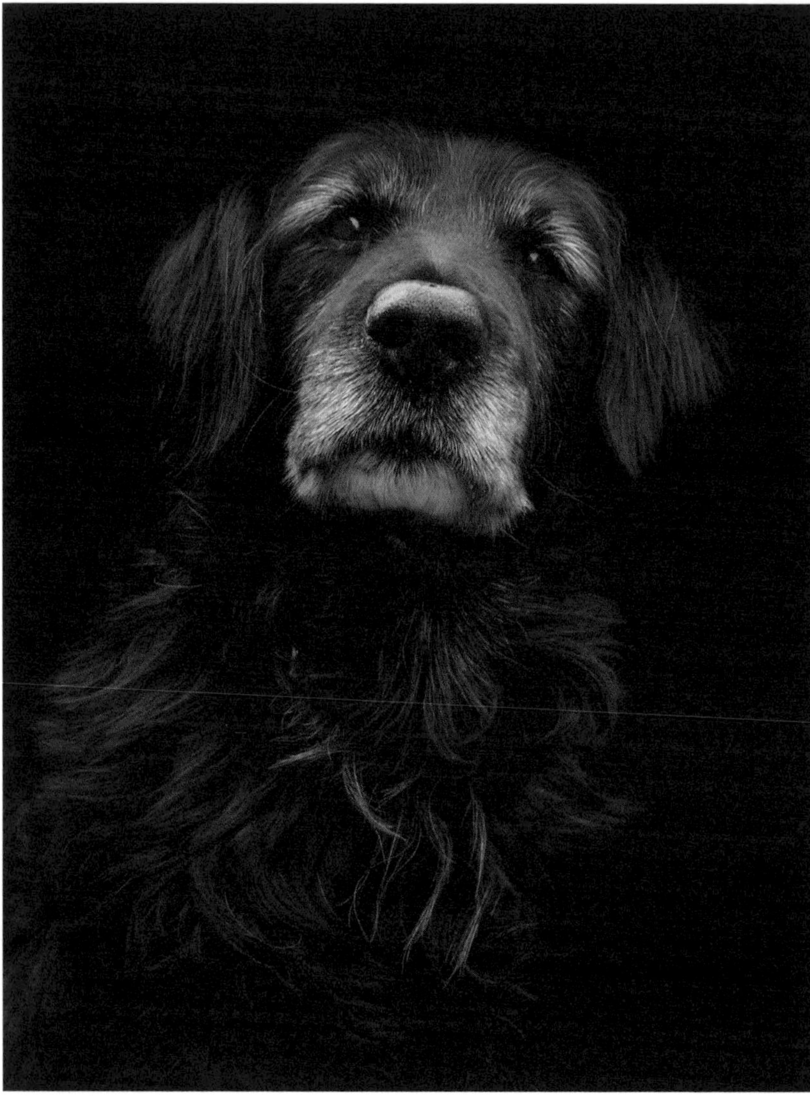

Above: *Dumbledore, Adopted*, 2006
Opposite: *Petey, Adopted*, 2006

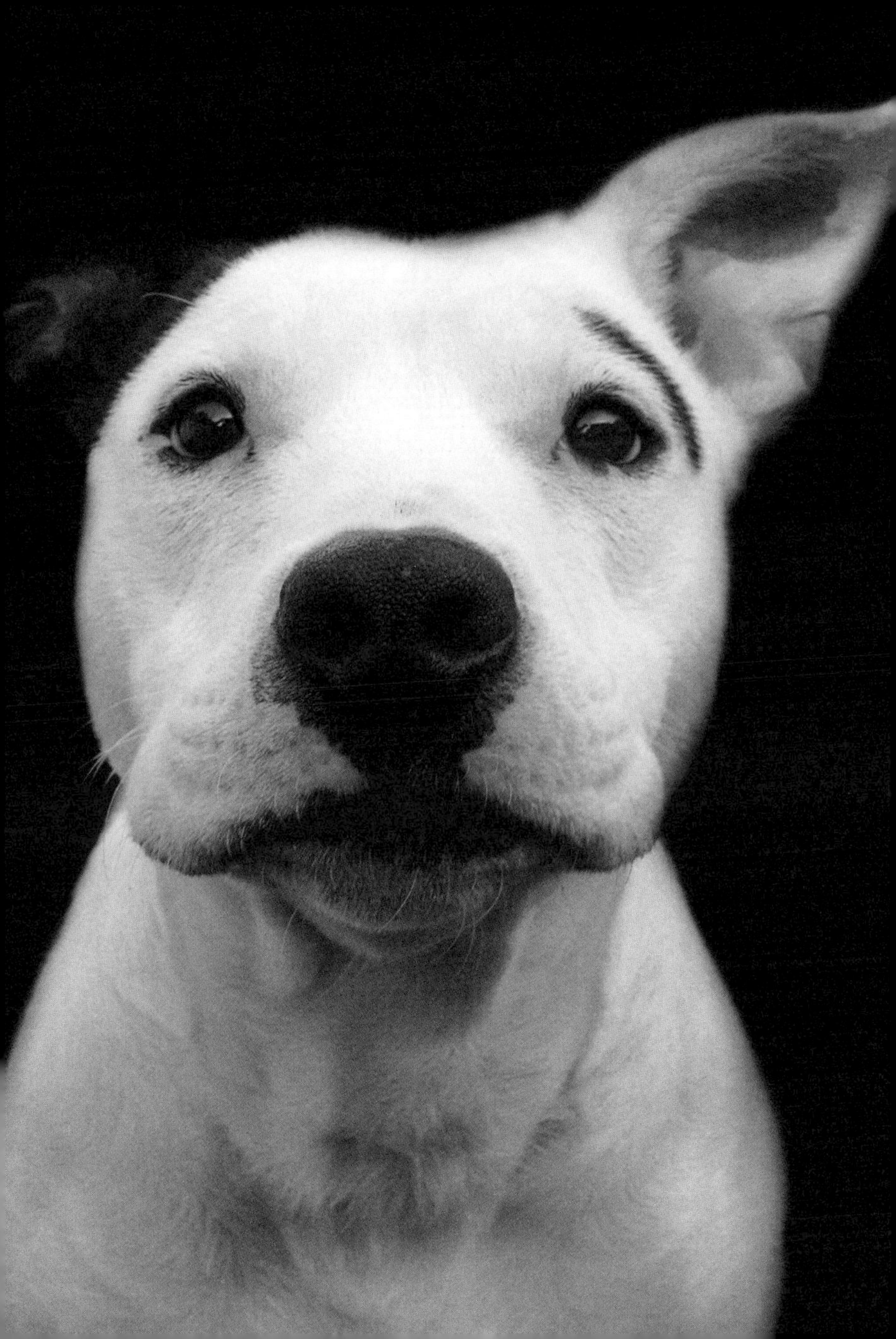

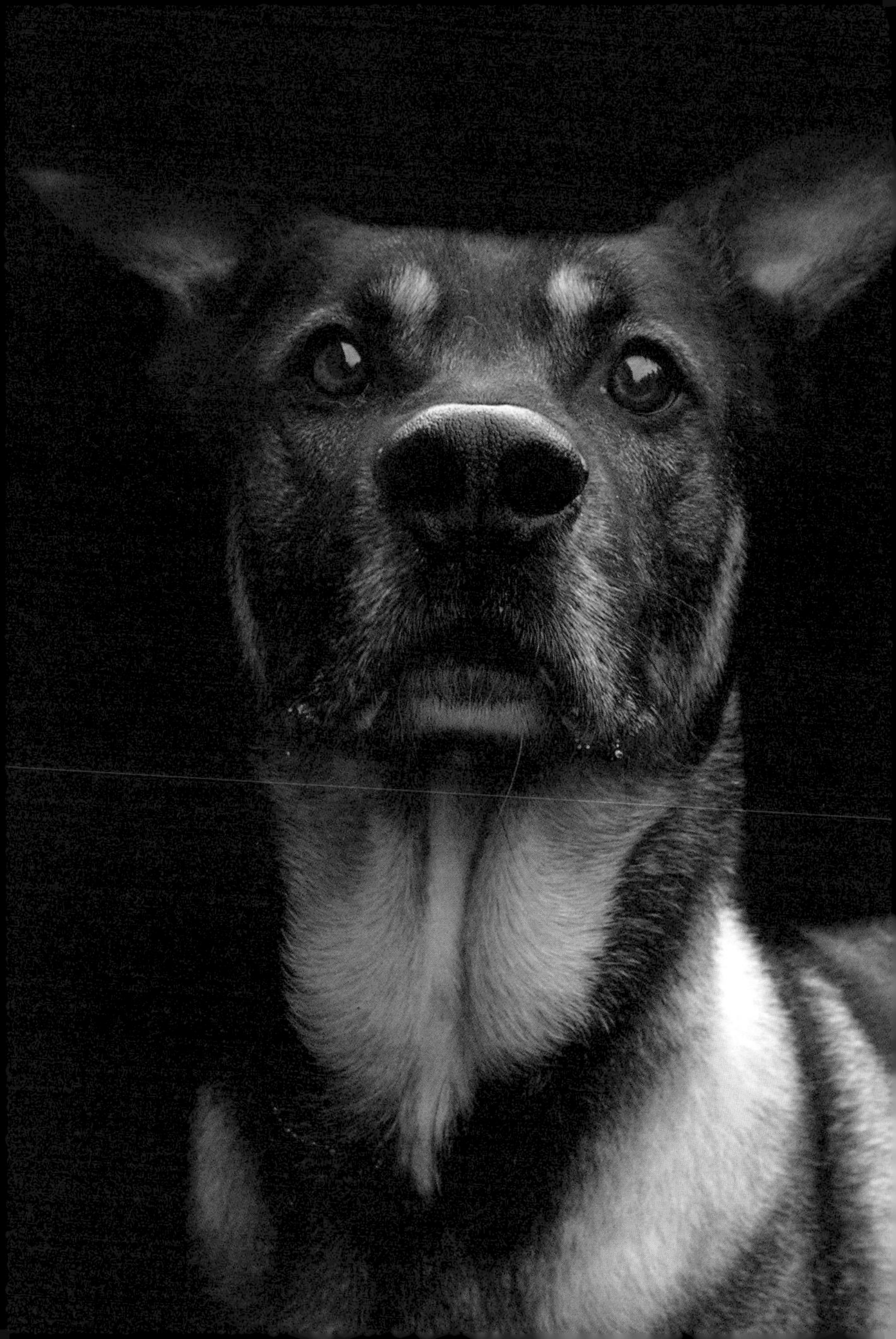

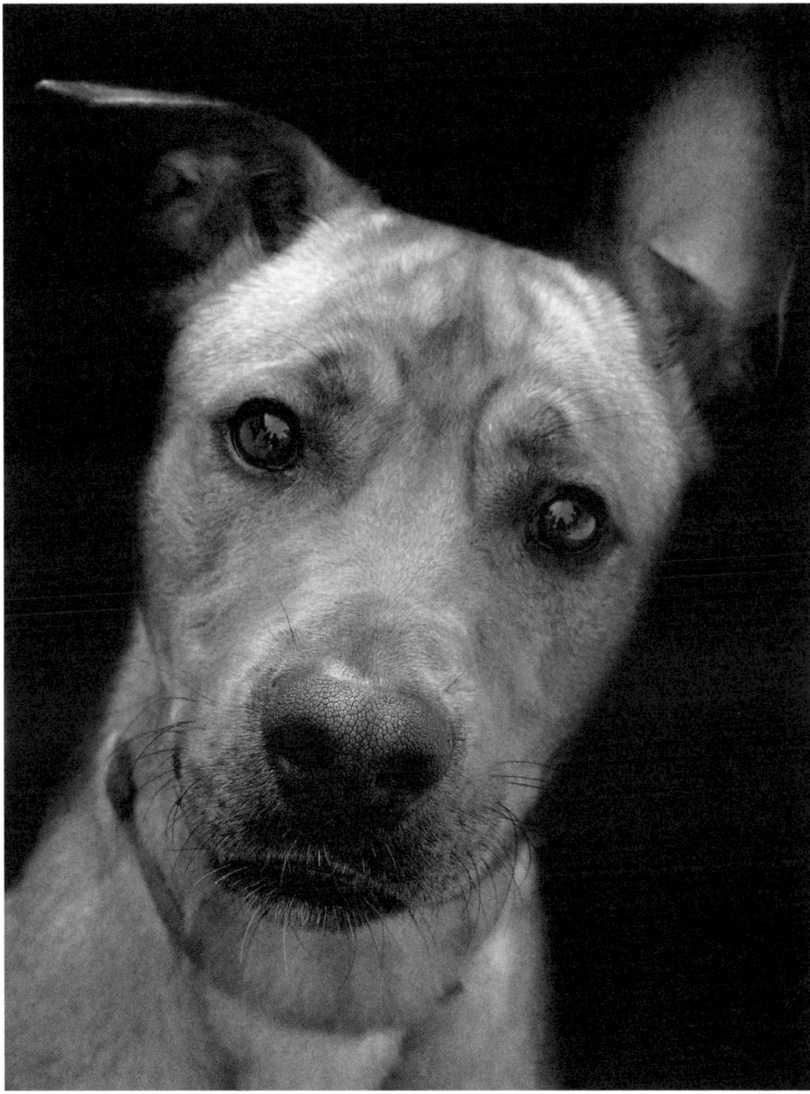

Above: *Riley, Euthanised*, 2006
Opposite: *Joshua, Adopted*, 2006

WHERE HUNTING DOGS REST

Martin Usborne

In photographs that are as beautiful as they are devastating, Martin Usborne portrays hunting dogs rescued from abandonment. Each year in Spain, tens – if not hundreds – of thousands are discarded when the hunting season ends, left behind or killed in gruesome ways once they are considered too old, slow or useless.

The most common breeds, Galgos and Podencos, were once deemed noble hounds, worthy of respect and protection. Usborne documents the tragic decline in their circumstances in photographs inspired by the quietly intense paintings of Spanish aristocracy by the 17th-century artist Velázquez.

Usborne photographed many of the dogs in shelters, pairing moving portraits with the landscapes of their abandonment – fields, rivers, roadsides, car parks and urban fringes. Some stand with tails tucked low; others shrink back or avert their gaze. Yet even in their vulnerability, the dogs retain a striking elegance. These resilient animals deserve, at the very least, a safe and comfortable place to lay their heads.

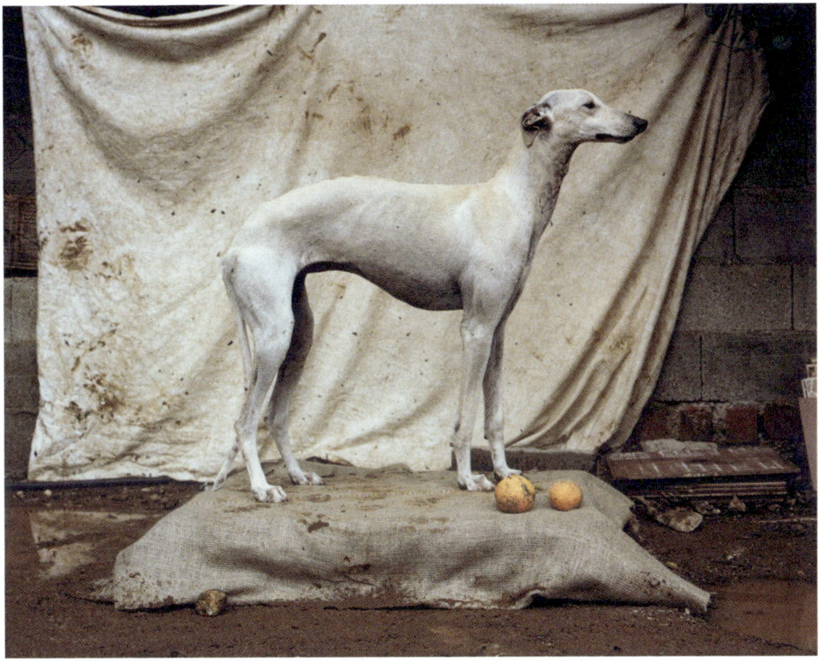

Galga, 2014

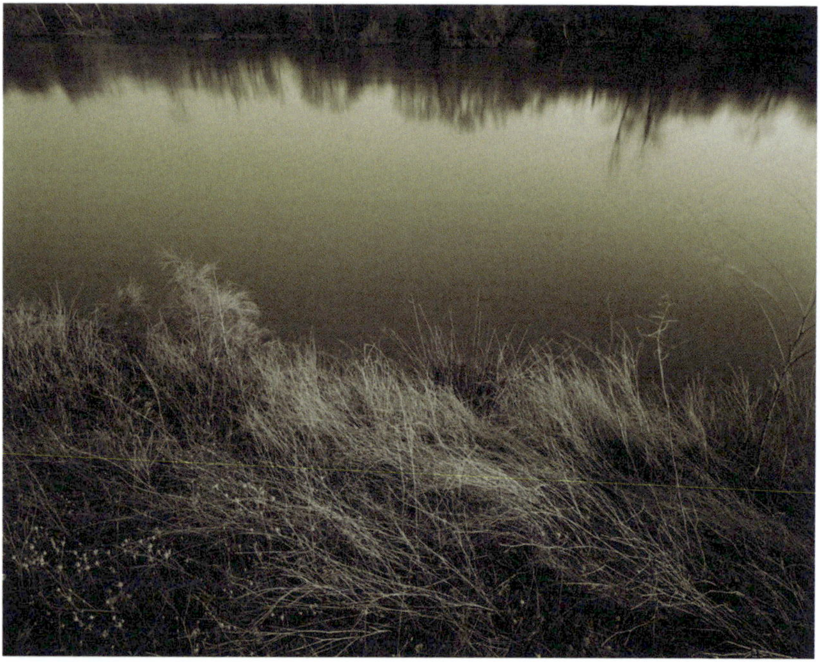

River, 2014

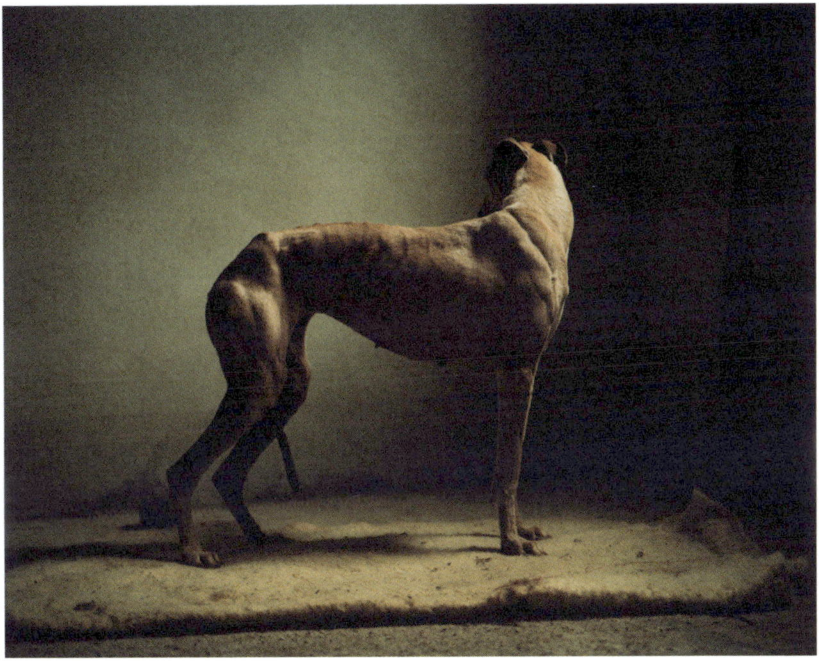

Above: *Galgo*, 2014
Overleaf: *Galga*, 2014

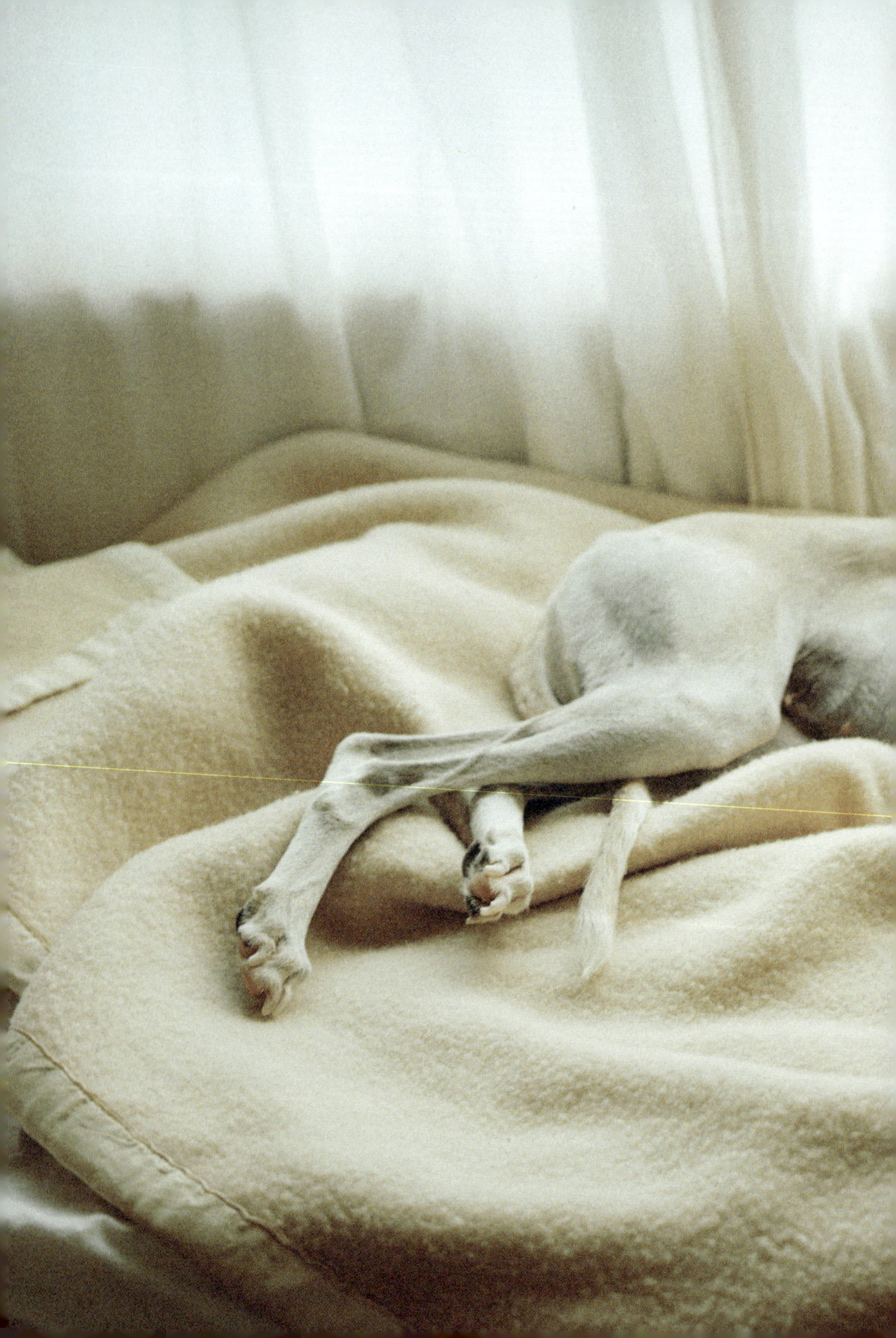

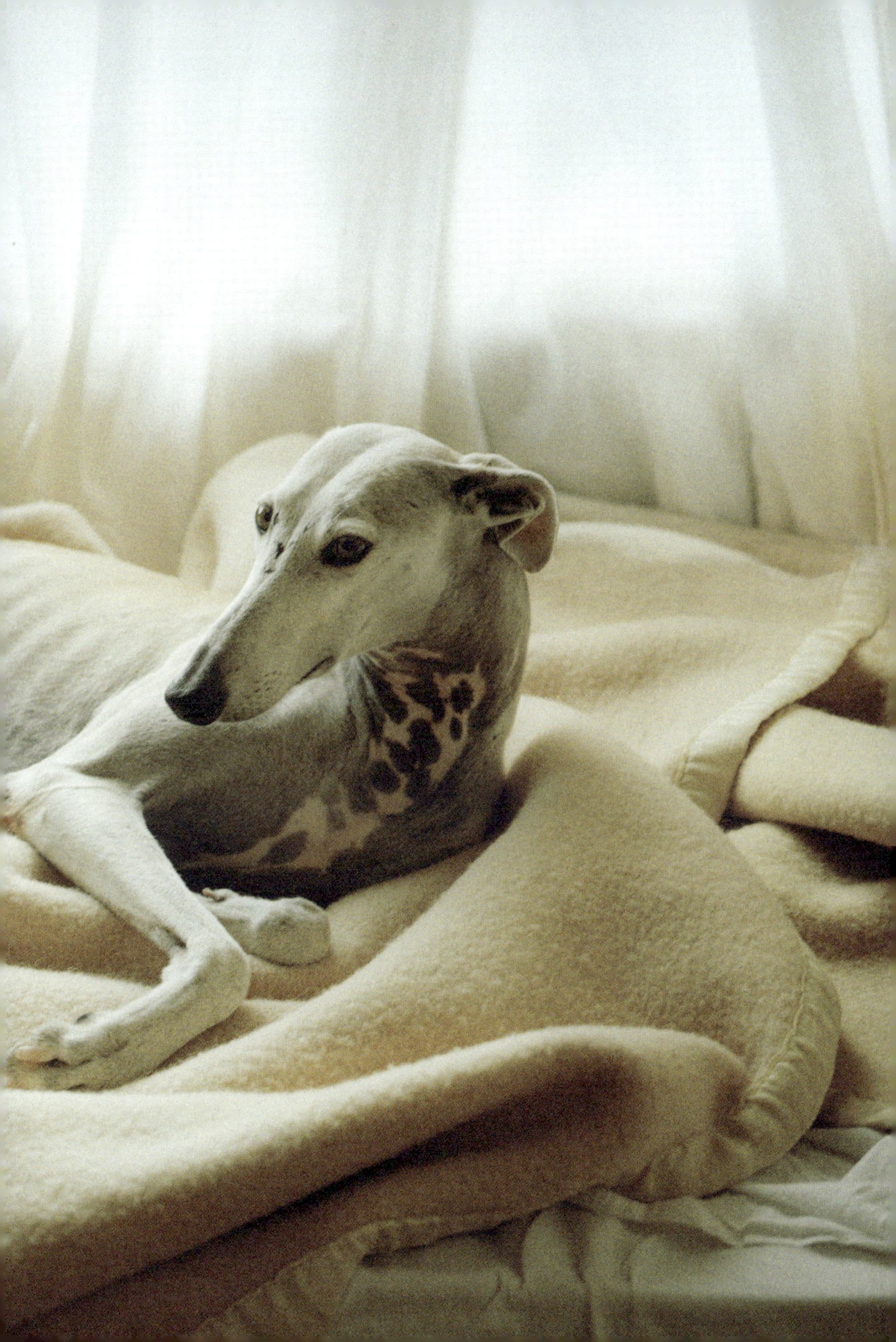

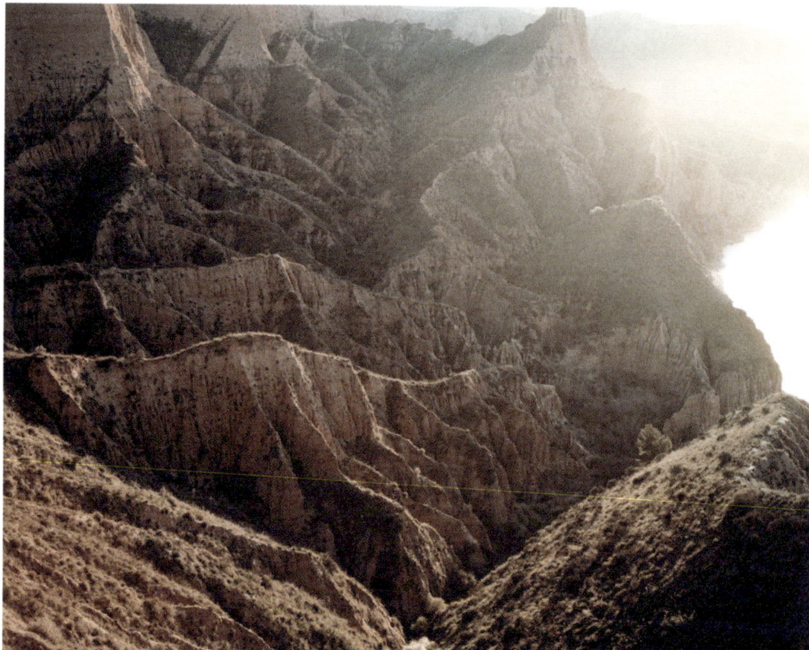

Ravine, 2014

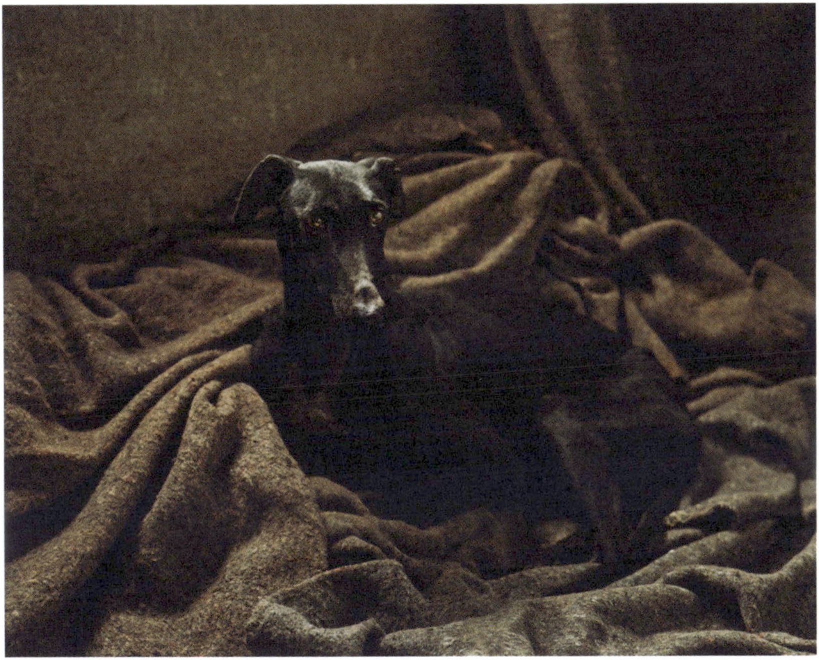

Galgo, 2014

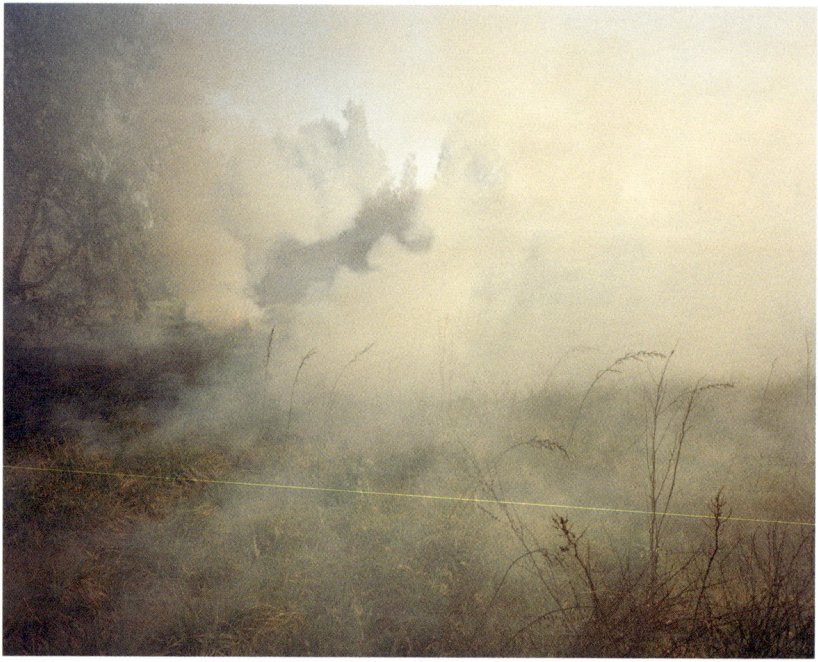

Fire, 2014

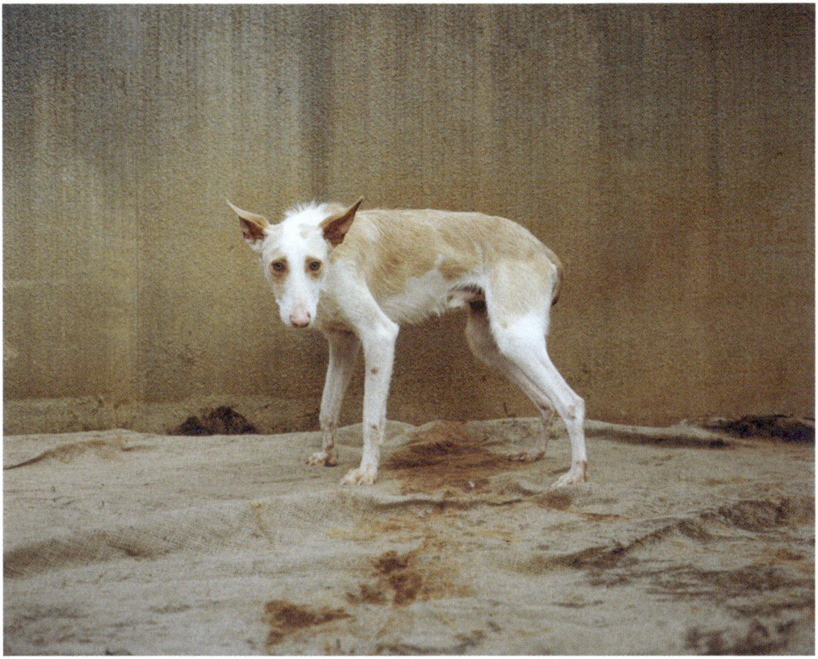

Podenco, 2014

DOGS AT HOME

Winnie Au

When people say, 'it's a dog's life', it used to mean a miserable or hard existence. These days? Not so much. The modern dog is a creature of comfort, whose biggest concern is finding the right spot for a snooze.

Winnie Au, an editorial and commercial photographer based in New York City, photographs dogs at home – portraying them as she would a human sitter. Growing up in rural Illinois, she was used to pets living outside, but today, dogs are fully fledged family members. 'They sleep in our beds, appear in family portraits, and even influence where and how we travel,' she says. 'My images capture this cultural shift.'

While some portraits are shot on commission for clients such as magazines and dog accessories brands, others form part of an ongoing personal project. In each image, Au applies the conventions of formal portraiture, giving her subjects the same care and attention she would afford any person. The dogs effortlessly rise to the occasion, every inch the family members they've become.

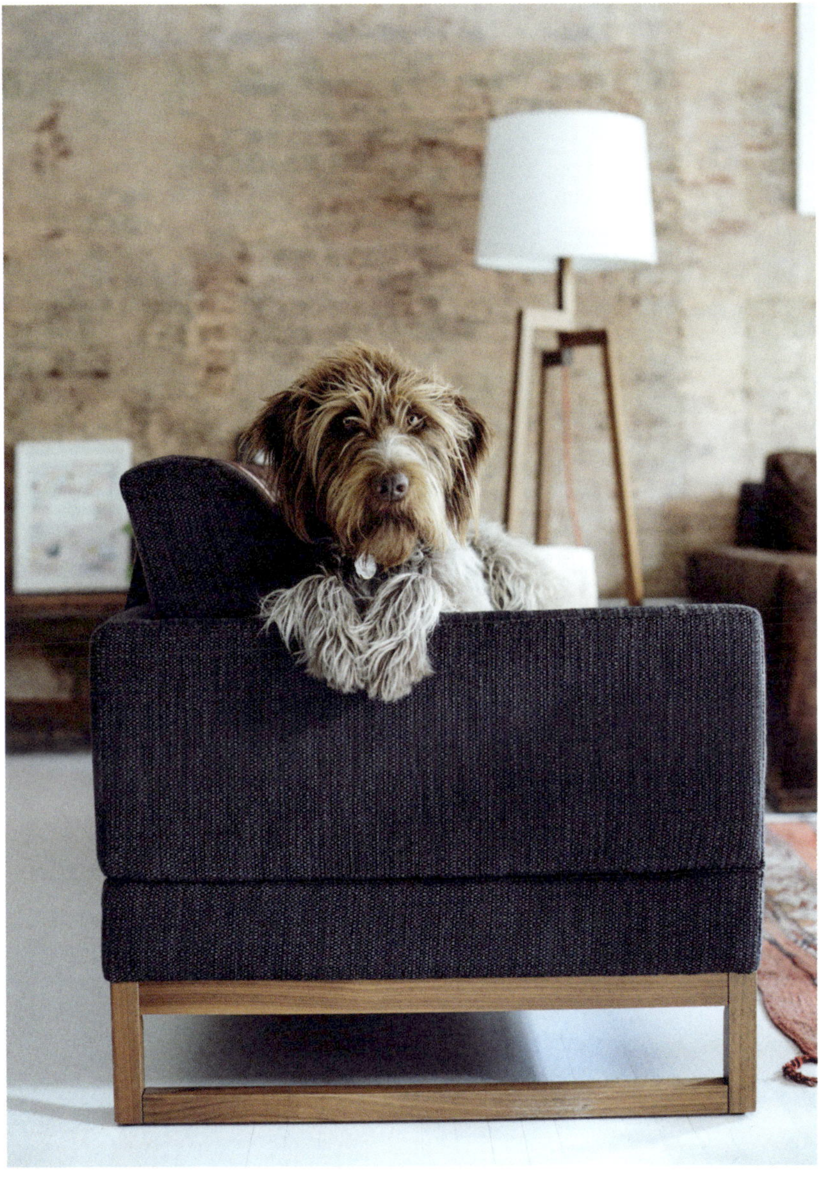

Darryl, 2016

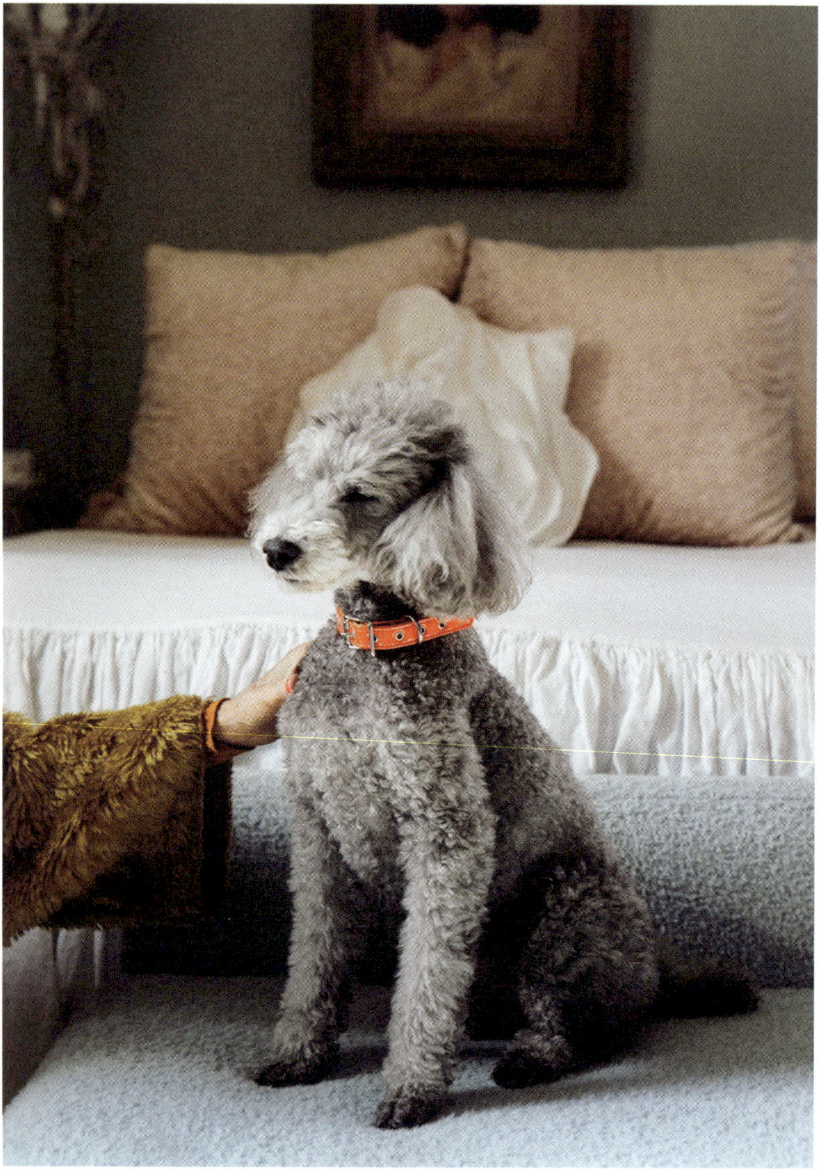

Winks, 2018

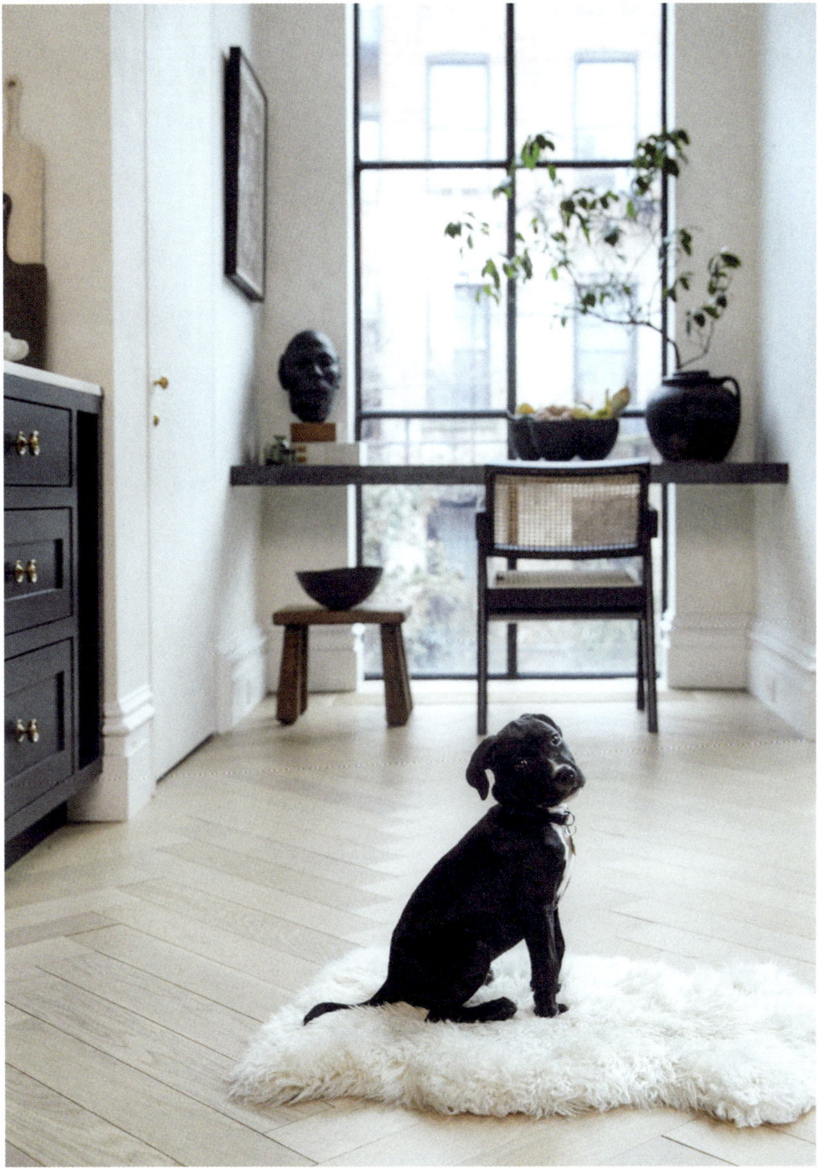

Tuco, 2019

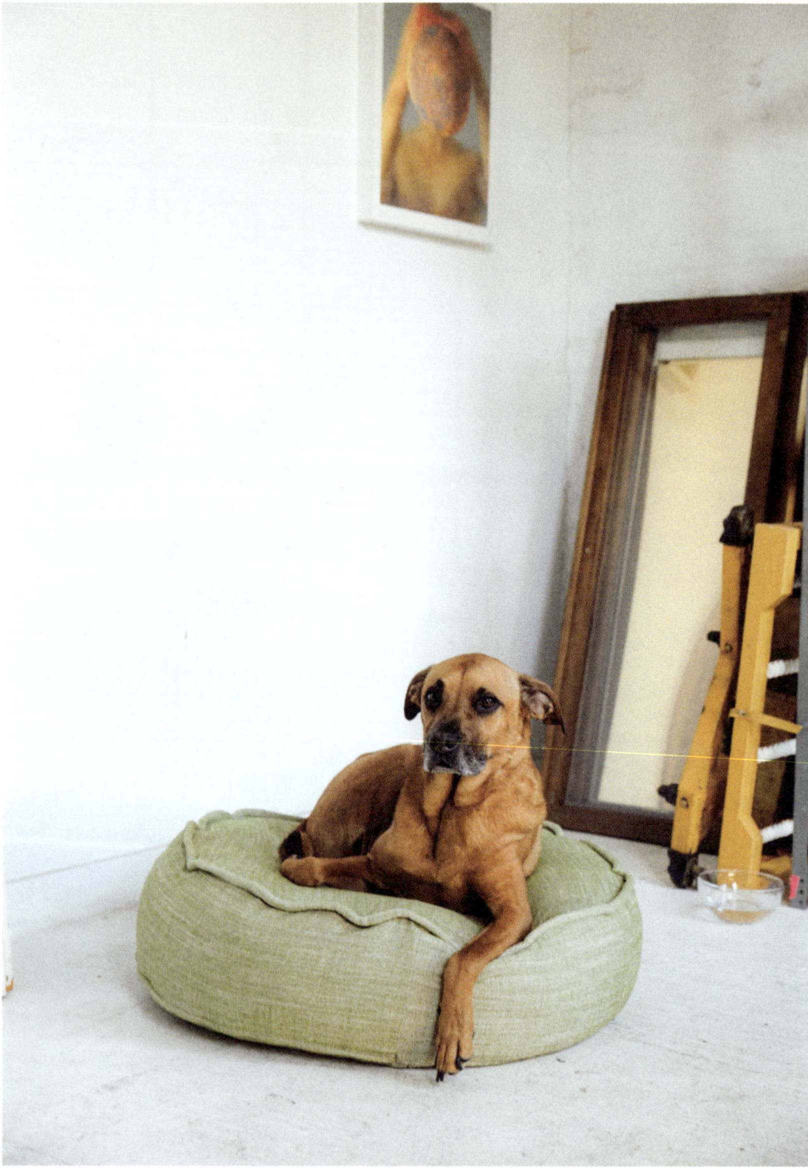

Arlen, 2019

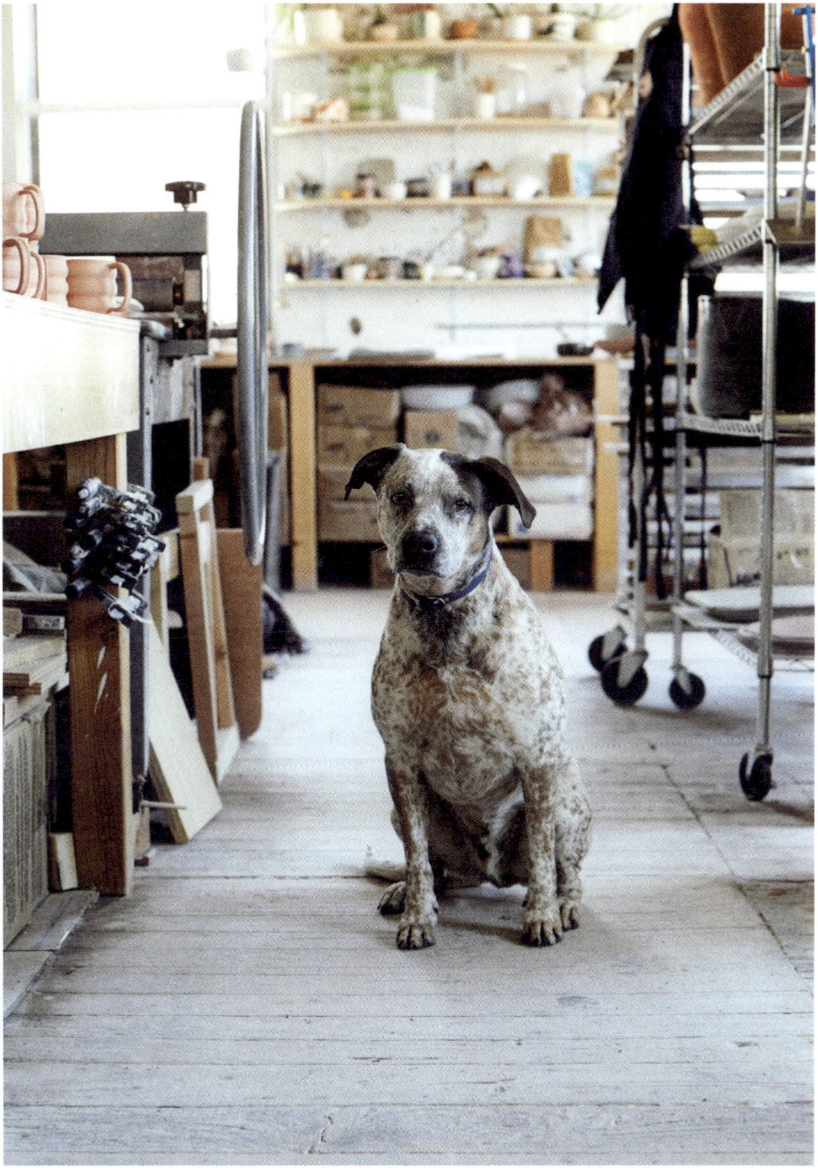

Billy, 2017

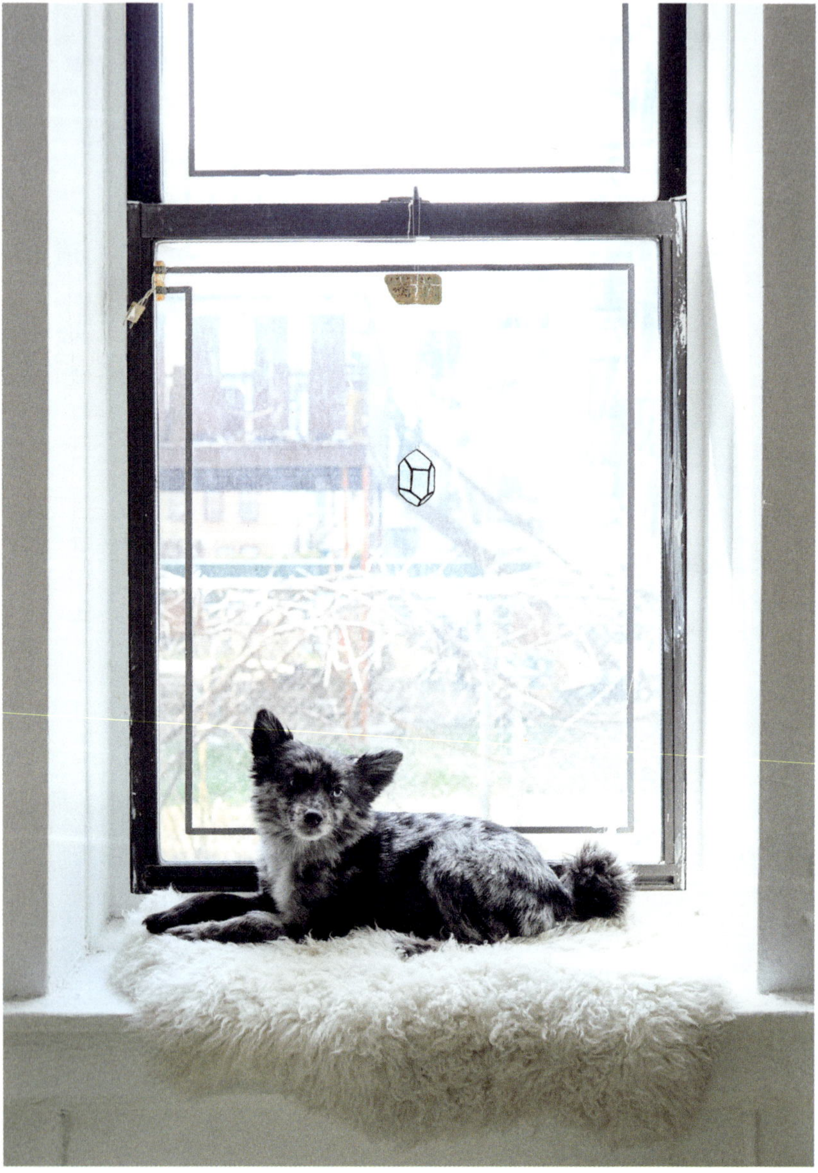

Powwow, 2015

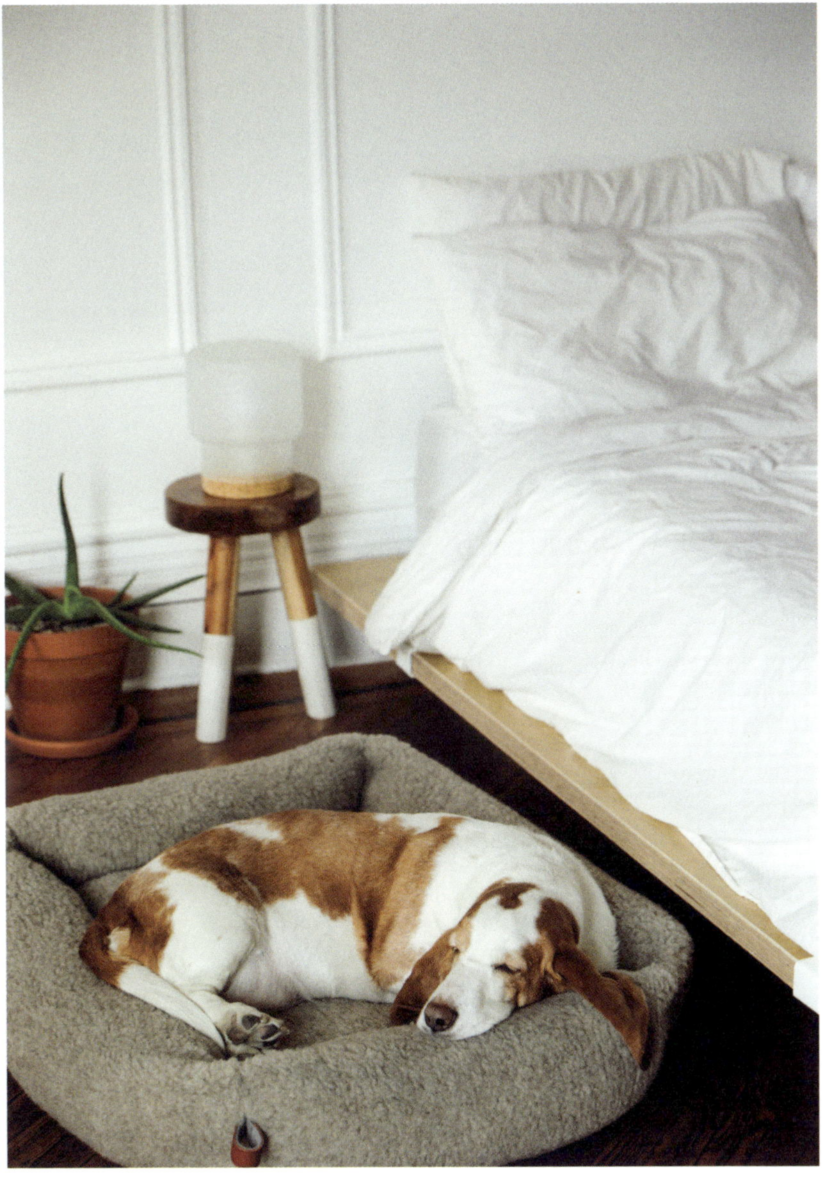

Clementine, 2019

THE LEVITATORS
Ruth van Beek

Artist Ruth van Beek hasn't had to set a single foot on the pavement or in the park to create these almost abstract canine figures. For years, she has collected photographs of dogs from newspaper clippings, amateur snapshots, family albums, old books and the internet, building an ever-growing archive in which she sees the history of the domestic dog reflected.

From this archive, van Beek crafts unique artworks that bring these canines back to life. By cutting, folding and reconfiguring the images, she transforms familiar animals into otherworldly creatures that seem to hover or float above the ground. Some are little more than flying fluff balls on a leash – barely recognisable as dogs at all.

Yet, in these small, precious collages, the dogs of yesteryear are reborn, animated with a new kind of spirit – playful, mysterious and a species entirely their own. If you came across one of these levitators in the wild, you'd probably blink twice.

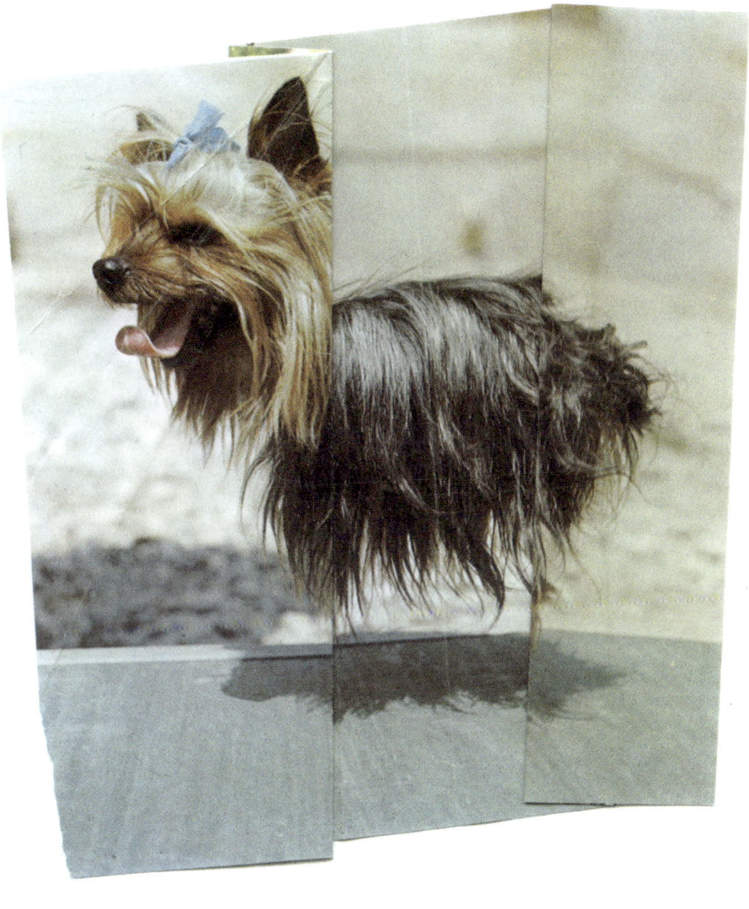

Untitled (The Levitators nr 35), 2013

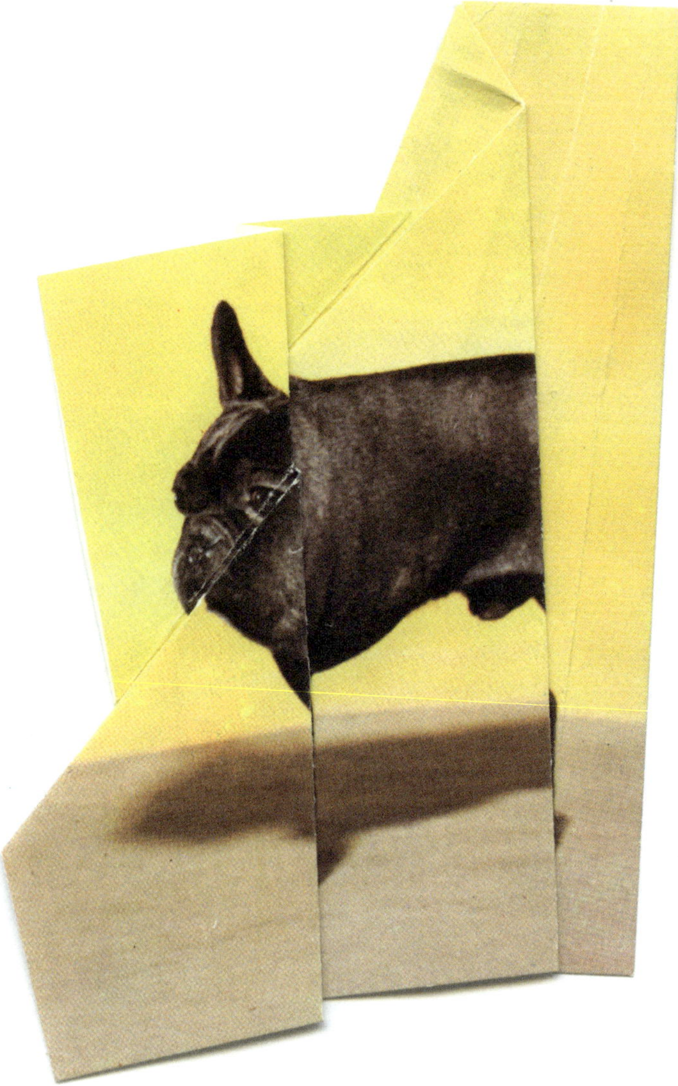

Untitled (The Levitators nr 19), 2013

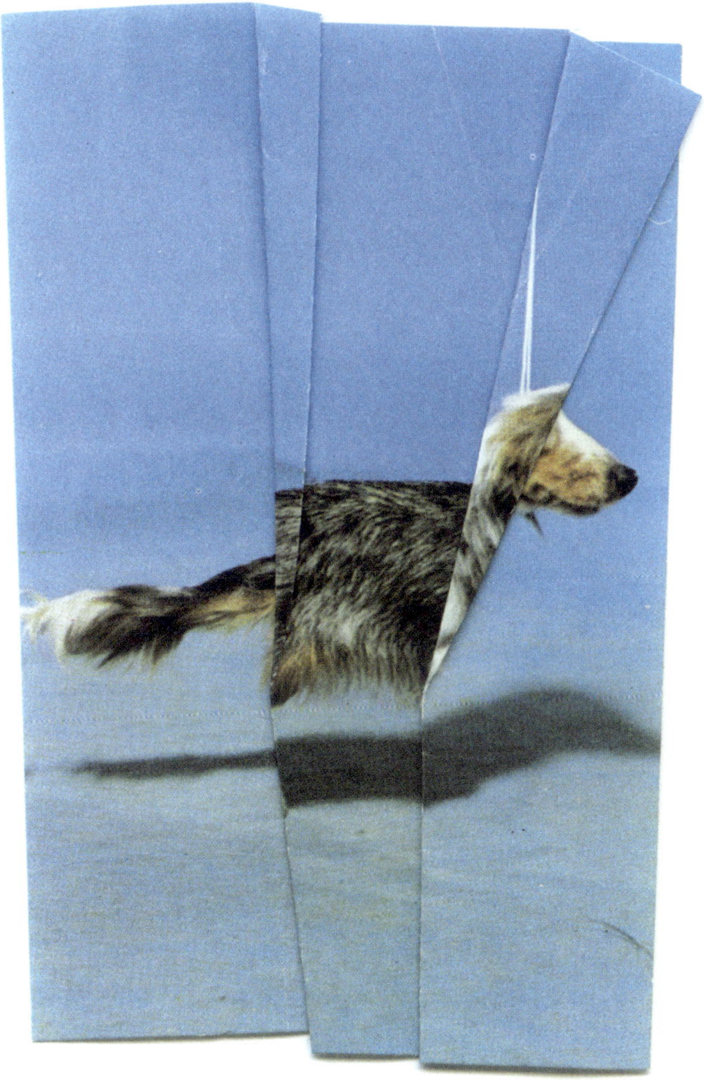

Untitled (The Levitators nr 20), 2013

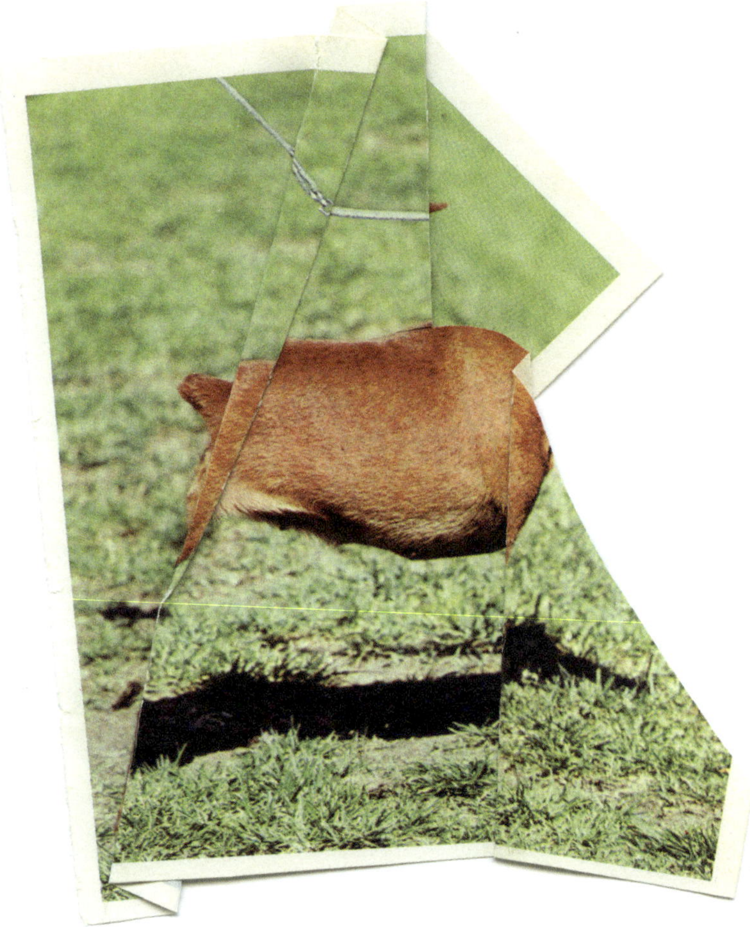

Untitled (The Levitators nr 27), 2013

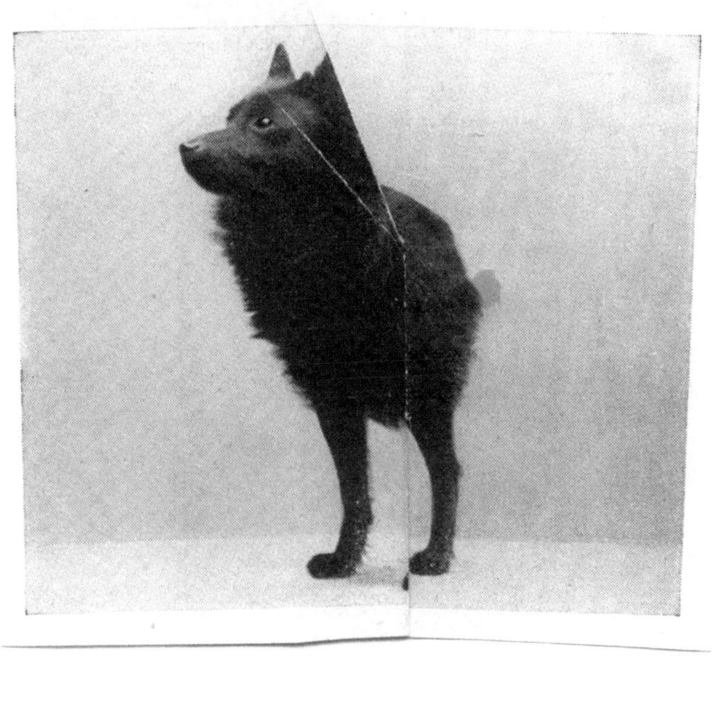

Untitled (The Levitators nr 29), 2013

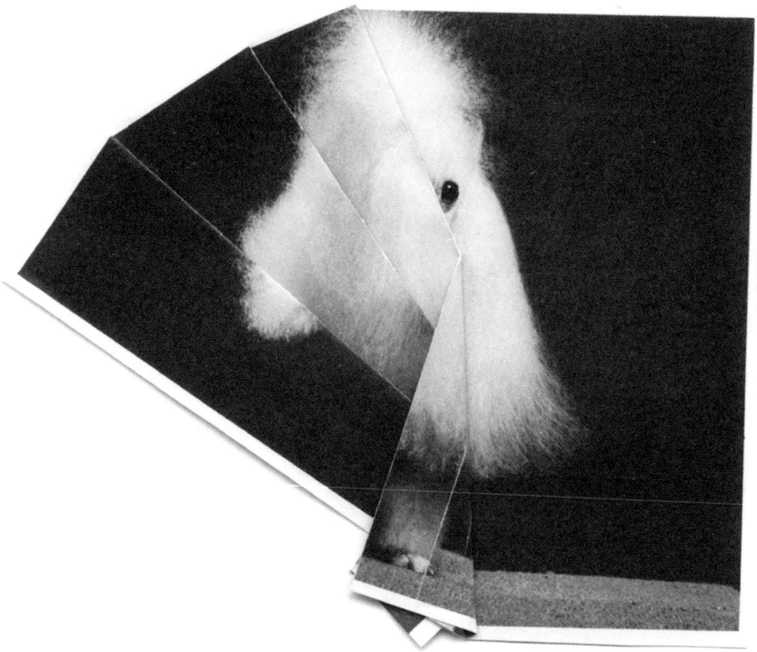

Untitled (The Levitators nr 14), 2013

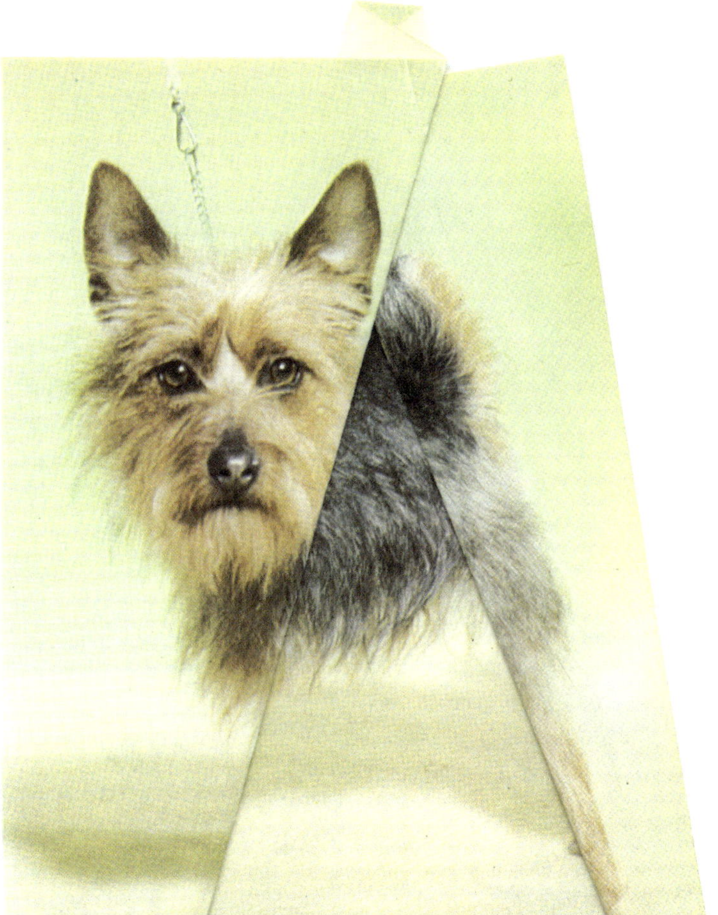

Untitled (The Levitators nr 7), 2013

DO YOU LOOK LIKE YOUR DOG?

Gerrard Gethings

We happily call our dogs 'fur babies' and treat them like offspring. Our four-legged companions are very much part of the family. They have evolved to mimic our expressions and mirror our traits, sometimes even adopting our physical features. No wonder the saying goes: 'like master, like dog'. But does the leash run both ways?

In his project, *Do You Look Like Your Dog?*, Gerrard Gethings portrayed 25 human–dog duos with striking similarities in hairstyle, facial features or expression. The idea of pairing people and pets for their likeness was inspired by his own dog Baxter, a Border Terrier, whom he's said to resemble.

Gethings cast his animal models first, then matched them with human lookalikes, finding them through open calls on social media or on the street. The series was made into a memory card game, inviting players to pair pups with their human doppelgängers. Bonus points for matching the only two real-life dog–owner pairs in the pack.

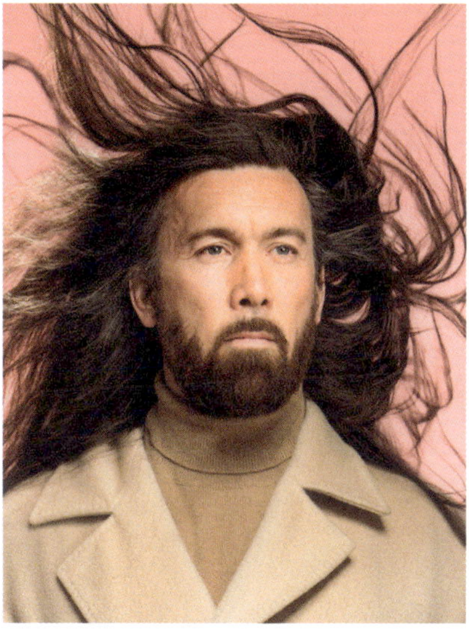

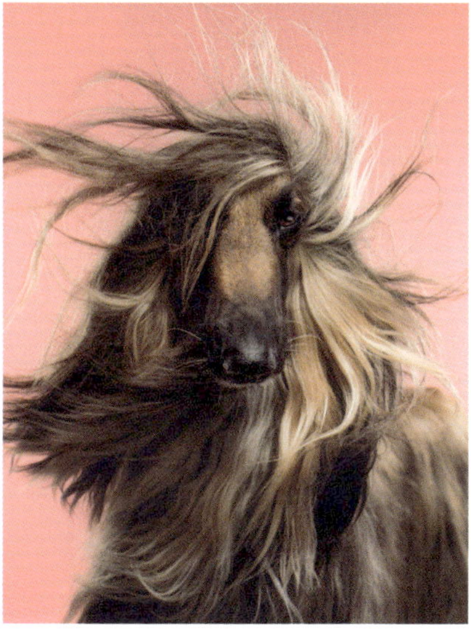

Henry and Hope, 2017

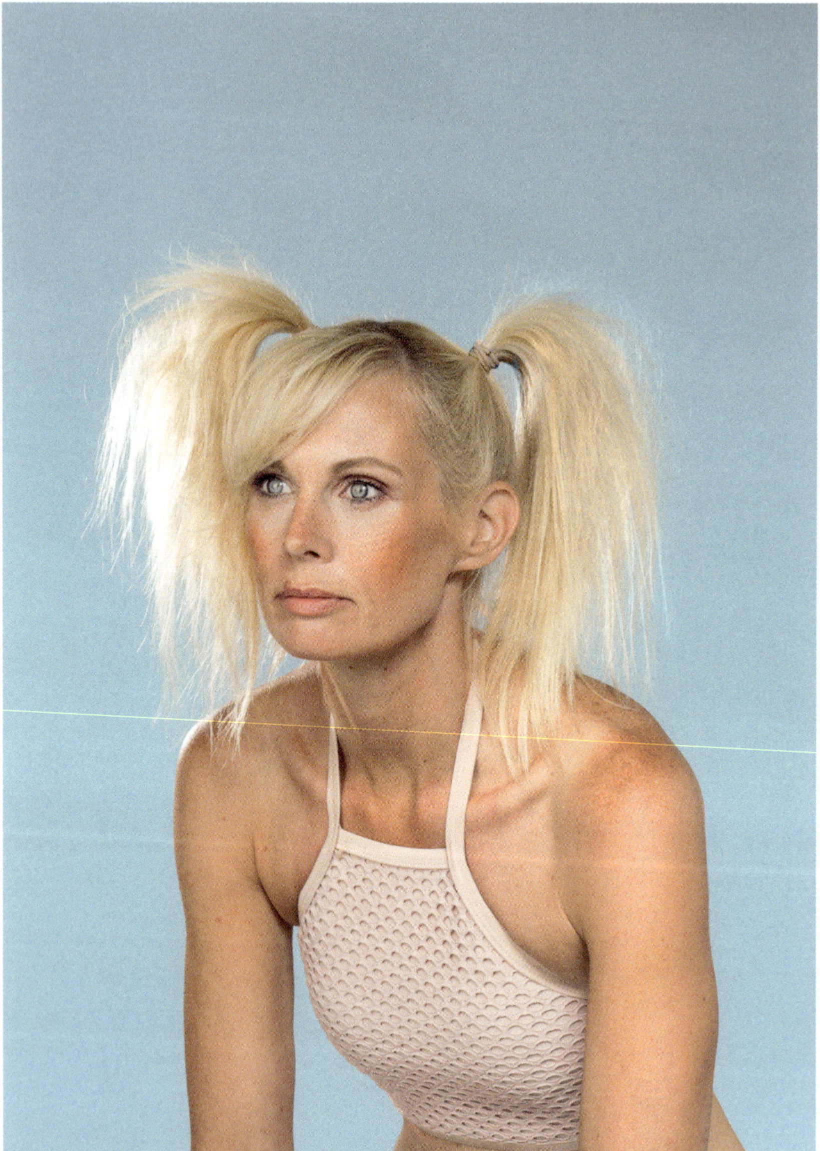

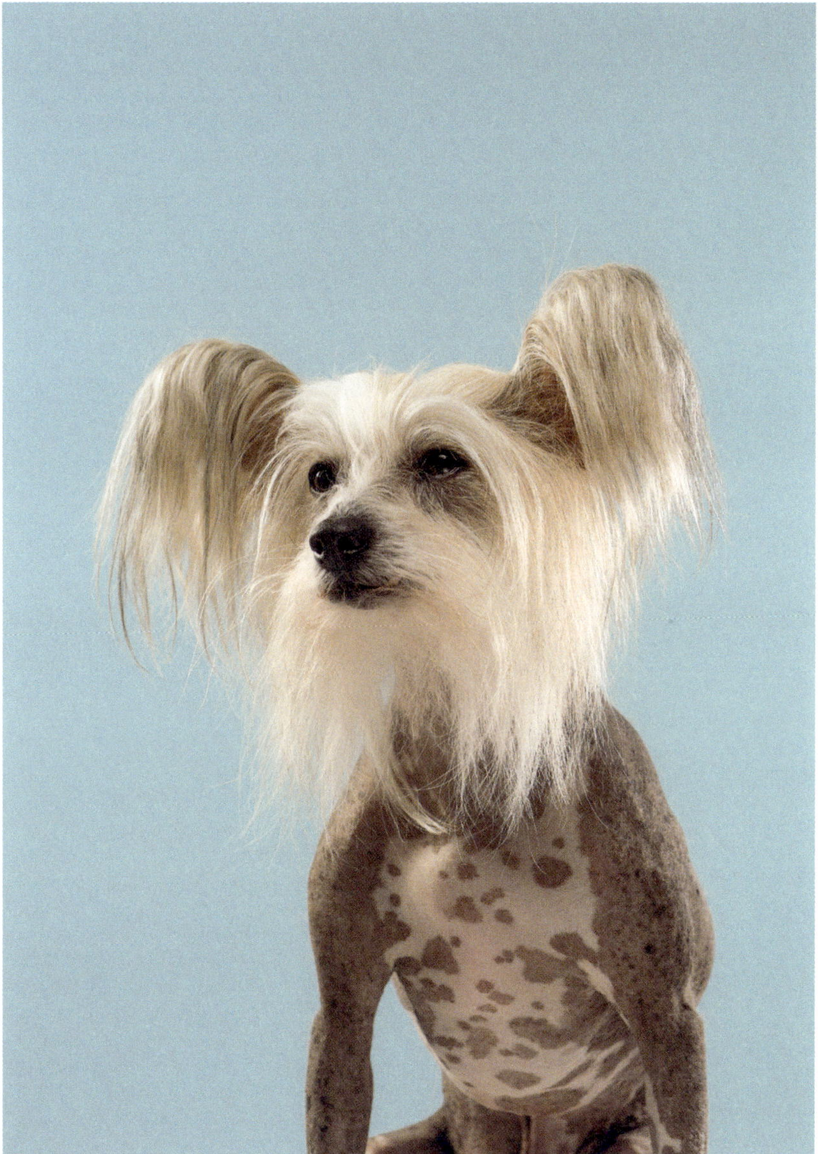

Charlotte and Caspar, 2017

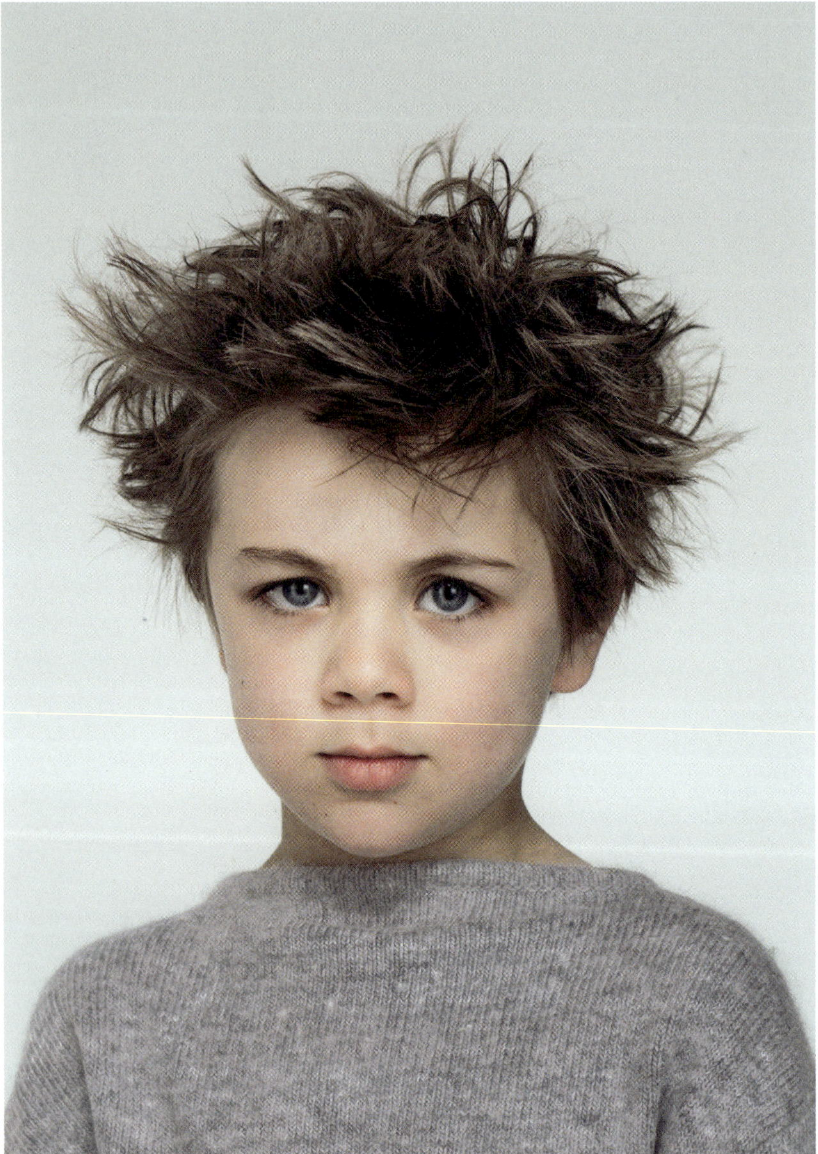

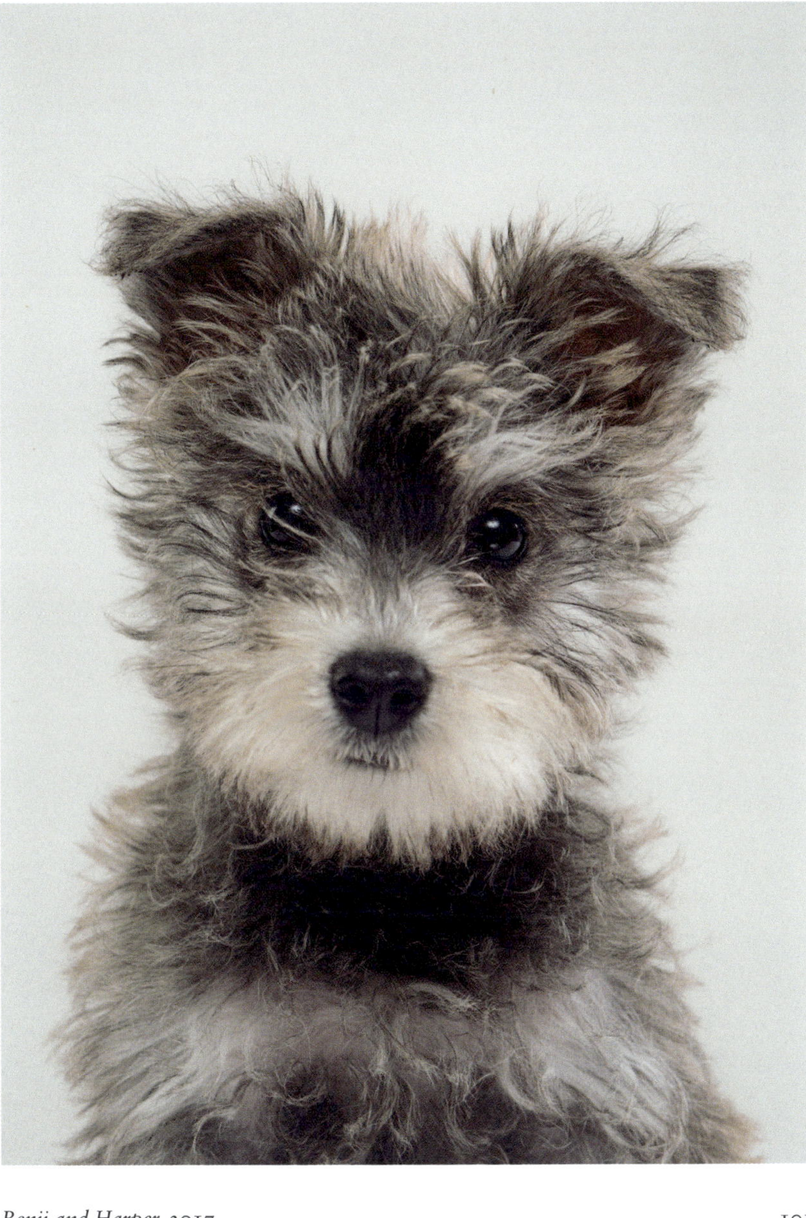

Benji and Harper, 2017

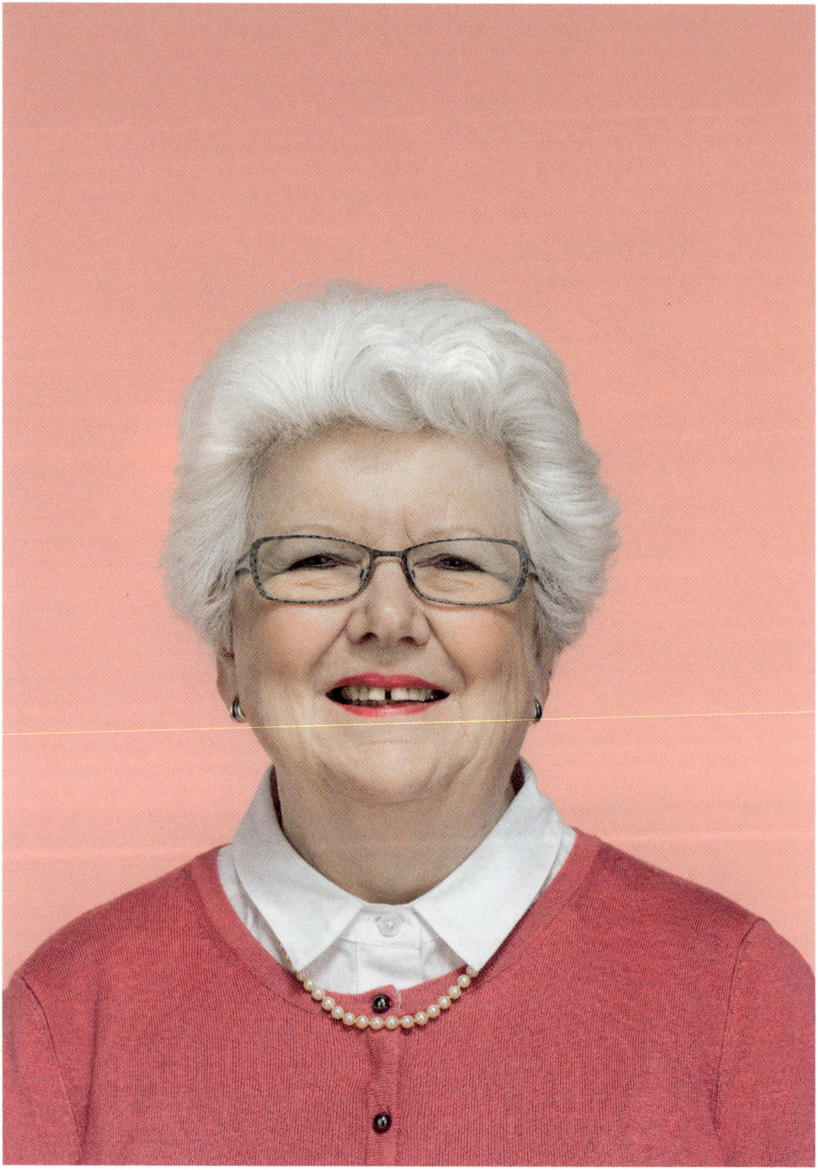

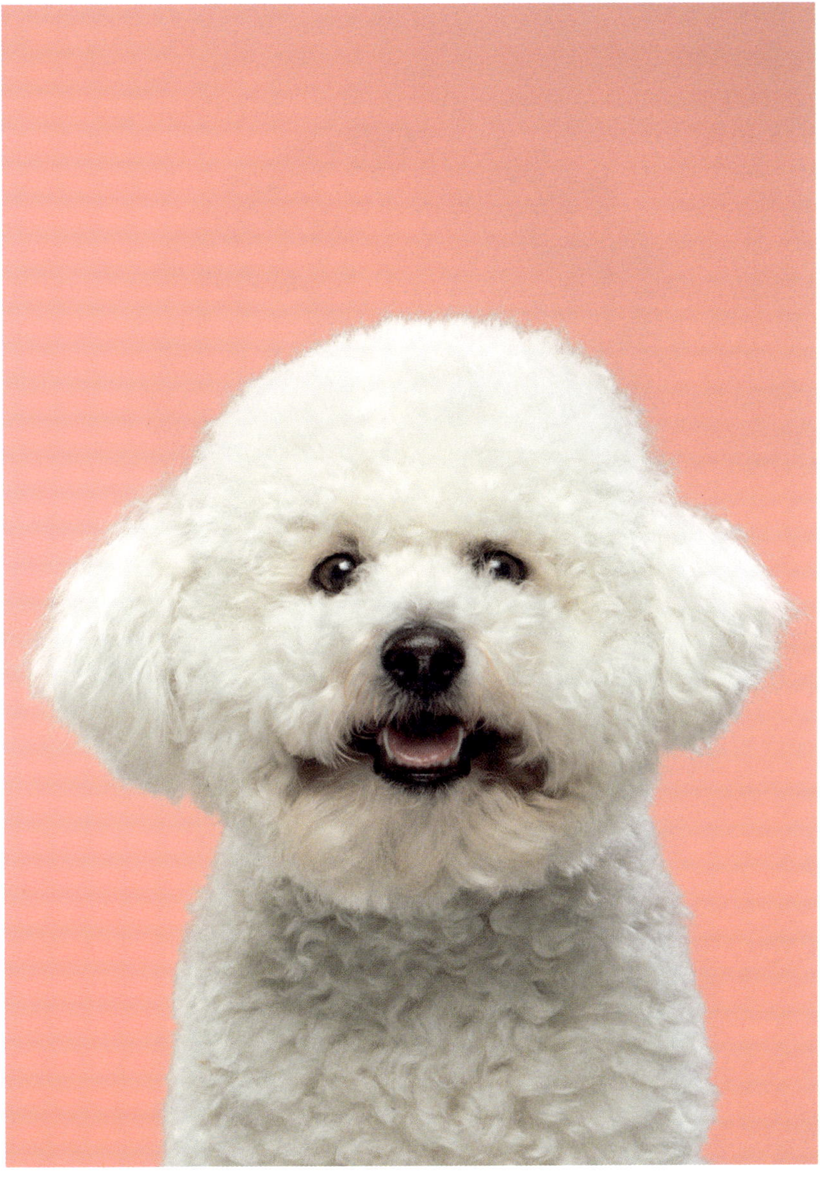

Jessica and Buddy, 2017

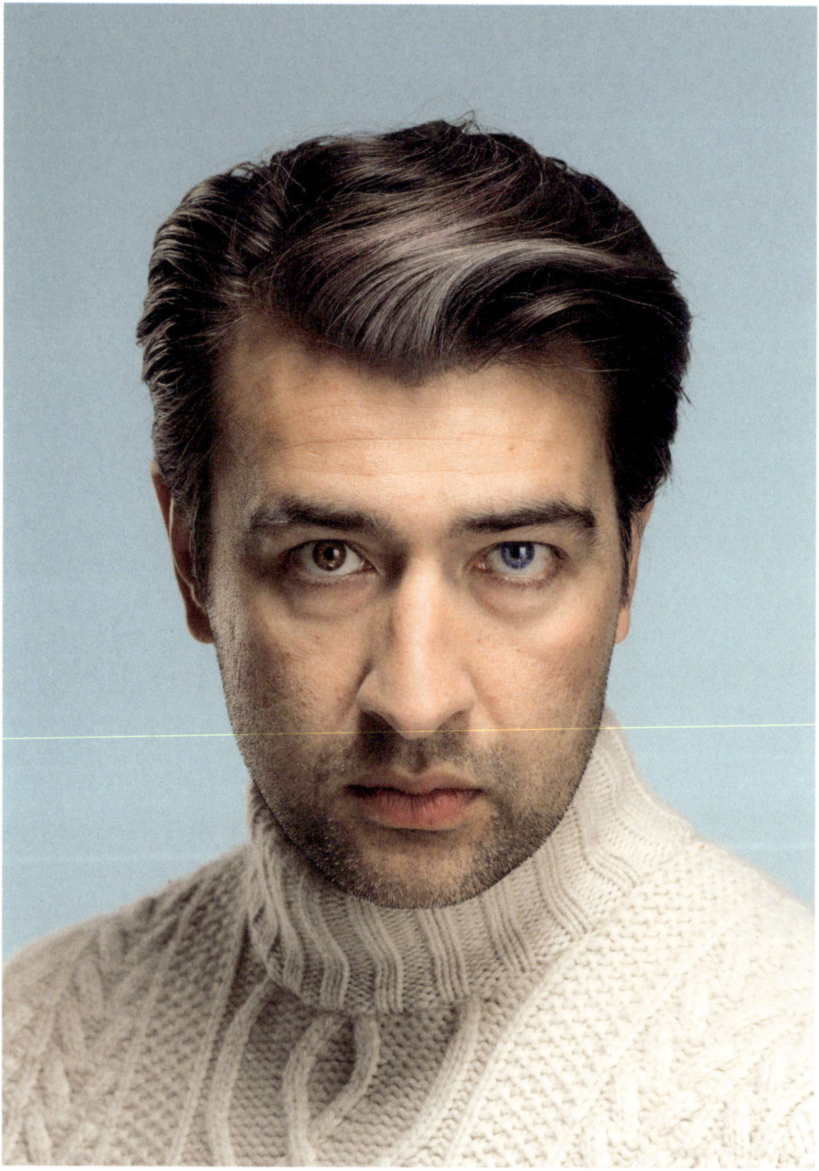

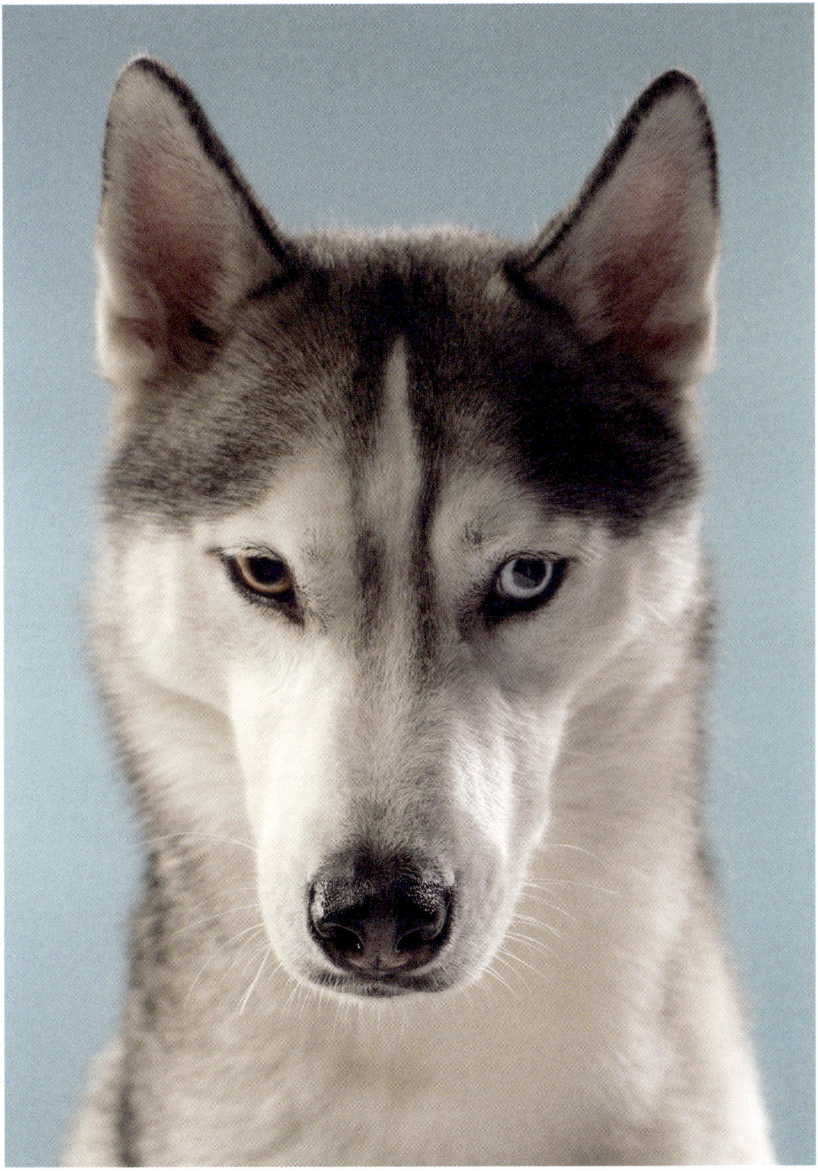

Sergei and Spike, 2017

A DOG'S LIFE
Alicia Rius

It may be a squeaky duck, a raggedy sheep spilling its stuffing or just a good old slipper – dogs are drawn to their favourite *paw-session*s in mysterious ways. With no spending power of their own, they nevertheless love to consume: fetching, chewing, stealing, swallowing and cherishing everything from prized treats and beloved toys to the downright disgusting and dangerous.

Barcelona-based animal photographer Alicia Rius arranges these objects into perfectly composed flat lays, revealing the material world of a dog. Knuckles, a seven-year-old Australian Shepherd, known as 'The Fetcher', is shown alongside the spoils of retrieval, while Lola Rose, a Maltese Shih Tzu pup, reveals a princess lifestyle complete with pink nail varnish and a 'Pawda' bag.

If these collections reveal the dogs' lives and personalities, it isn't all fun and games. Spare a thought for 'The Neurotic' and 'The Senior', whose worlds are defined by pills, scraps and the undeniable evidence of destruction. After all, they say, you are what you chew.

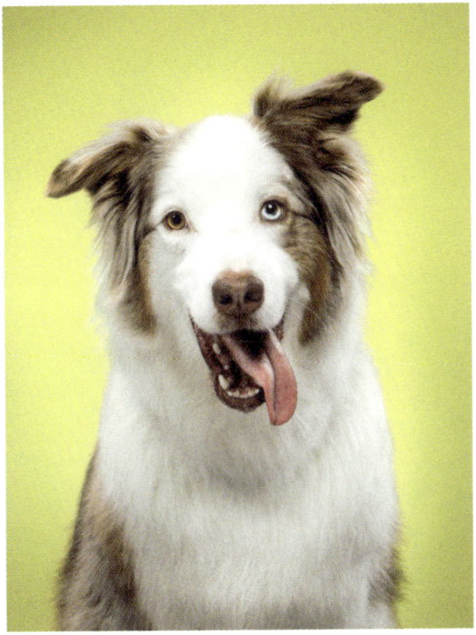

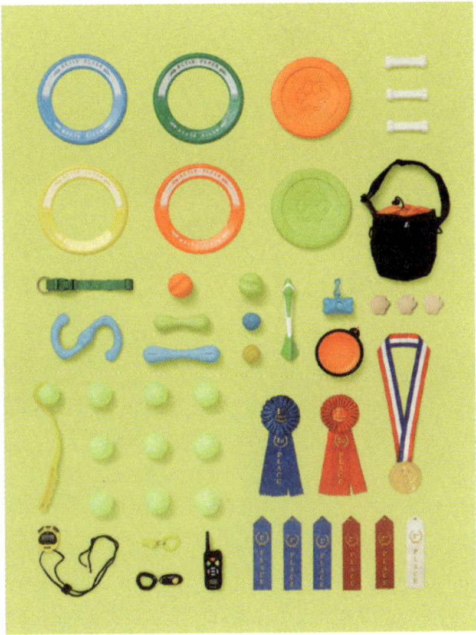

The Fetcher, 2018

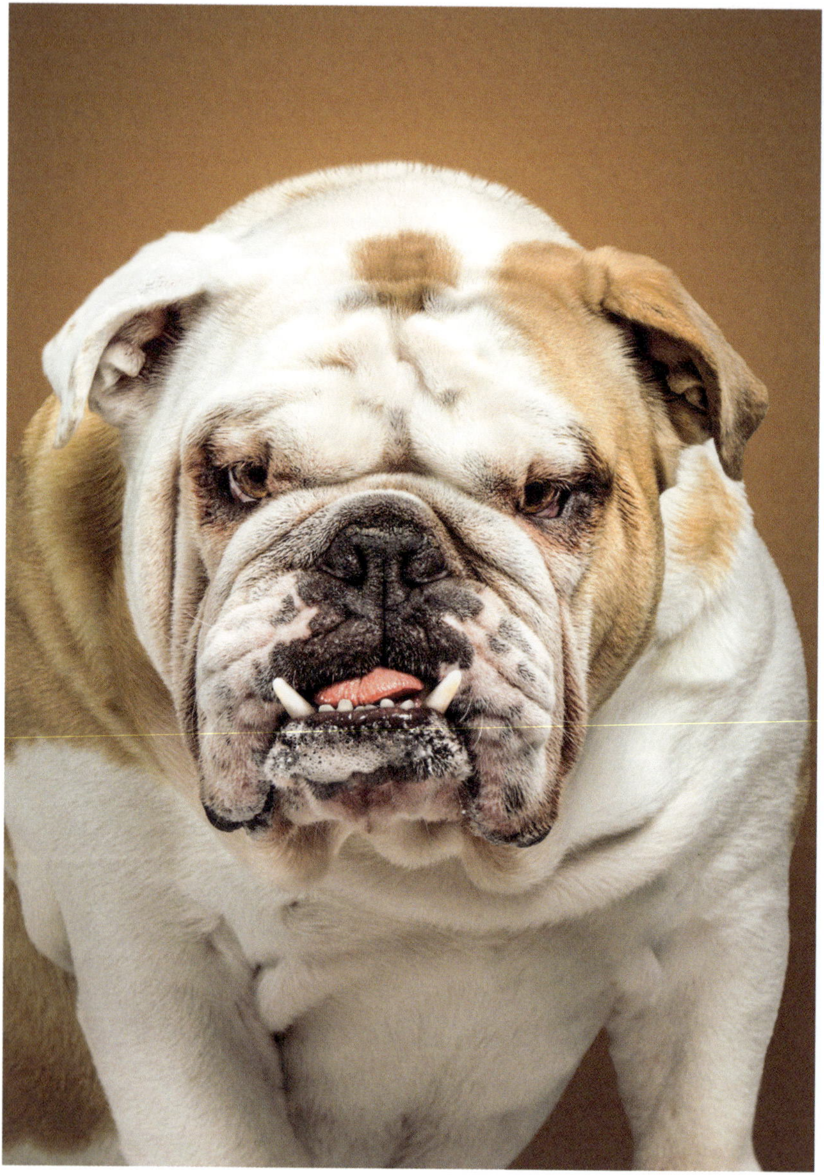

The Neurotic, 2018

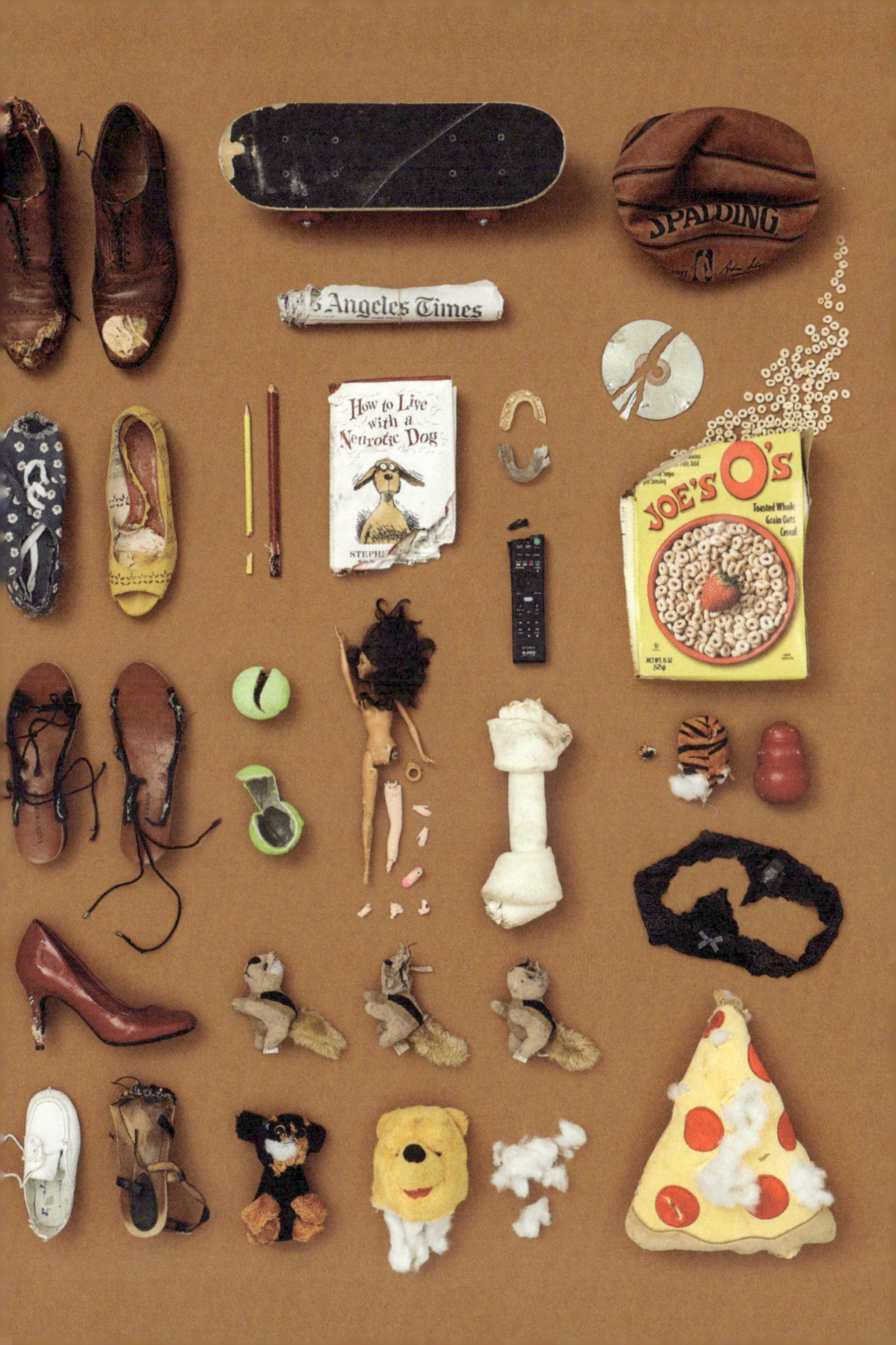
SPALDING
Angeles Times
How to Live with a Neurotic Dog
JOE'S O's
Toasted Whole Grain Oats Cereal

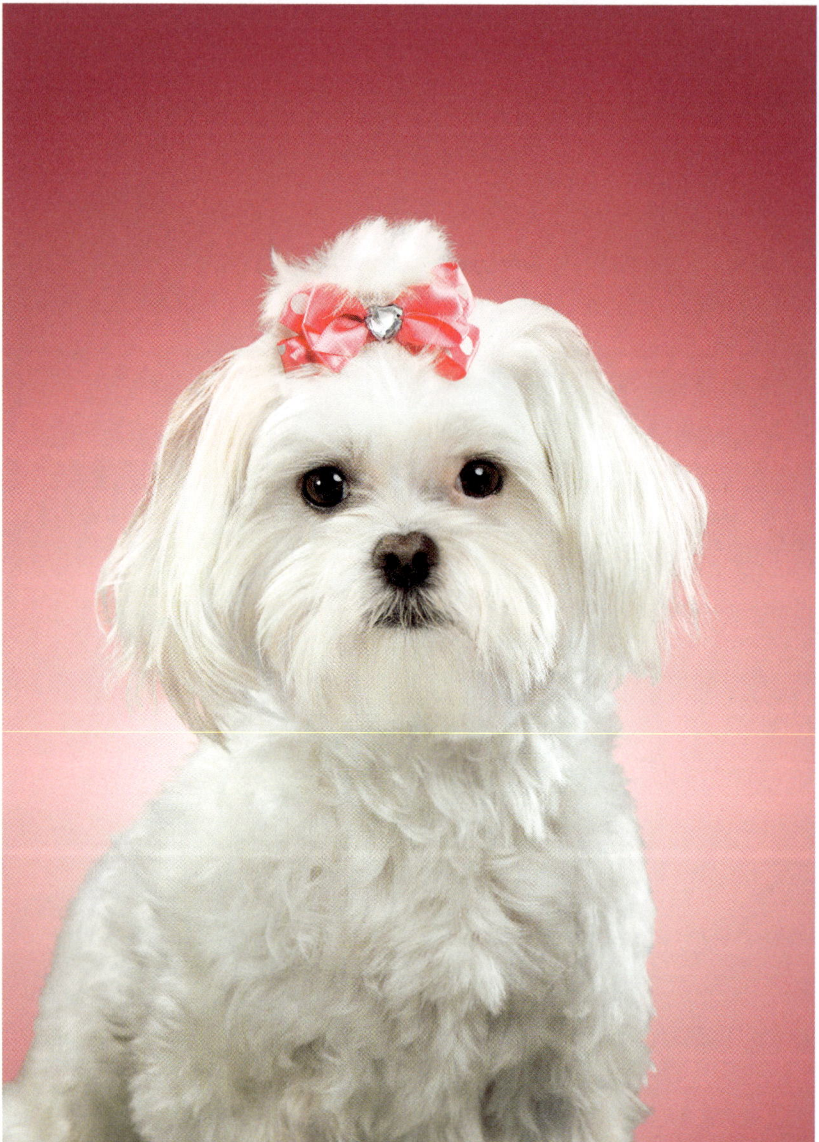

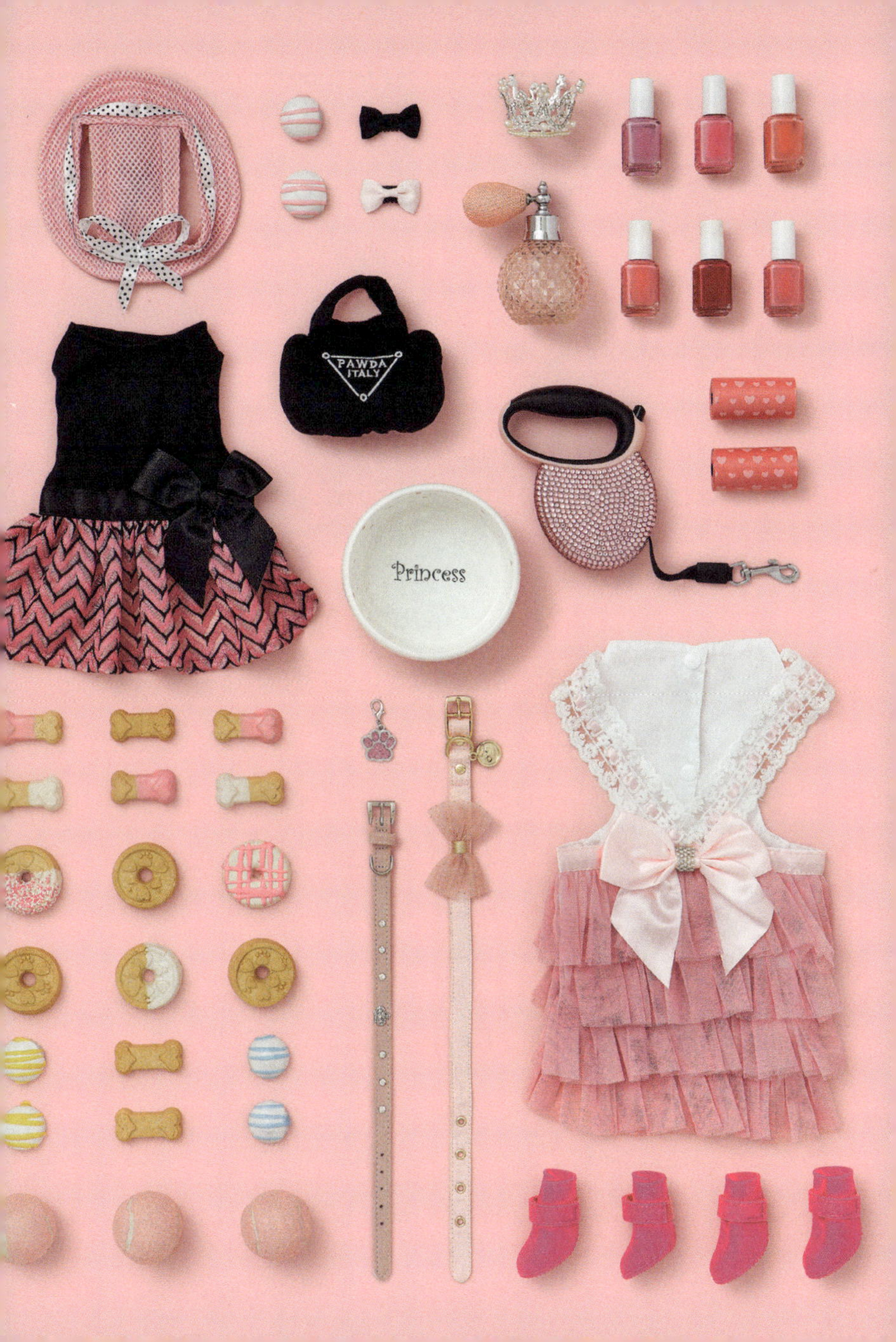
PAWDA
ITALY
Princess

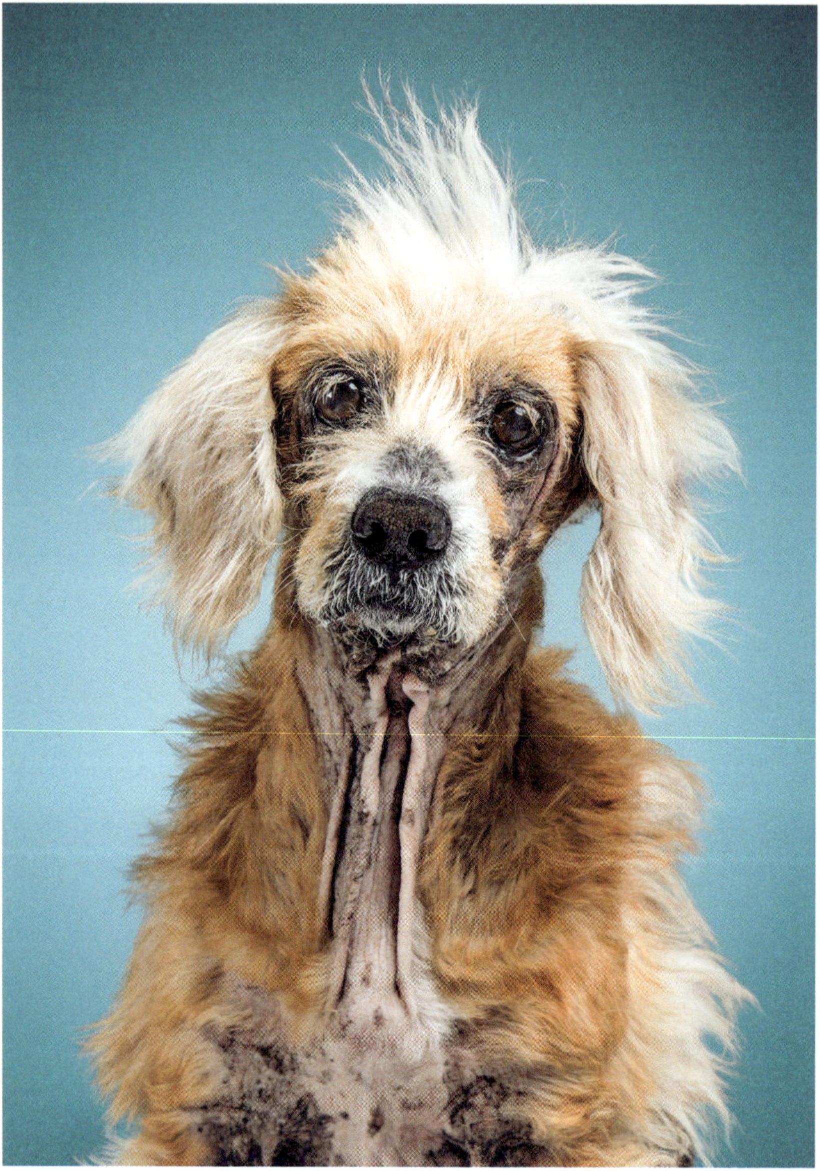

The Senior, 2018

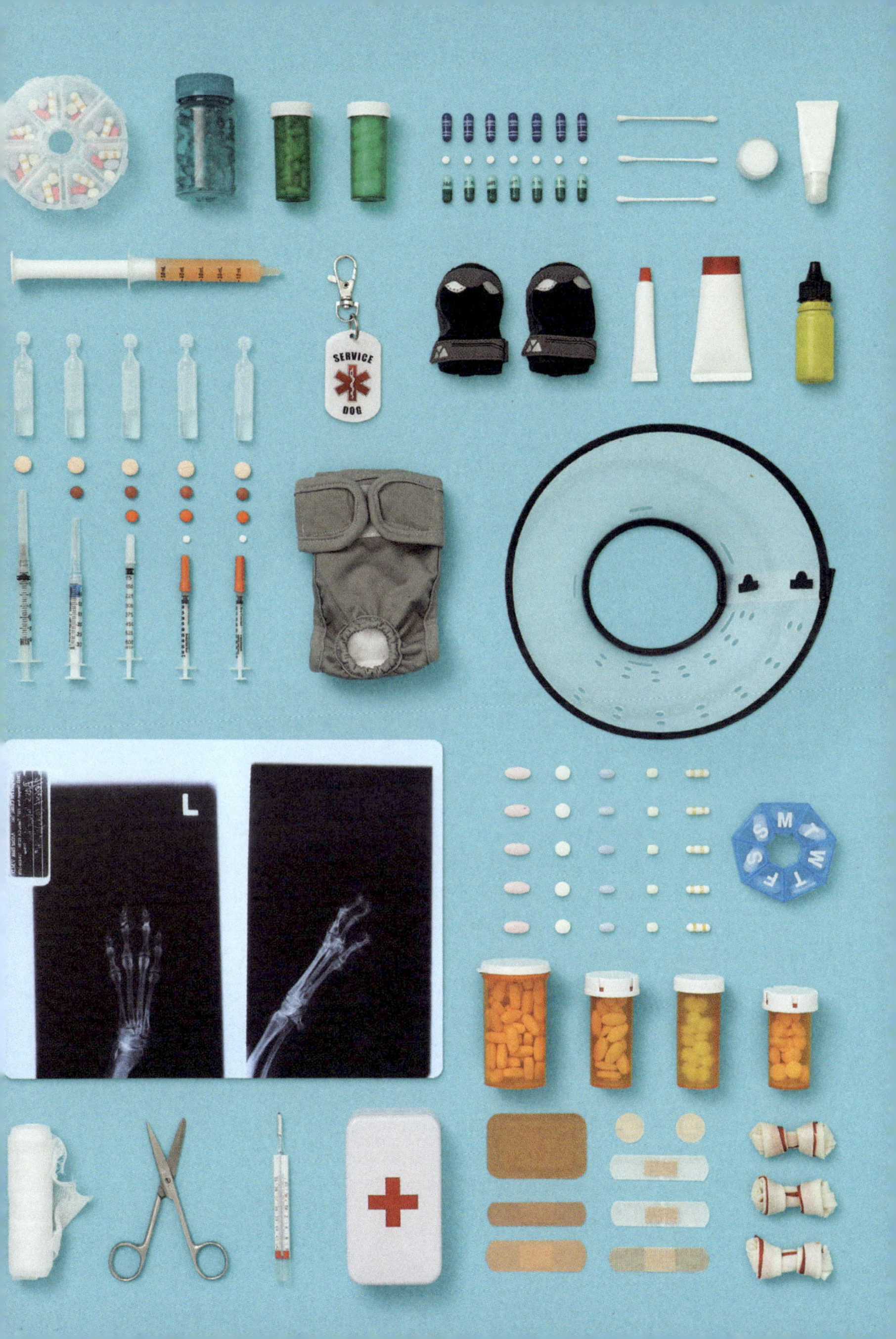
SERVICE
DOG
L

A HANDBOOK FOR DOG WALKERS

Tomáš Werner

The four-year-old Pomeranian known as Q and Slovakian photographer Tomáš Werner are a match made in – well, the Art Deco heaven of Miami. The pair met through a friend, and what started as a casual dog-sitting favour quickly blossomed into a sun-soaked collab where canine photography meets the colourful landscape of Floridian architecture.

A willing and evidently self-assured model, this pooch has perfected the art of the perch – demonstrated across more than 100 images published in Werner's 2015 book, *A Handbook for Dog Walkers*. Fountains, pipes, statues, letterboxes, ice vending machines and air-conditioning units – if it can be sat on, Q has claimed it. And not only this, he does it all with a smile: that flash of tiny pink tongue is a sure sign he's entirely in on the joke.

Pomeranians, as it happens, used to be quite a bit larger than they are today, before they were bred down to their current – let's say, more perchable – proportions. According to Werner, Q loves to strike a pose and is excellent at following directions: 'It almost seemed like he was waiting to be photographed.'

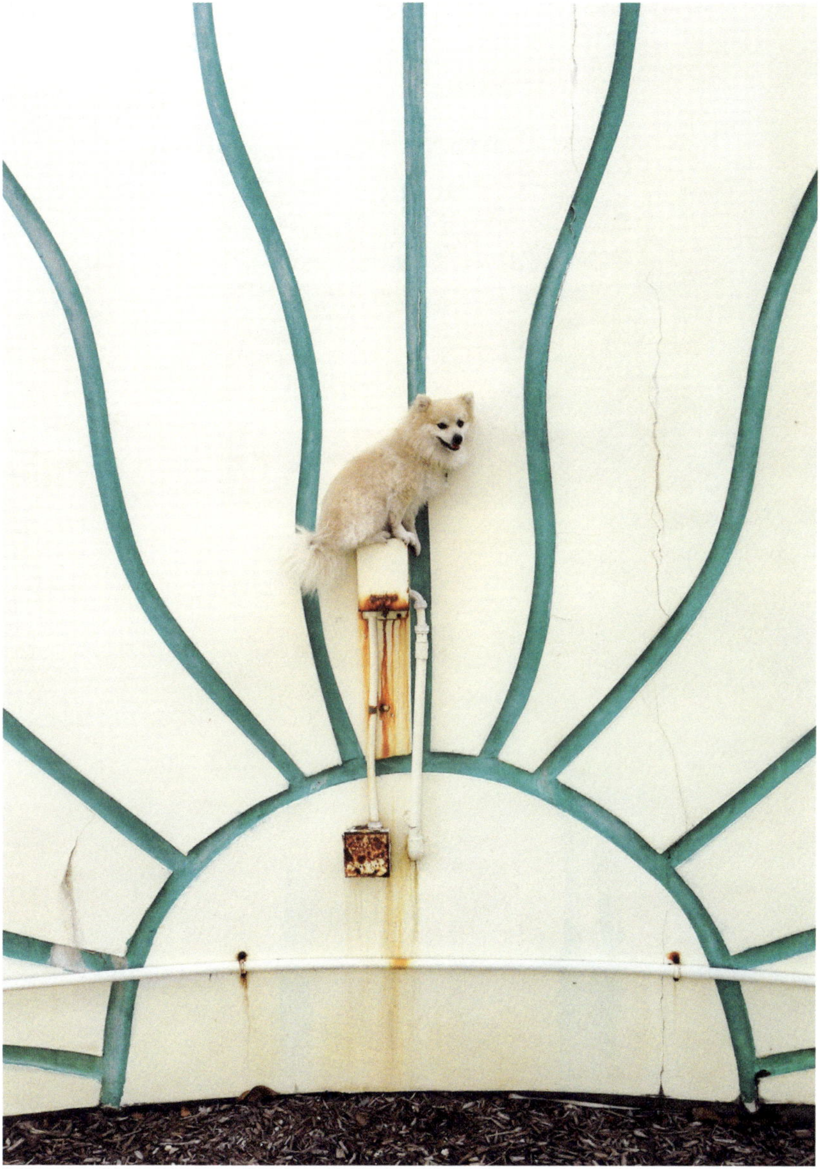

Swimming Pool, 2015

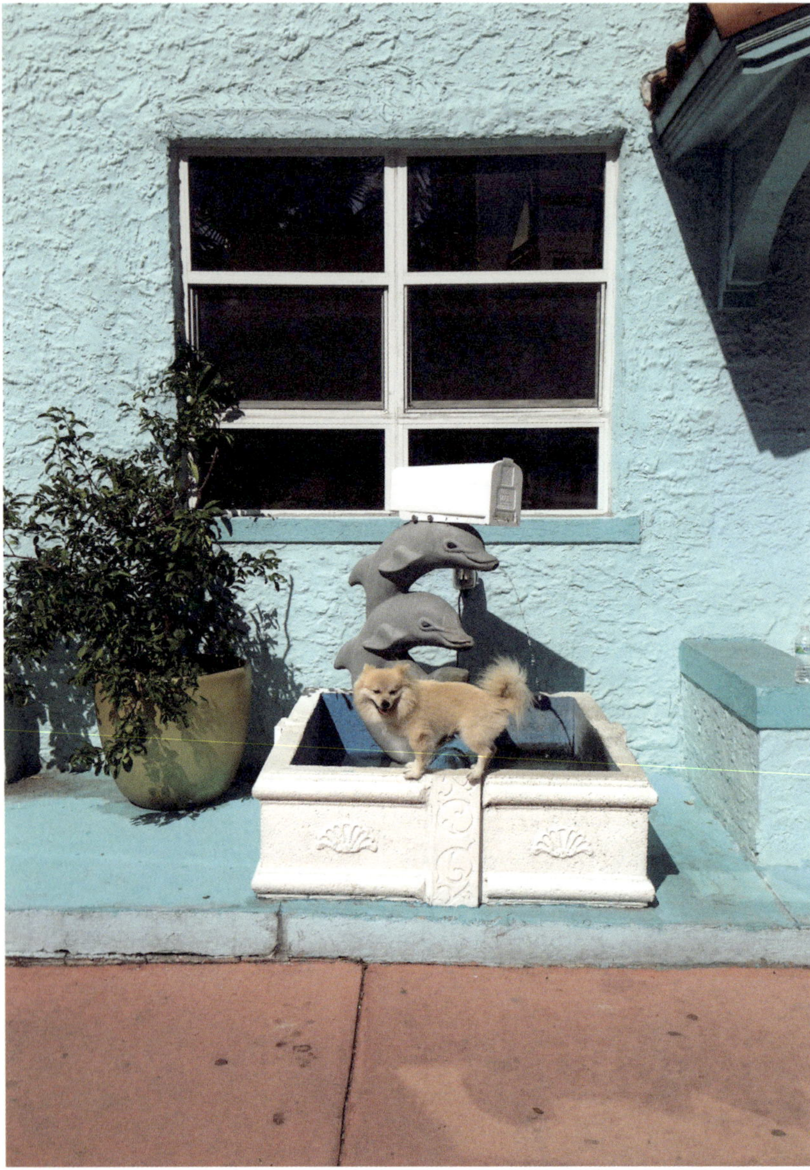

Above: *Dolphins*, 2015
Opposite: *Red Ladder*, 2015

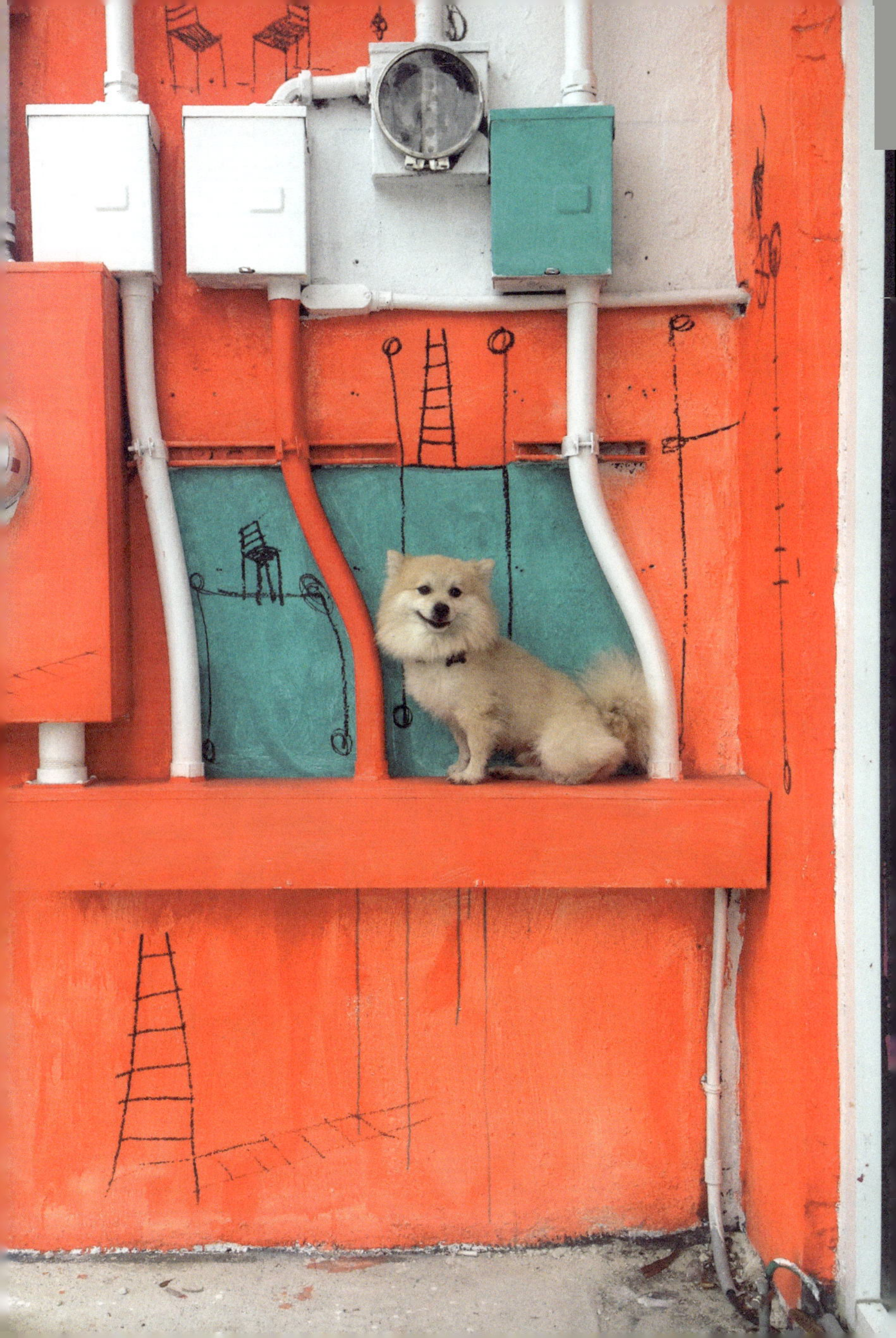

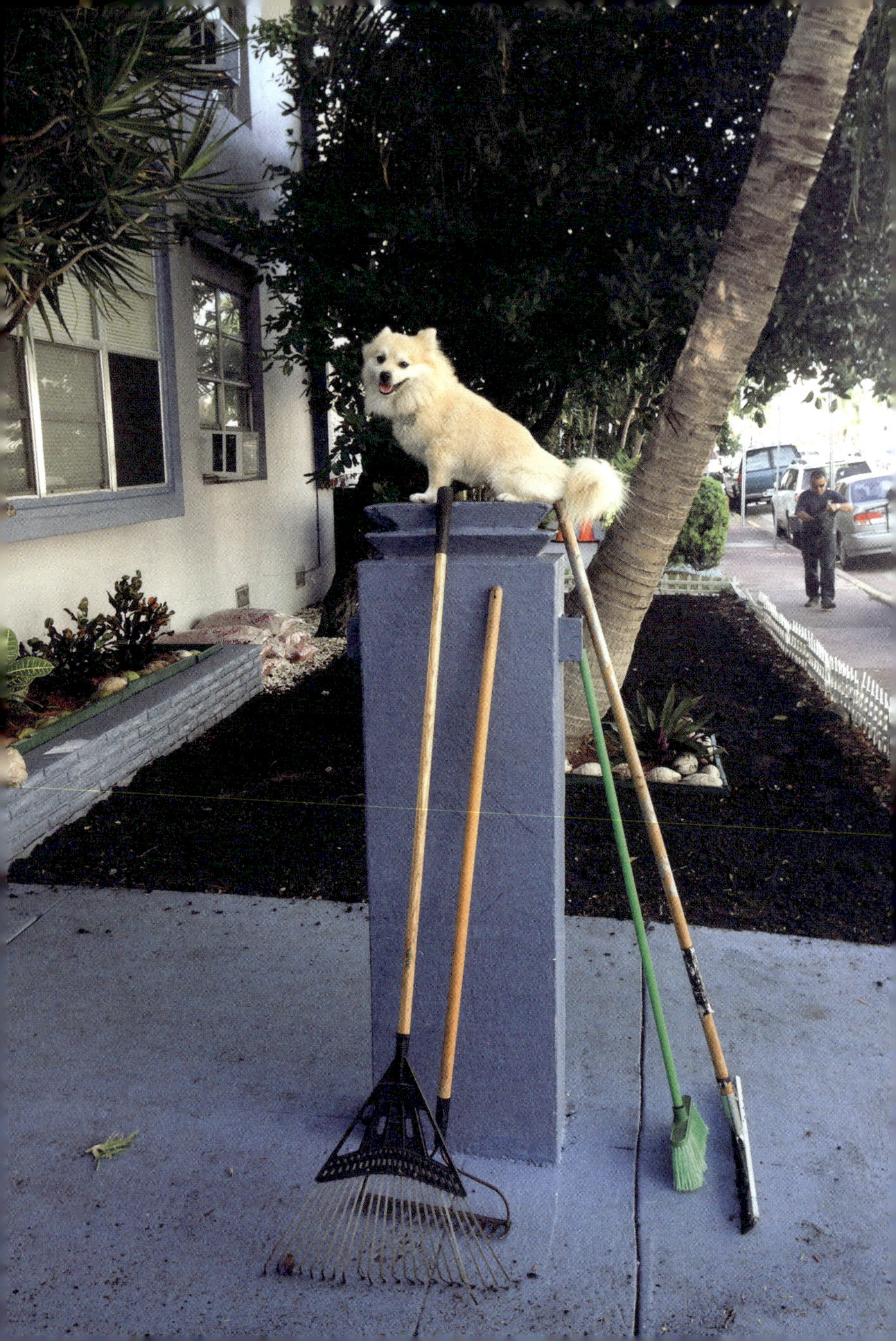

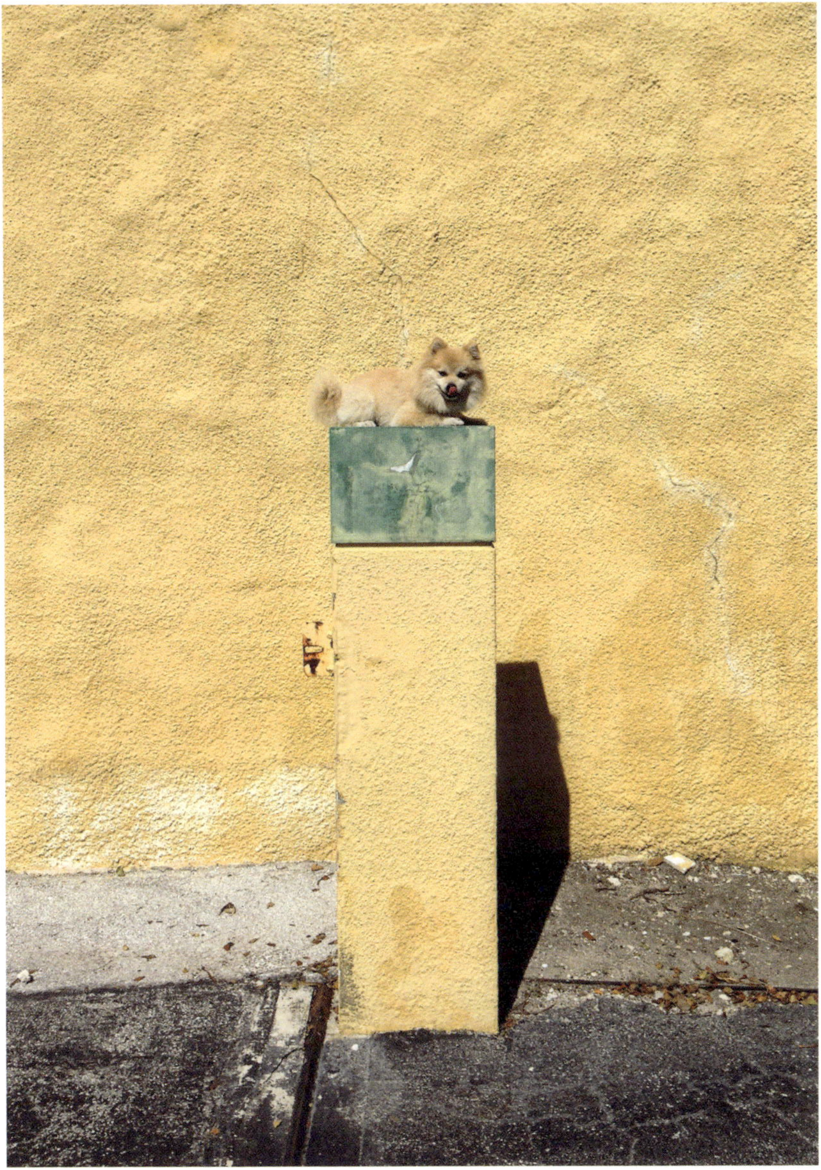

Above: *Yellow Plinth*, 2015
Opposite: *Cleaning*, 2015

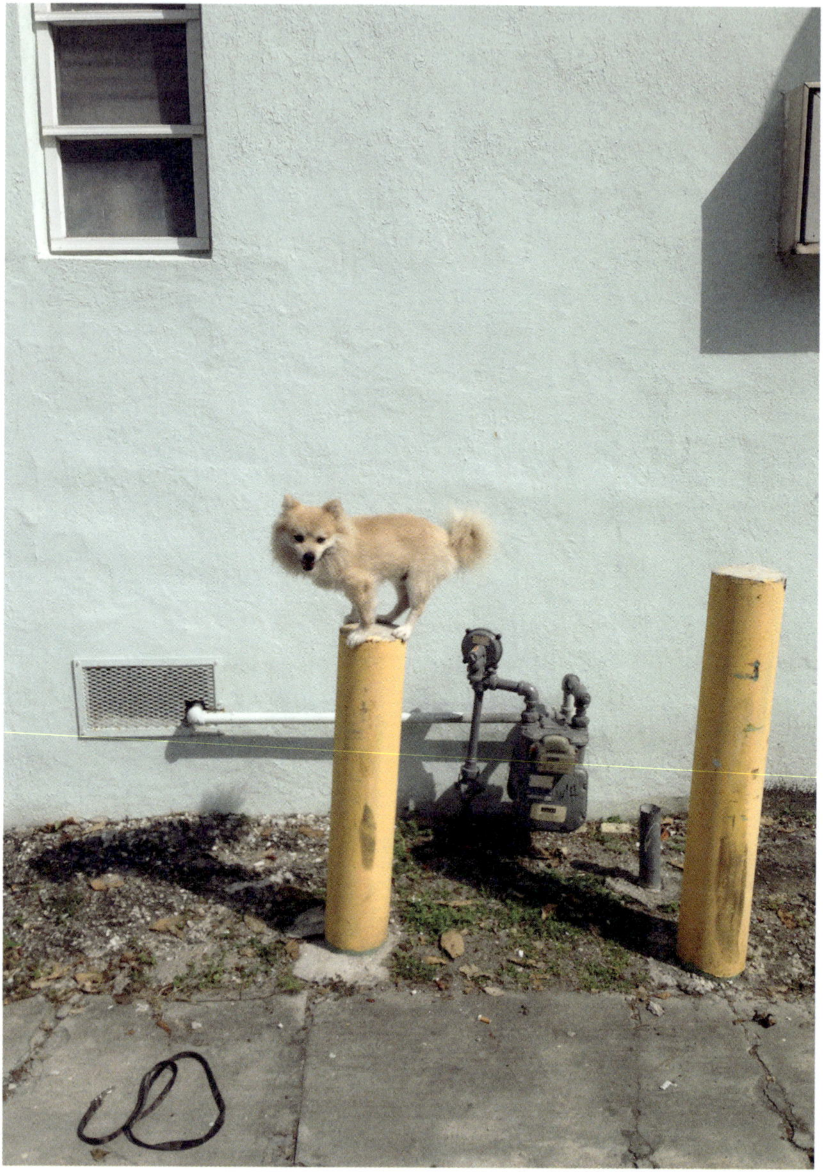

Above: *Yellow Bollard*, 2015
Opposite: *Telephone*, 2015

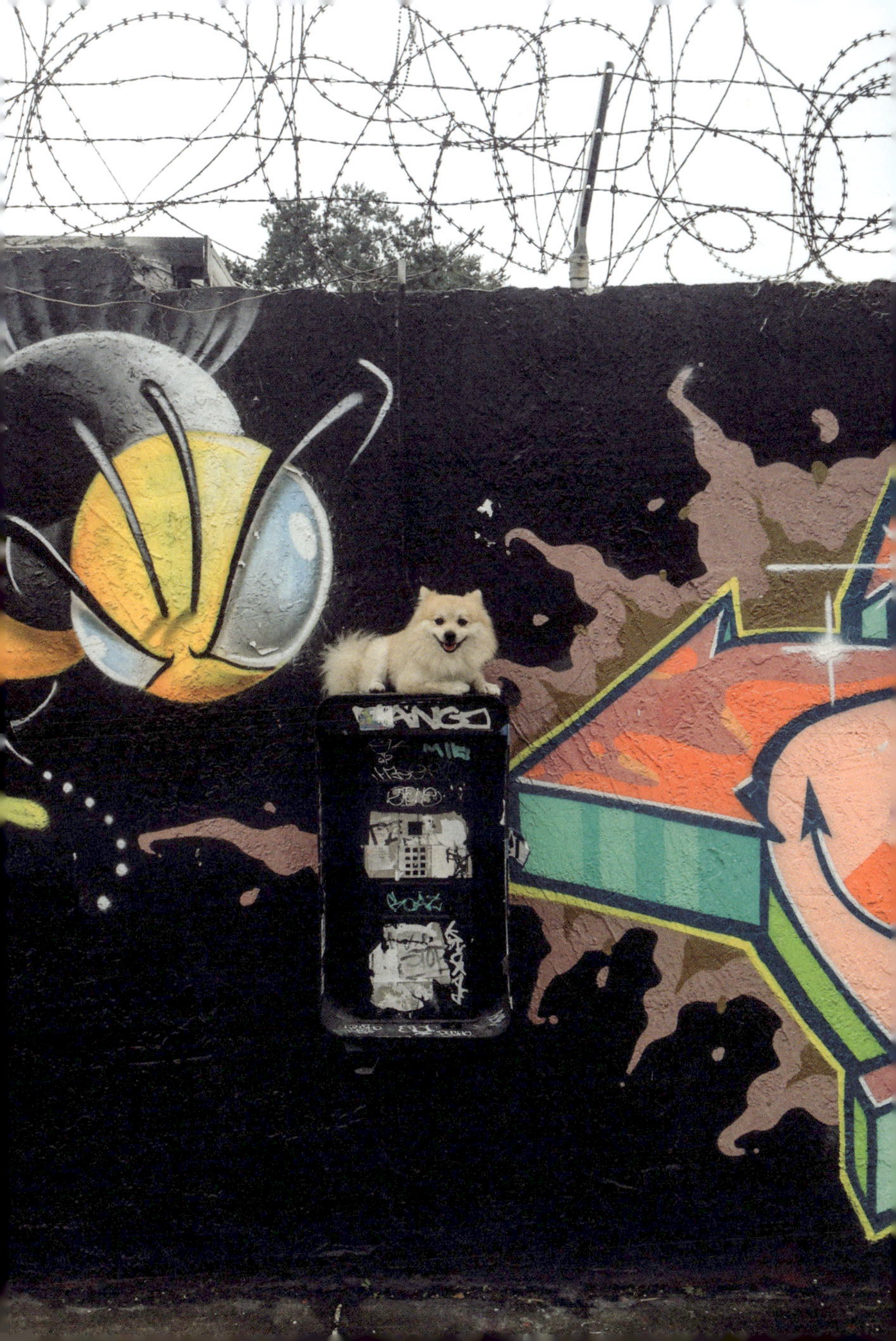

DOGSONALITY
Elke Vogelsang

Elke Vogelsang could very well be a dog whisperer. For more than 15 years, she's been celebrated for her hilarious and characterful portraits of dogs. A raised eyebrow, a sly tilt of the head or a cautious grin is all it takes to glimpse the full spectrum of canine character: from wisdom and sensitivity to goofiness and mischief.

Her journey began with her beloved rescue dogs, Noodles and Scout, two Spanish Galgo mixes, during a period of personal stress and uncertainty. Photography became both a distraction and a creative escape, helping her through difficult days. Vogelsang honed her craft and evolved into a full-time commercial and editorial pet photographer. 'Photography is not only my job,' she says, 'it's my hobby gone wild, my daily creative outlet, my therapy and, next to the dogs, my favourite pastime.'

Vogelsang's models have a knack for making you smile. With zero self-consciousness or hesitation, they candidly expose their very beings with expressions that teeter between the comedic and the profound. Try not to laugh. (Spoiler: it's impossible.)

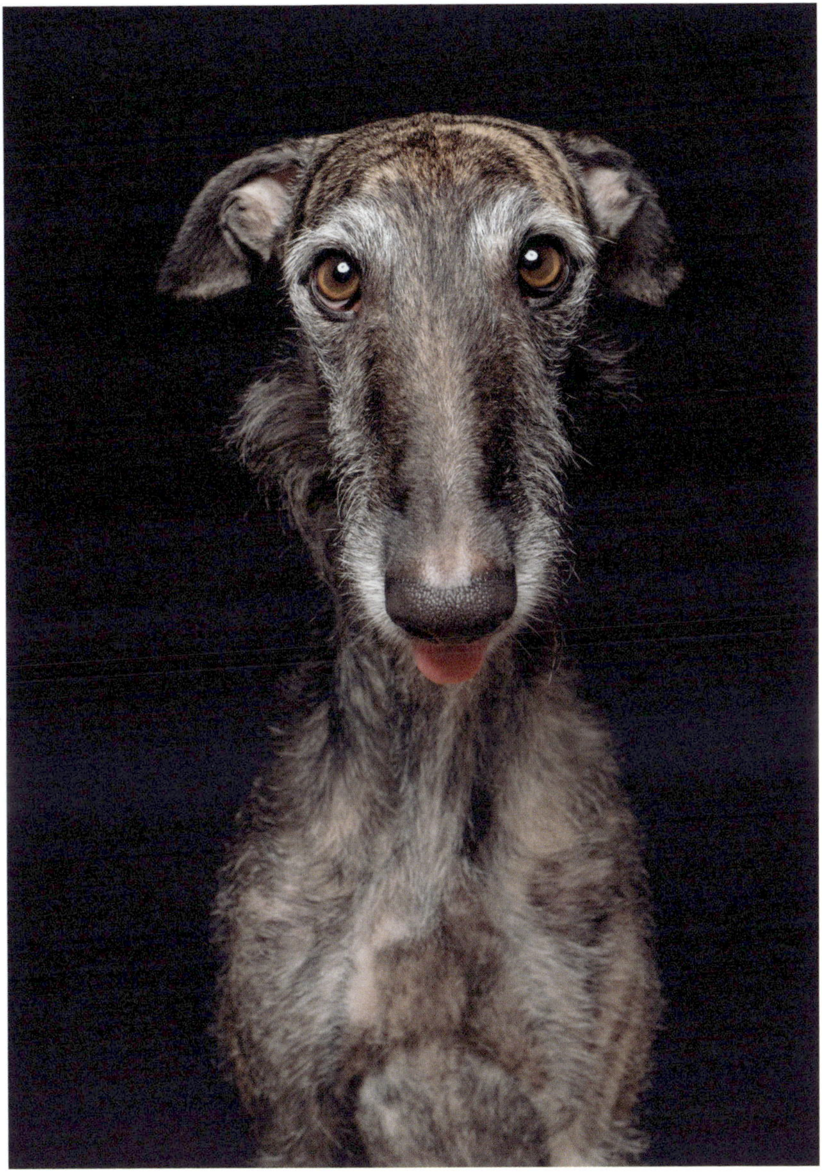

The Cheeky Galgo, 2025

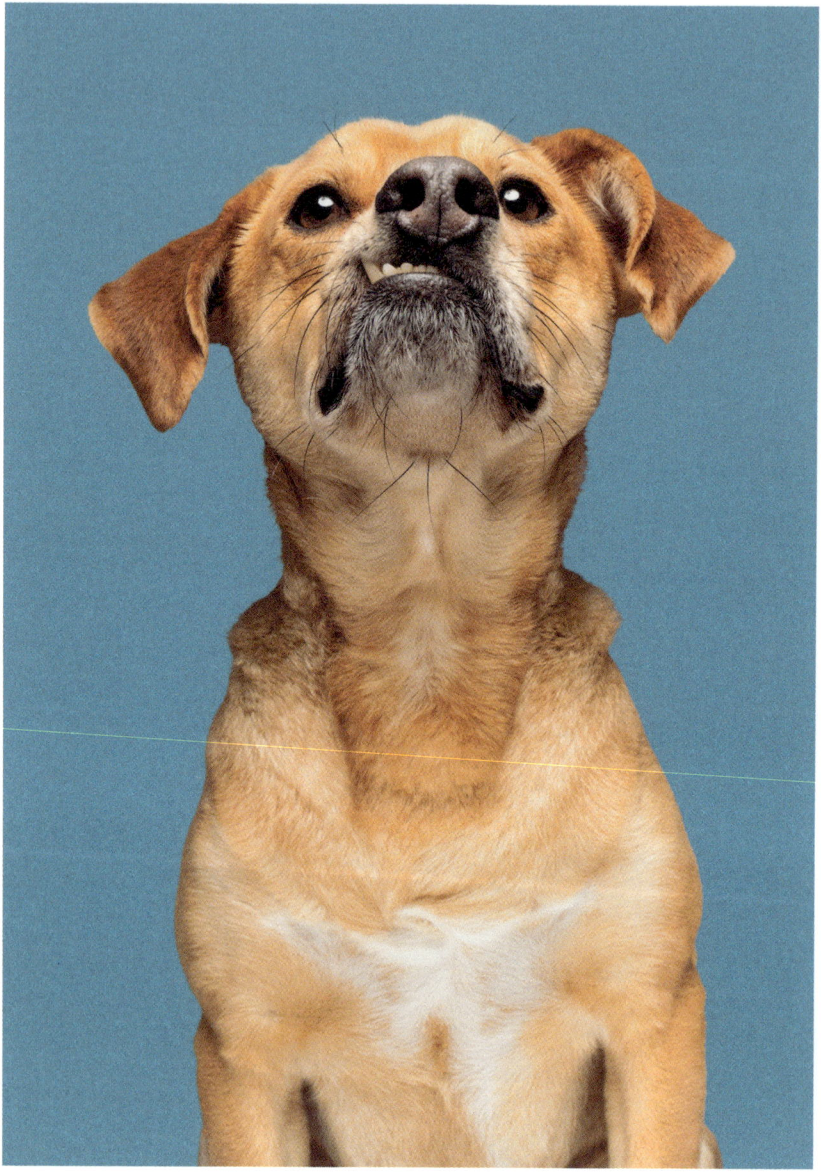

Cutest Underbite, 2025

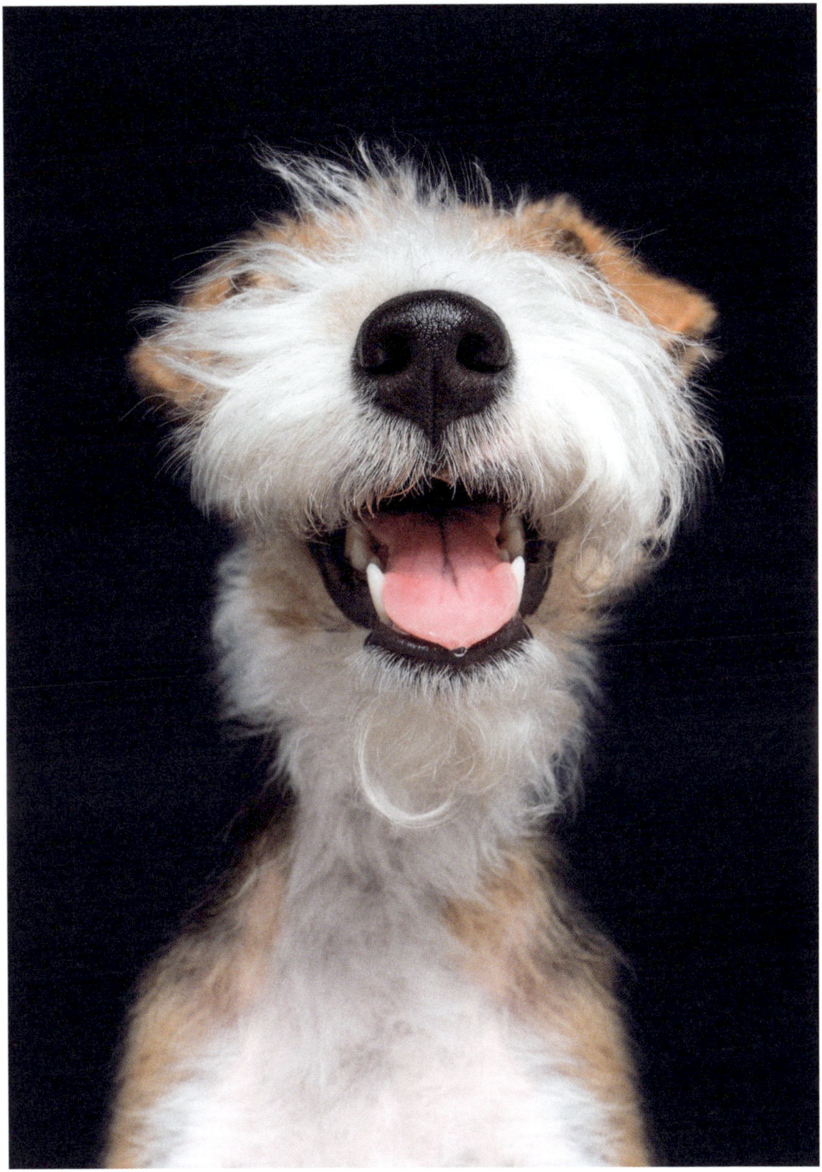

Muppetational, 2018

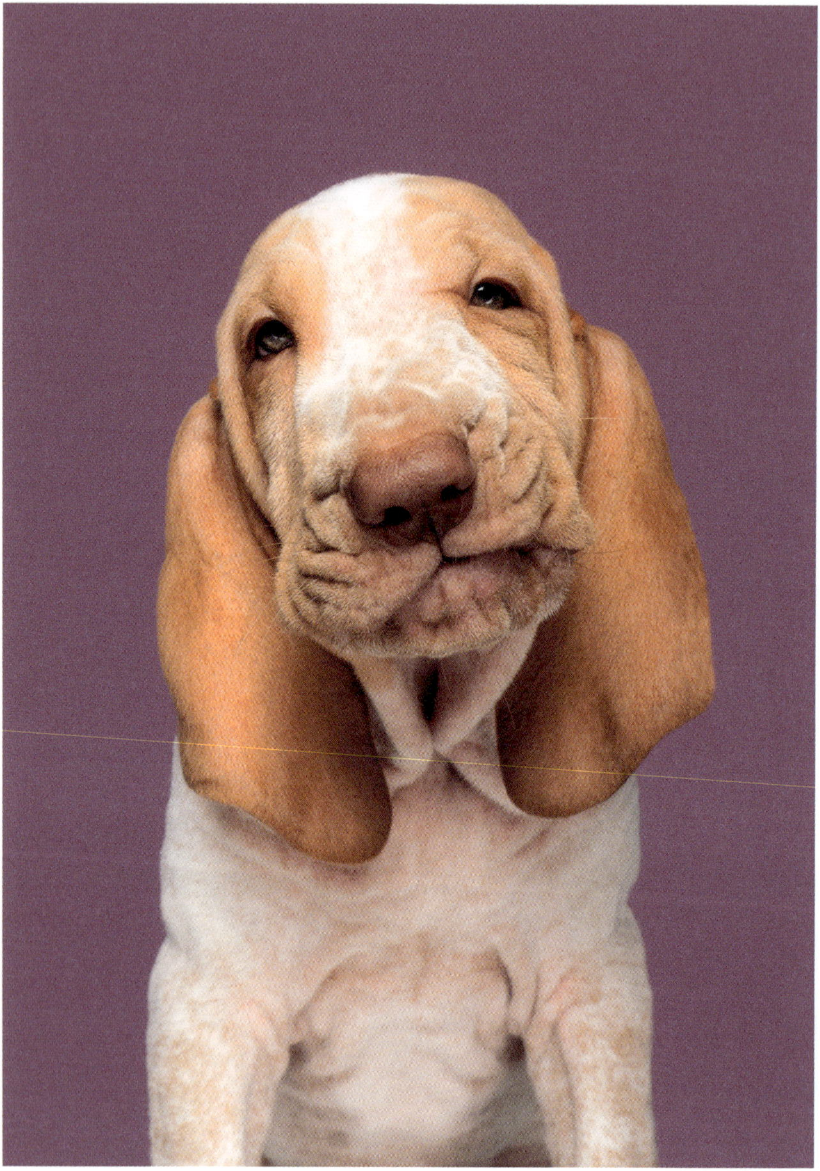

Cool Girl Trude, 2022

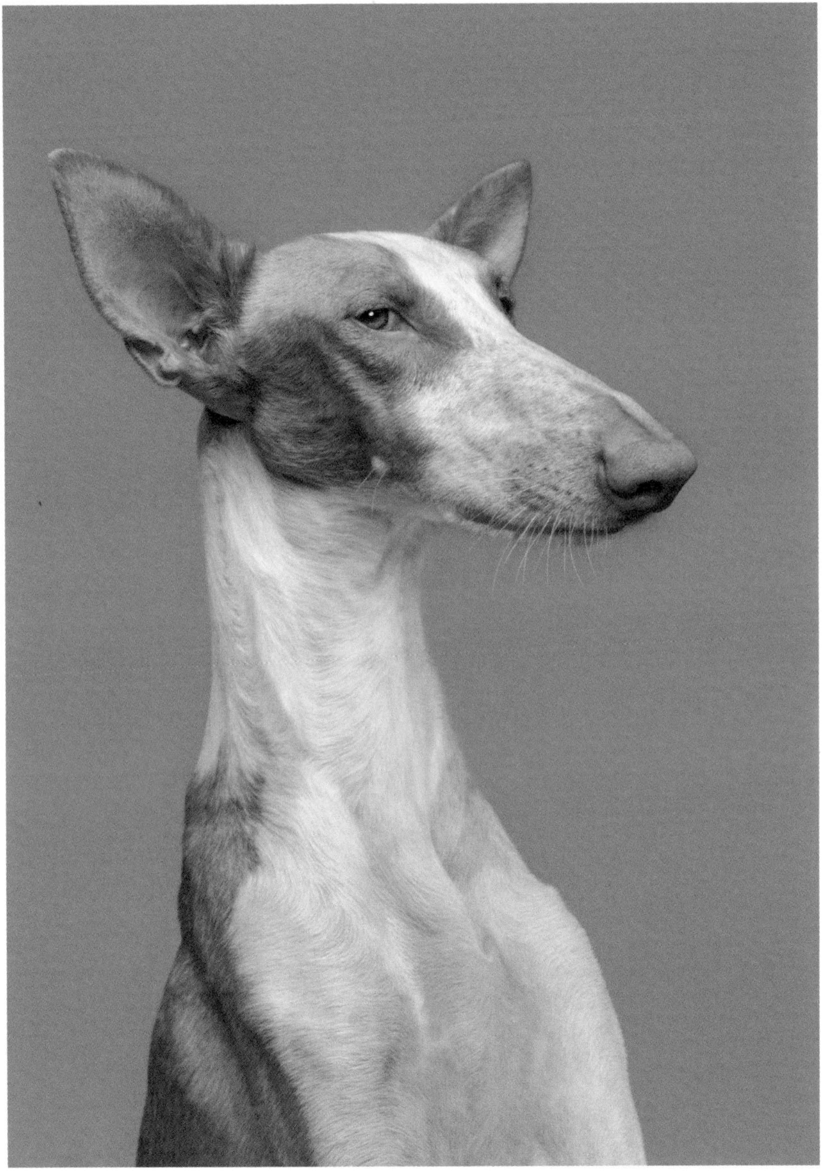

Side-eye for the Hunters, 2024

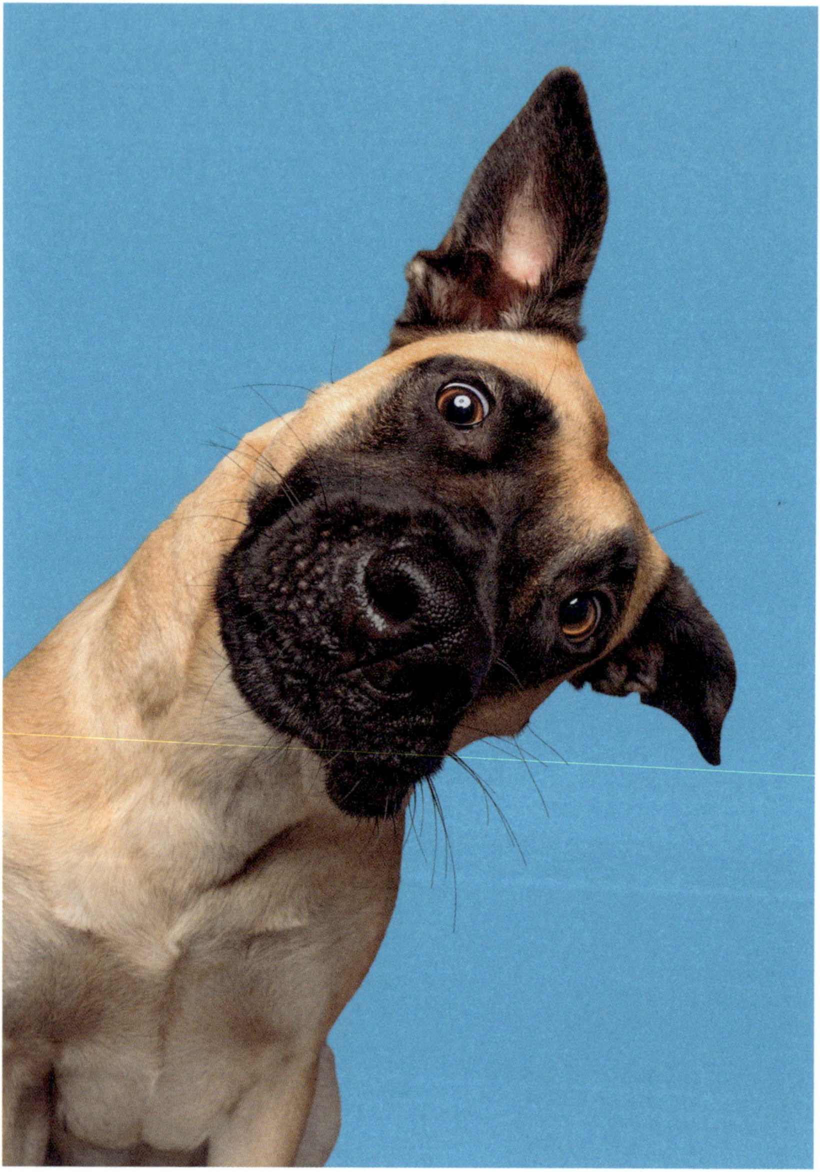

Checking On Us is Dakota, 2025

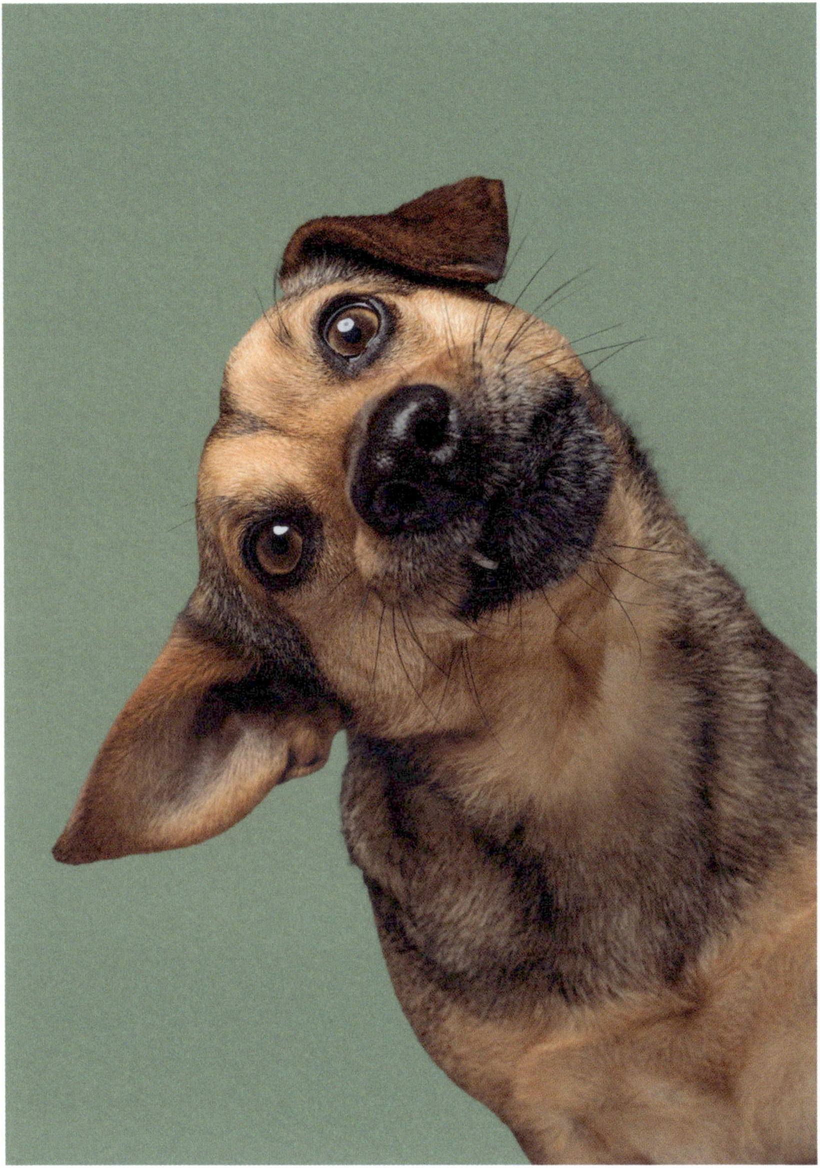

Faces of Toni, 2025

WET DOG
Sophie Gamand

There's something both hilarious and slightly tragic about a wet dog. From Labradors launching themselves into muddy ponds in pursuit of a stick to fluffy poodles shrinking to half their size, water has a remarkable way of rewriting their identity.

Most dogs are not fans of baths, and artist and animal advocate Sophie Gamand chose precisely this least glamorous of moments to click the shutter. Captured in grooming salons across New York City, her subjects are caught in their most vulnerable state: mid-shampoo, mid-spray, mid-betrayal, in that dreaded ritual of hose, lather and blow-dry so familiar to the modern, well-pampered dog.

Gamand's subjects look exposed, fragile, vaguely offended – and, frankly, deeply unimpressed. Who can blame them? They didn't sign up for this. Gamand wonders: 'Are the wet dogs beckoning us the same way humanity reaches out for her own gods, asking the Almighty the reason for their suffering?'

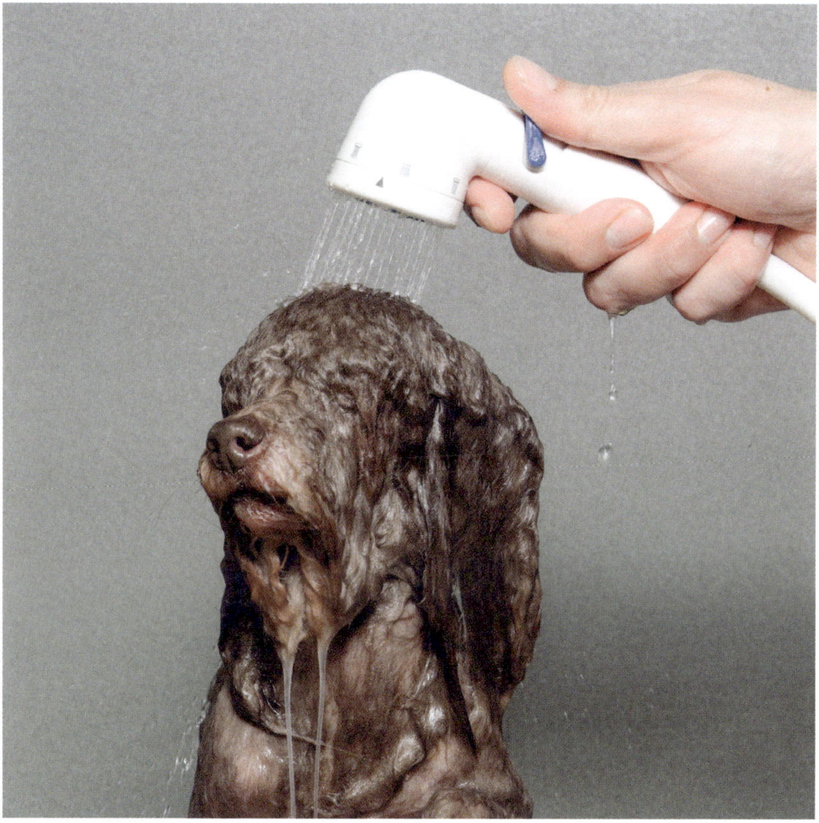

Britney, 2013

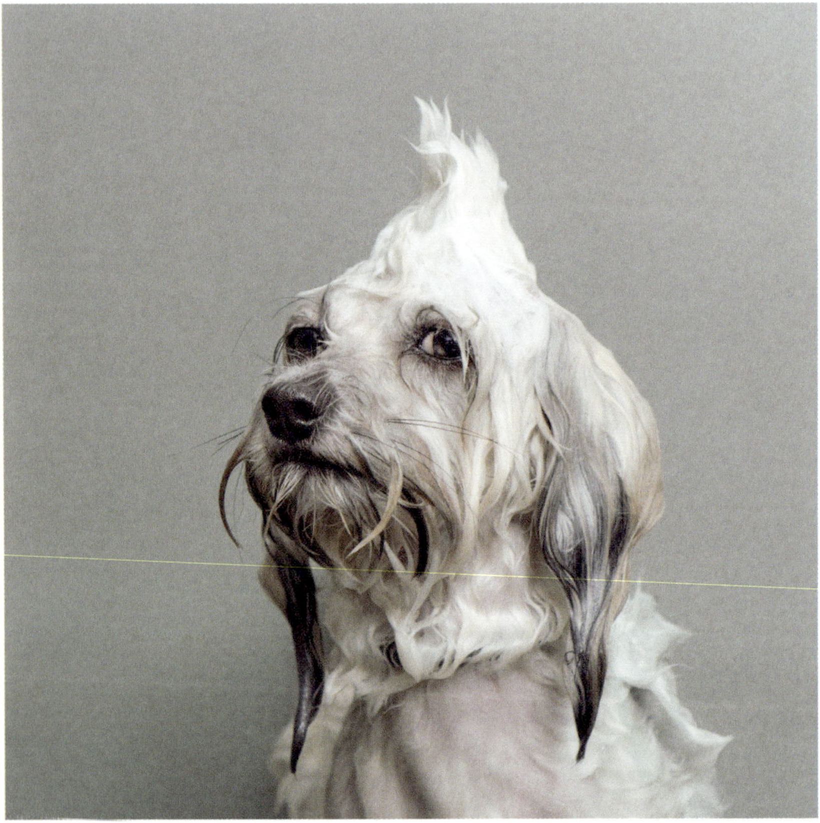

Oscar, 2013

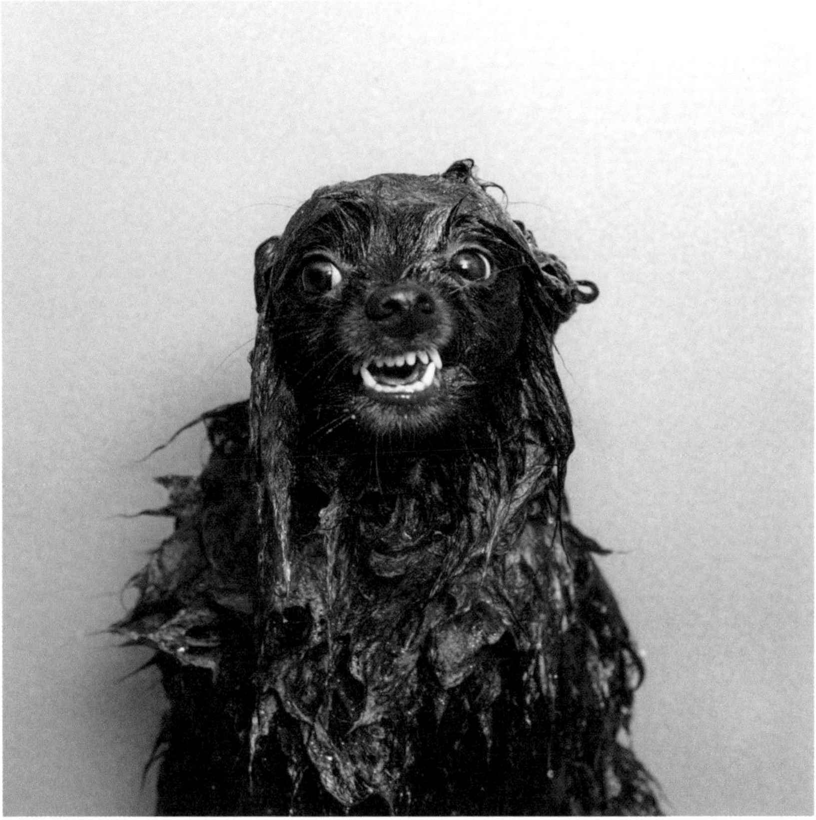

Joy, 2013

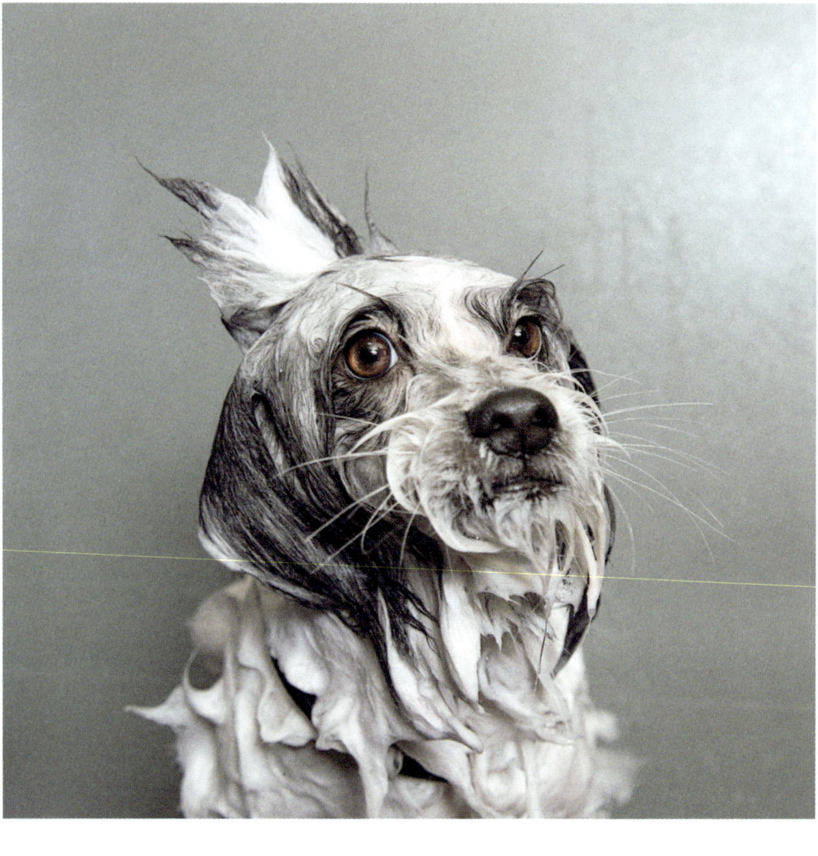

Mia, 2013

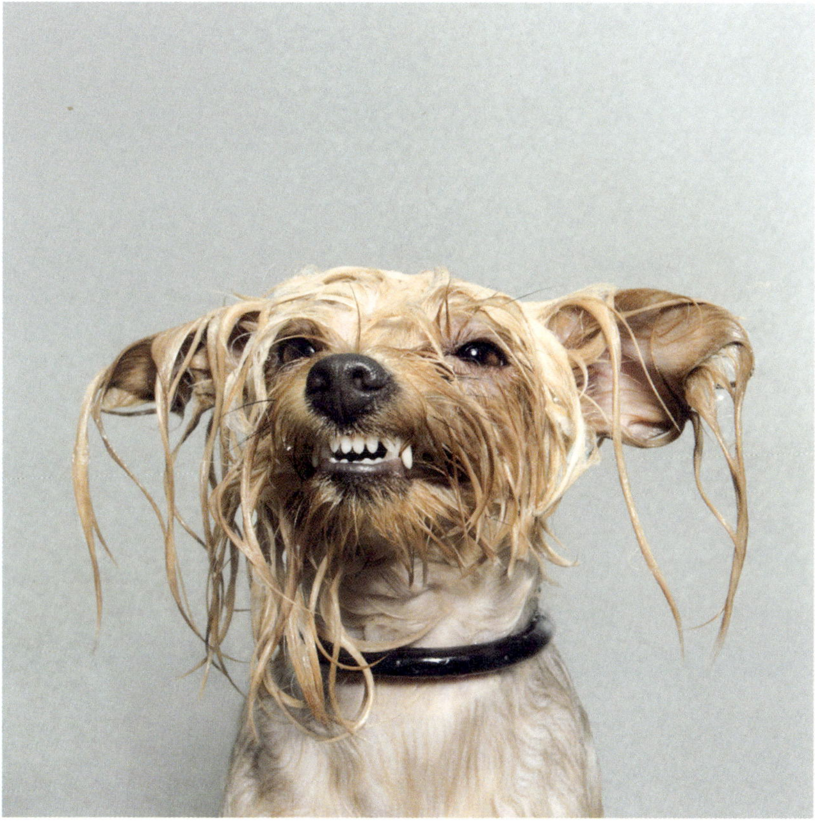

Diamond, 2013

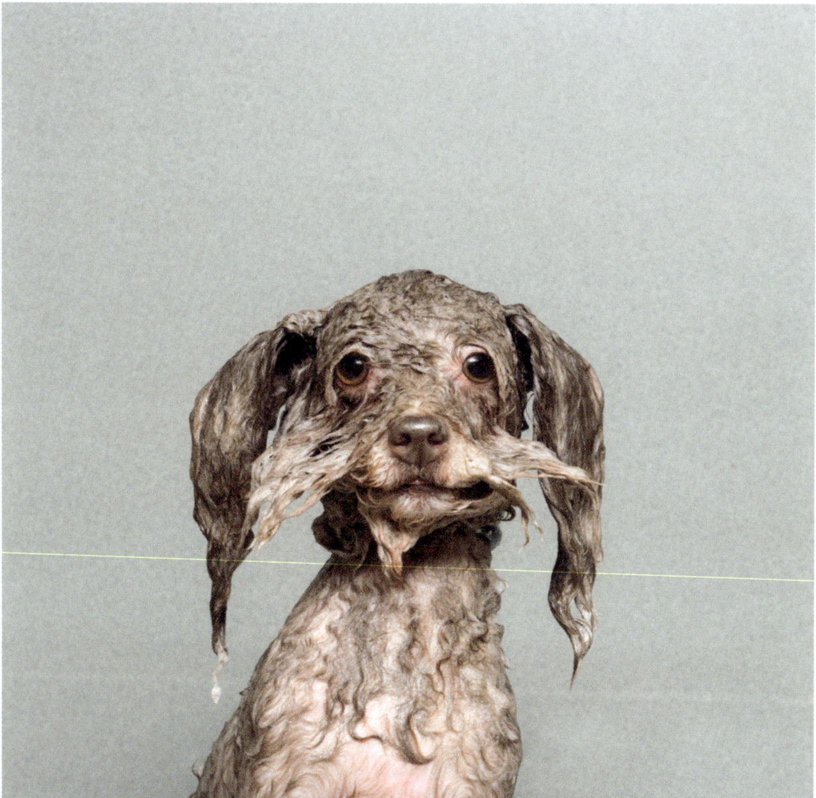

Britney, 2013

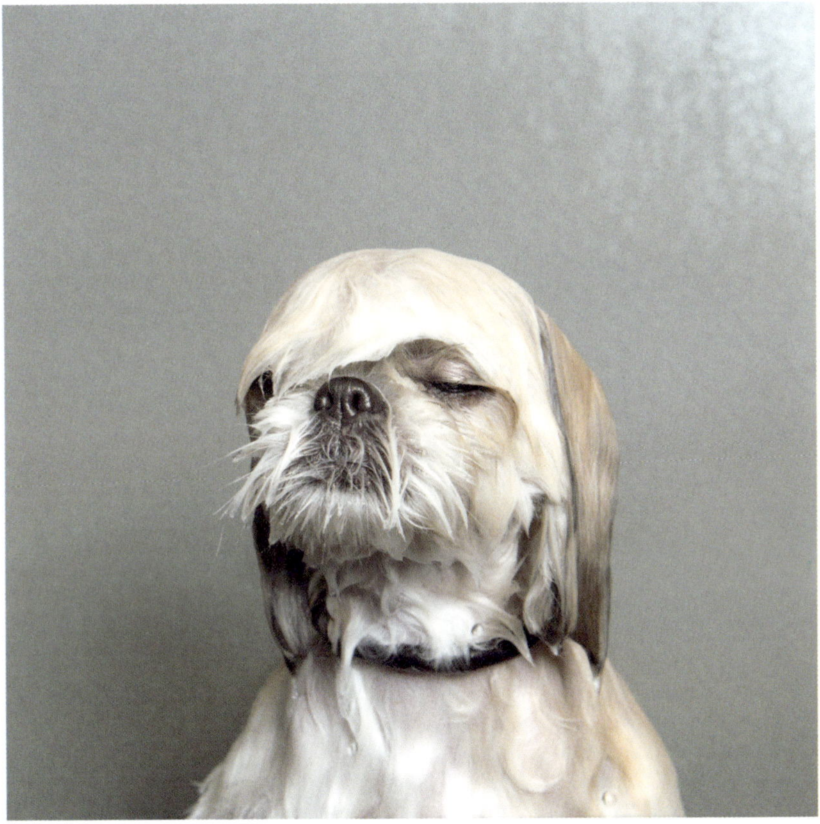

Crunchy, 2013

SHAKE DOGS
Carli Davidson

Drool, fur and water droplets fly in every direction as cheeks, ears and tongues flap wildly: these dogs are having a good old shake. Davidson's own dog, Norbert, a Dogue de Bordeaux, was known for smearing the walls of her house with drool. One day, she picked up a high-speed camera and what began as an experiment with Norbert grew into a project in which she caught more than 60 dogs mid-action.

Davidson grew up beside a nature preserve and later worked in animal care and conservation at the Oregon Zoo in Portland, where she lives. This experience led her to work with animal models, including exotic animals and pets with disabilities. Even so, she can't always control the outcome. Of the many dogs she scheduled to shoot for *Shake Dogs*, not all could be coaxed into shaking.

In these freeze-frame portraits, the dogs' faces are all scrunched up, some hilariously still trying to maintain eye contact with the camera. They are hard not to laugh at.

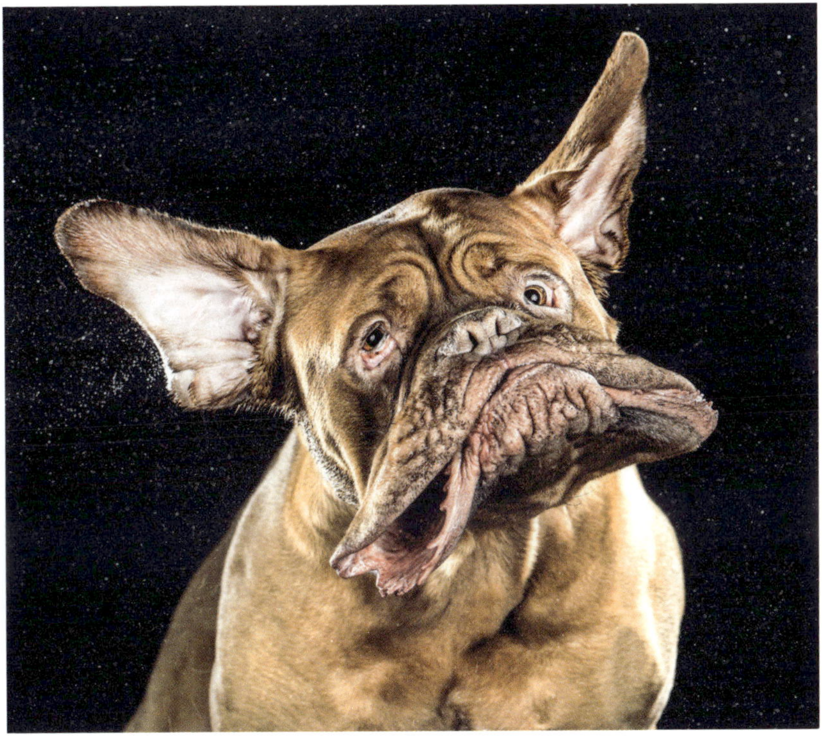

SHAKE-135, 2012

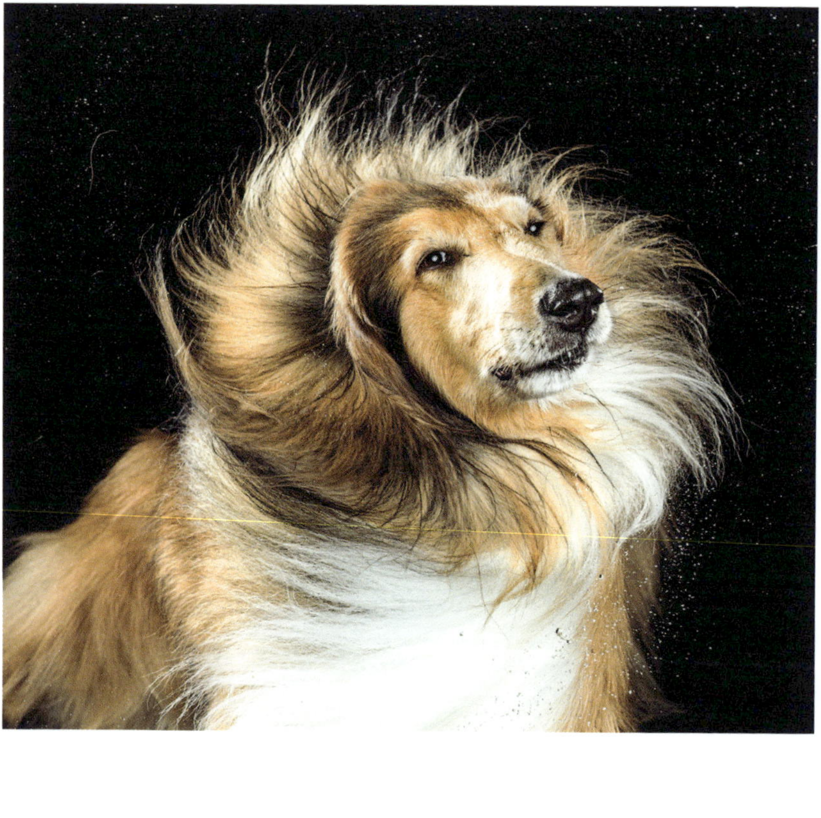

SHAKE-18, 2012

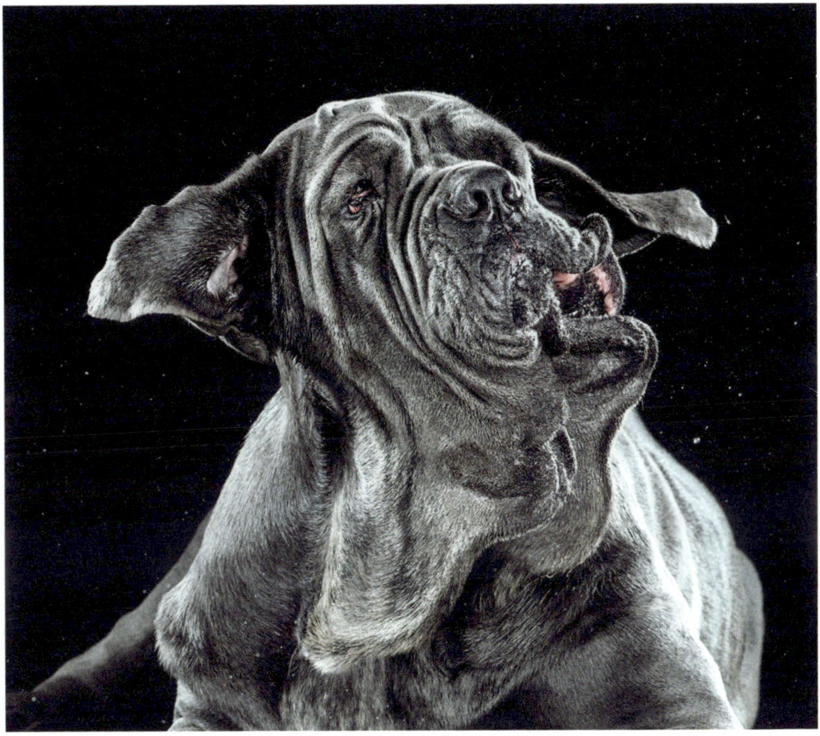

SHAKE-49, 2012

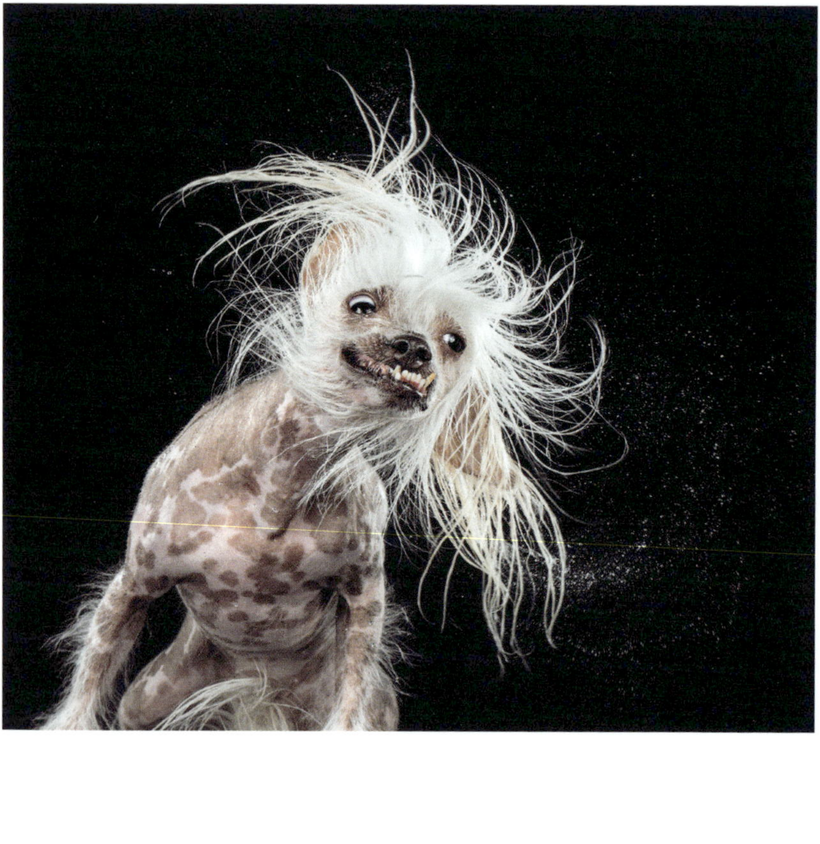

SHAKE-5, 2012

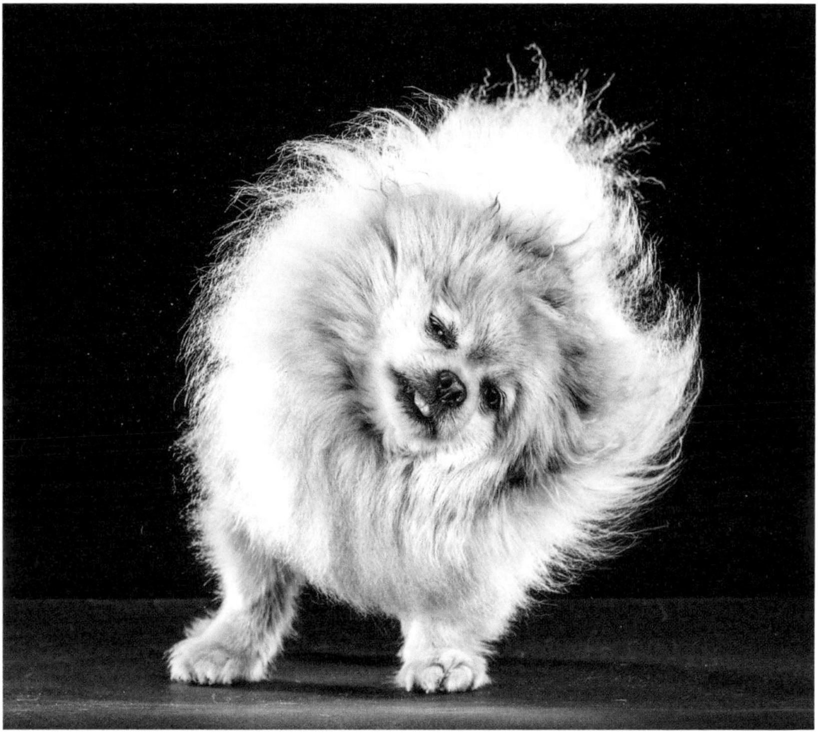

SHAKE-23, 2012

AMELIA & THE ANIMALS
Robin Schwartz

We're all part of the animal kingdom, but how often do we get to see eye-to-eye with other species? When her daughter Amelia was three, photographer Robin Schwartz made it her mission to introduce her to as many animals as possible. Over the following decades, she has recorded Amelia's encounters with both wild and domestic creatures.

Monkeys, elephants, llamas, ponies, big cats and, of course, dogs have become part of their photo-based menagerie. Thankfully, Amelia hits it off with most. She's intuitive and a great collaborator, as much at ease with a dog as with a kangaroo. In pictures that often resemble fables or fairy tales, dogs appear as protectors, friends, playmates and confidantes.

Tender, affectionate and sometimes funny, Amelia's portraits with dogs reflect an intimacy that can perhaps only be shared with man's best friend. If this is an ode to interspecies connection, dog lovers everywhere will surely agree that no other animal can beat the bond between a human and a loyal hound.

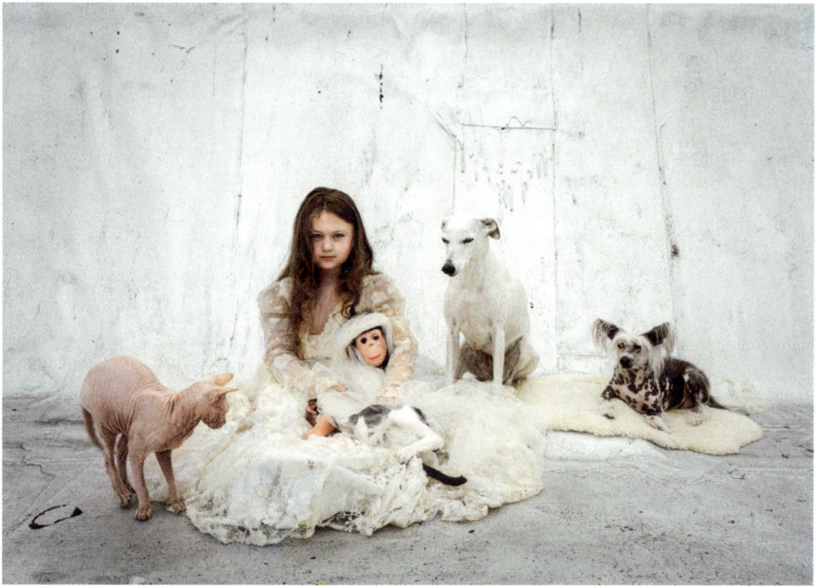

Roof Top Wedding, Our Pack: Jacob, Amelia, Ming, Hannah, Rebecca and Nora, 2010

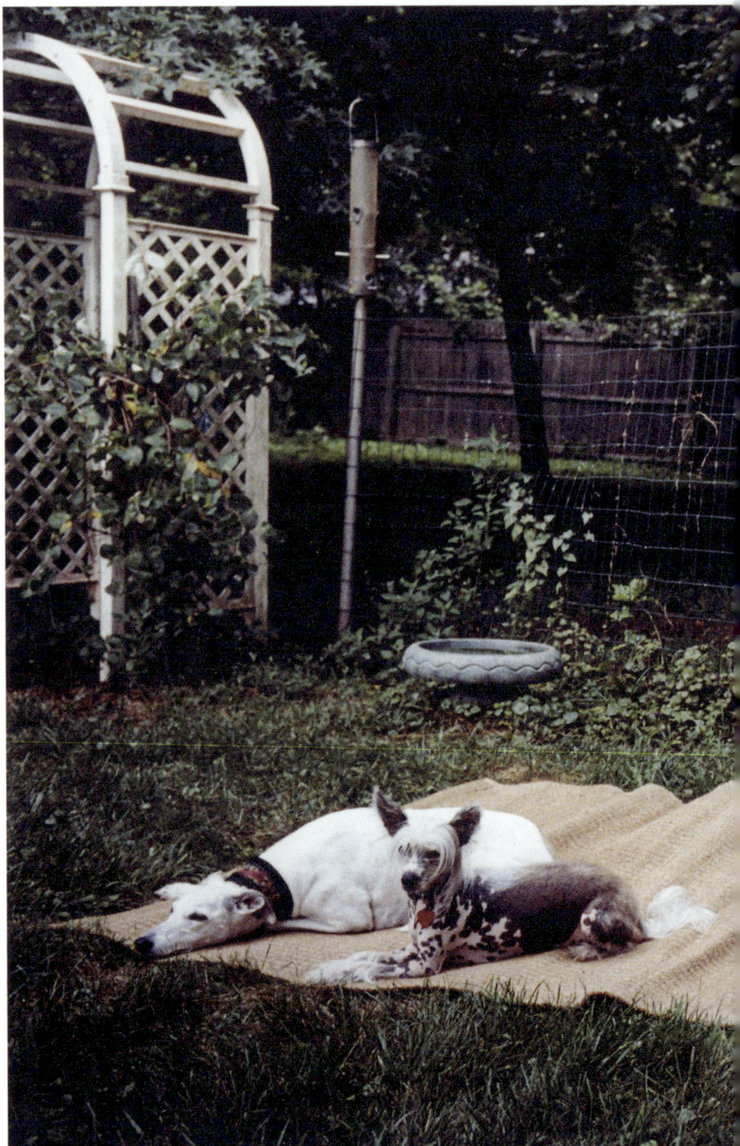

Linda's Backyard, Rebecca, Nora, Jonah and Amelia, 2008

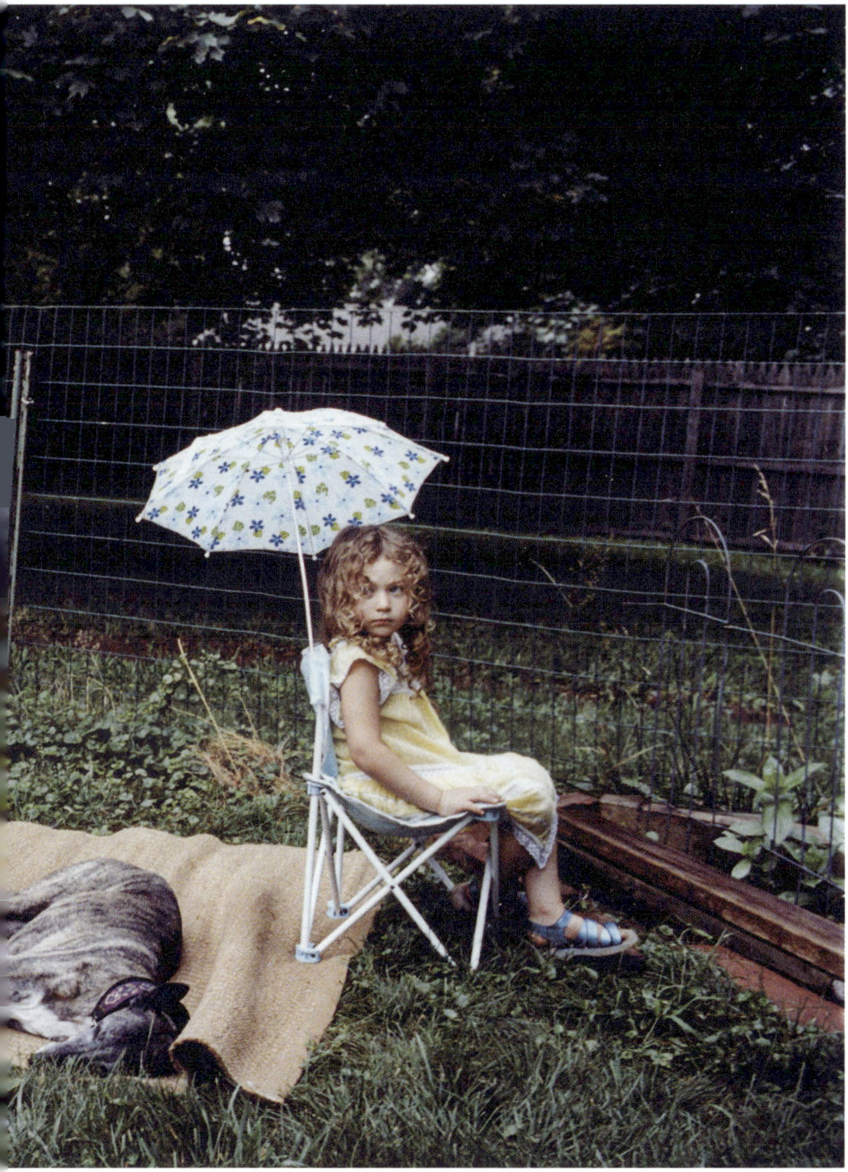

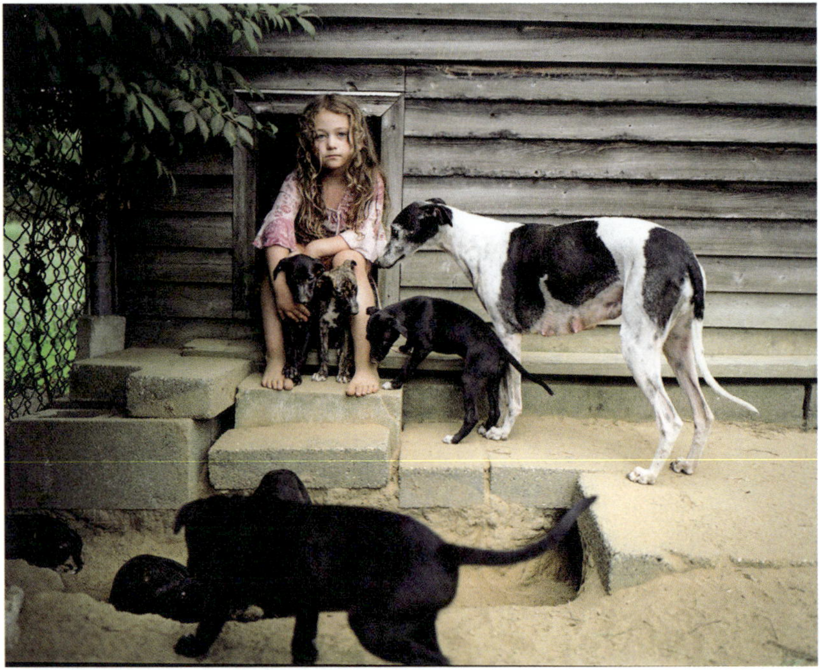

Amelia and Jetta puppy, Ariel's Whippet's puppies, 2005

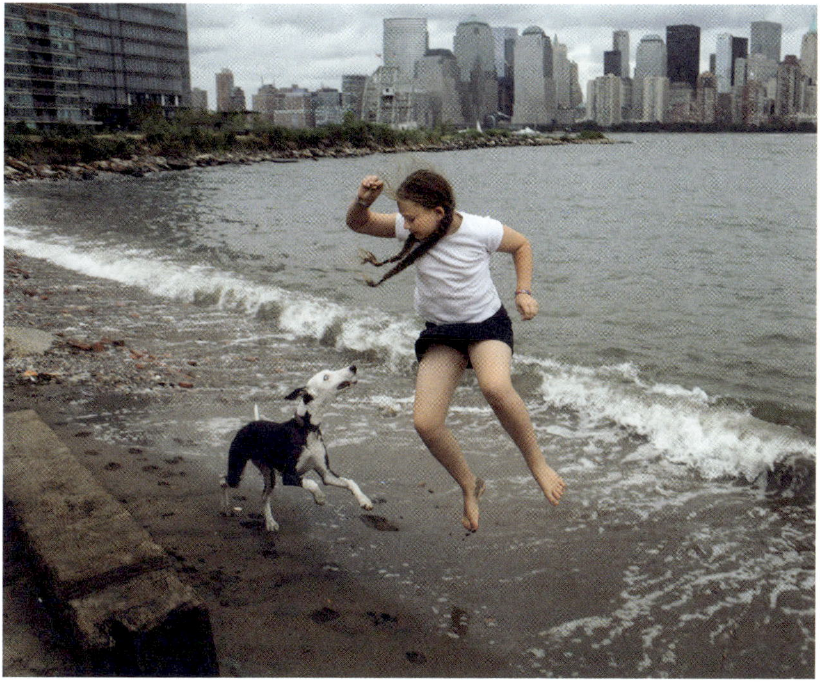

Above: *Ruby Whippet and Amelia, Across from World Trade Center,* 2010
Overleaf: *Baby Ruby Whippet and Amelia,* 2010

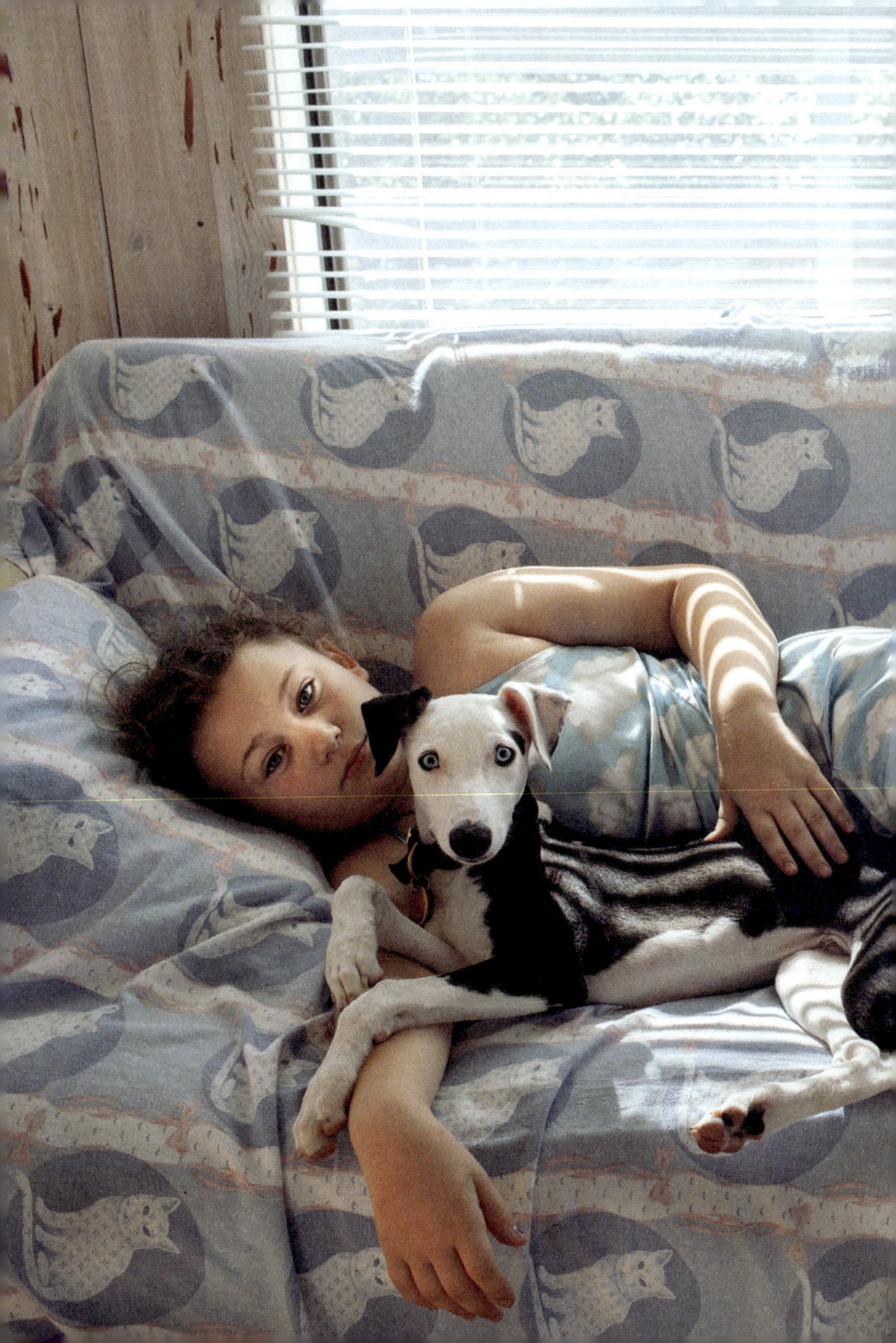

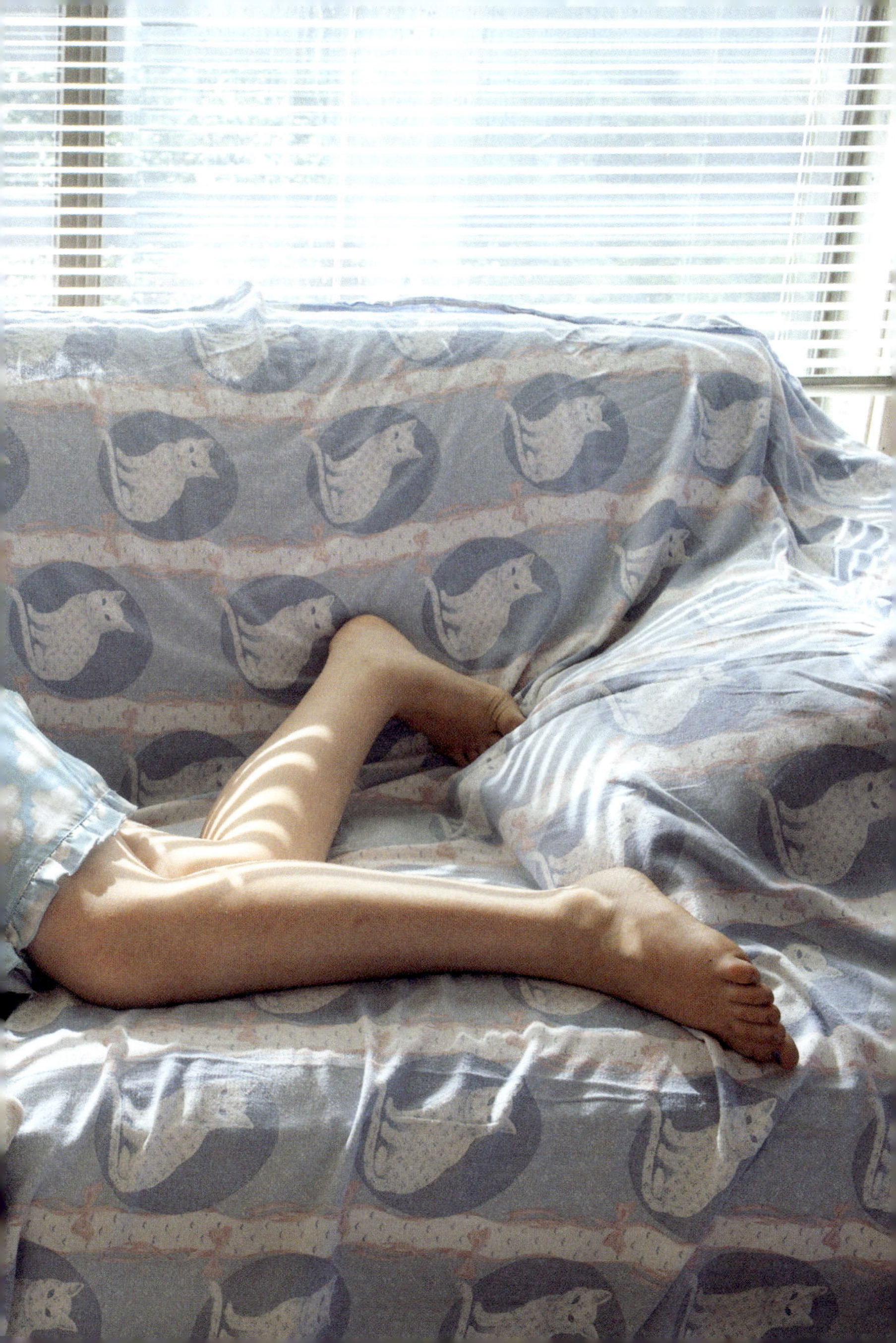

DOGS OF NEW YORK
Dietmar Busse

Michael and Alex, with TamTam, perch on two small stools, posing for the camera in an otherwise bare room. It's a perfect family portrait – one of a series of photographs by the artist Dietmar Busse, shot in his Manhattan studio between 2006 and 2014.

Having begun his career in the 1990s shooting fashion and portraiture for well-known magazines, Busse invited friends, artists and fellow New Yorkers into his studio, photographing them against whitewashed walls and worn wooden floorboards. Some brought their dogs along, and they soon became subjects in their own right.

Ask Busse why he loves photographing these four-legged companions and he'll tell you they keep you on your toes: you have to be quick to hold their attention. But more than that, a dog's honesty is disarming – they simply are who they are. Unlike their owners, they never ask to see the shots afterwards.

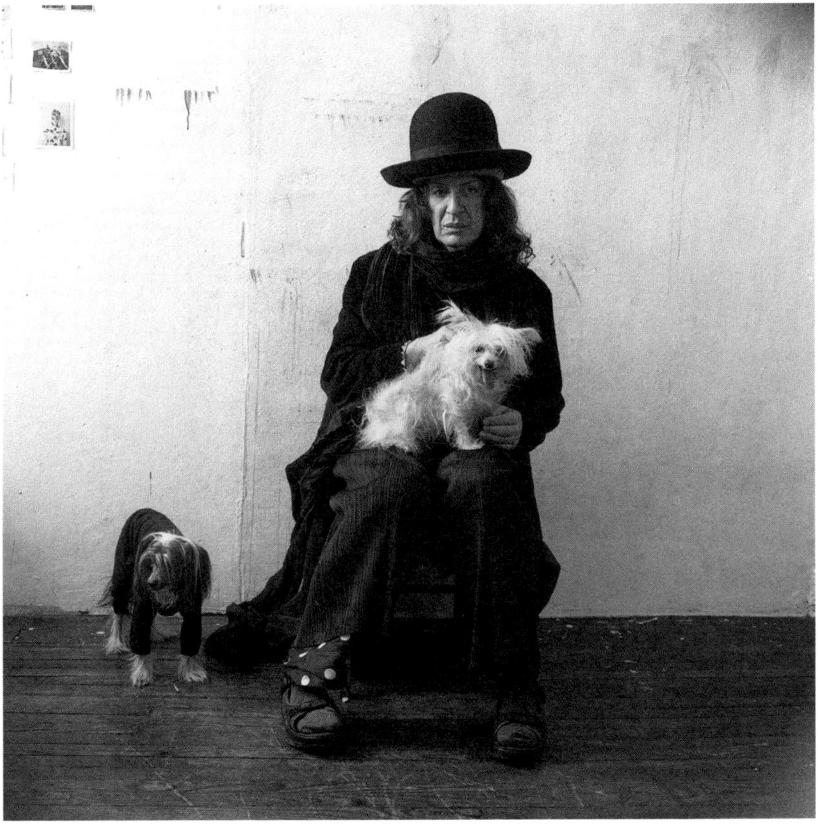

Johnny Rosza with Hobson and Stella, 2014

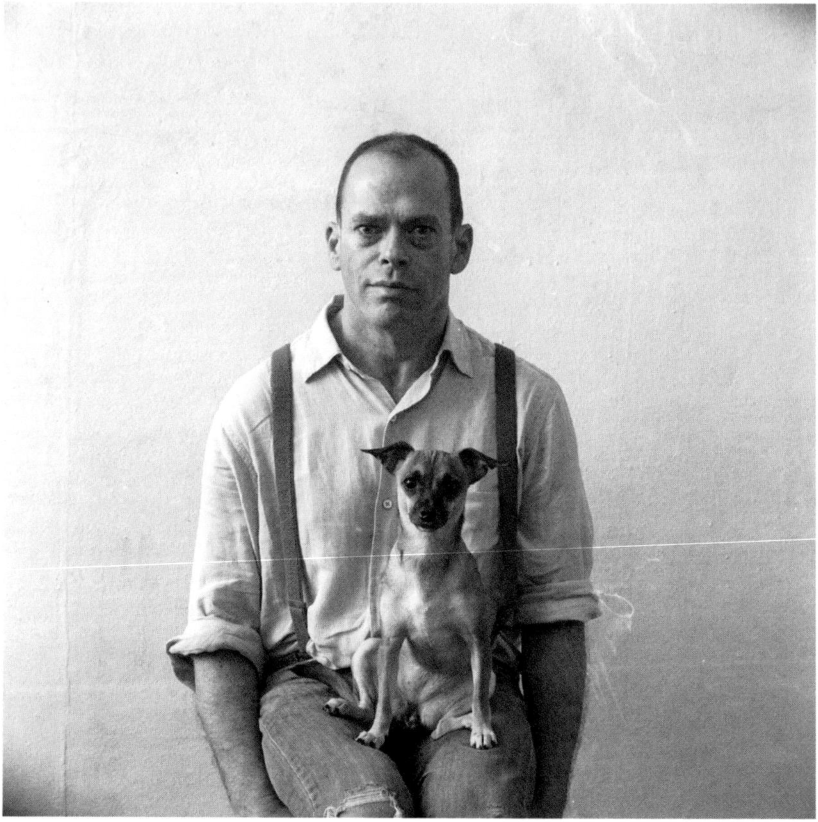

Eric Rhein with Scout, 2012

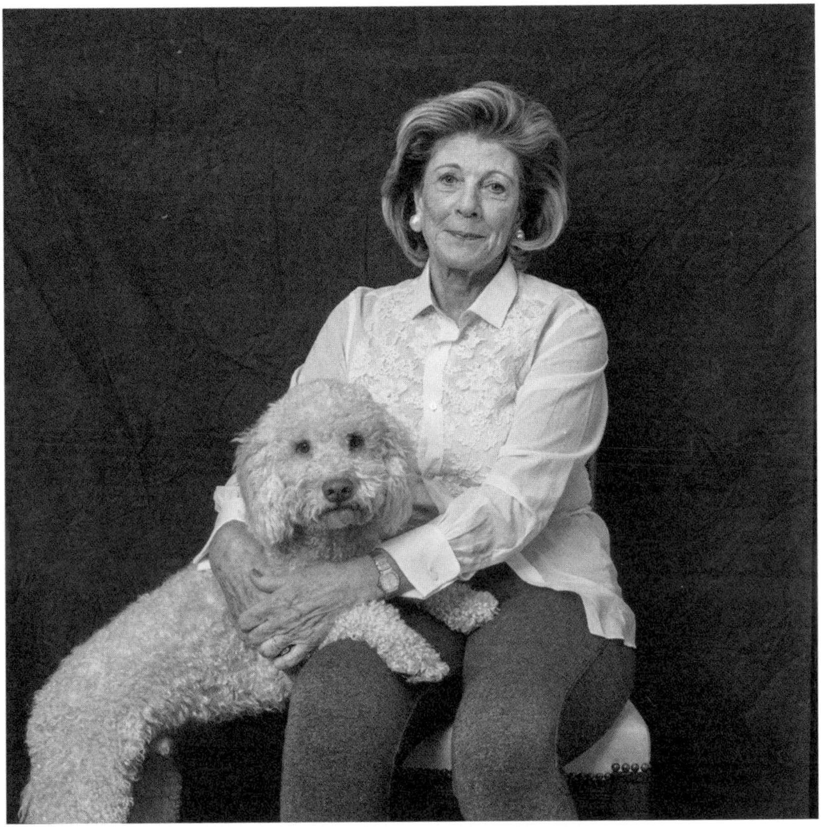

Agnes Gund with Bronzino, 2014

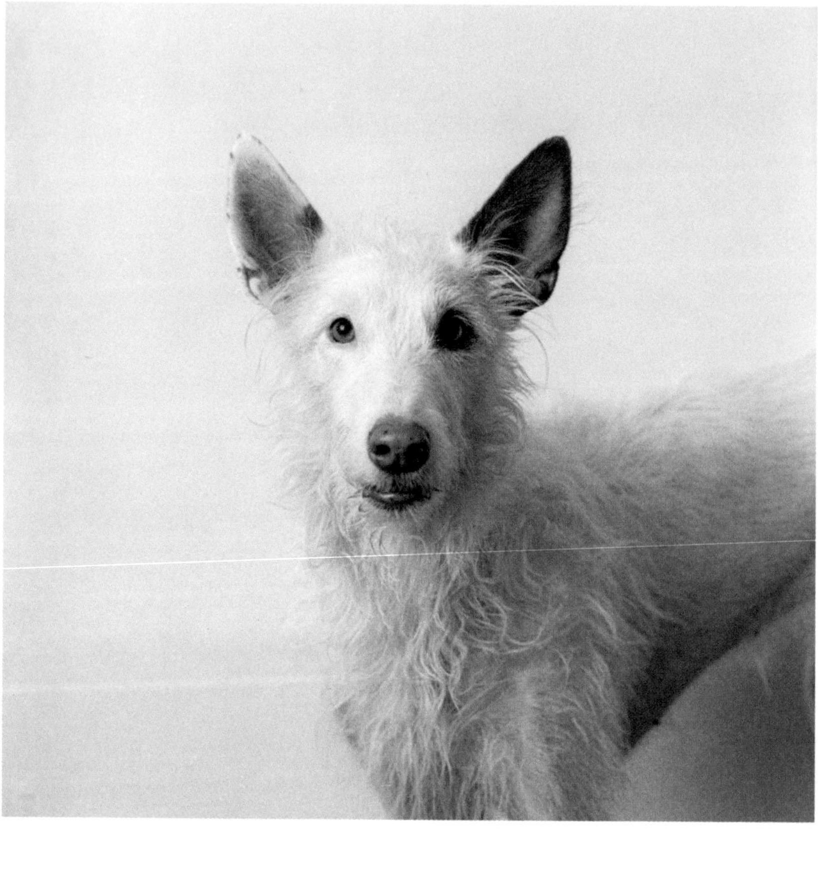

Ibizan Hound, 2008

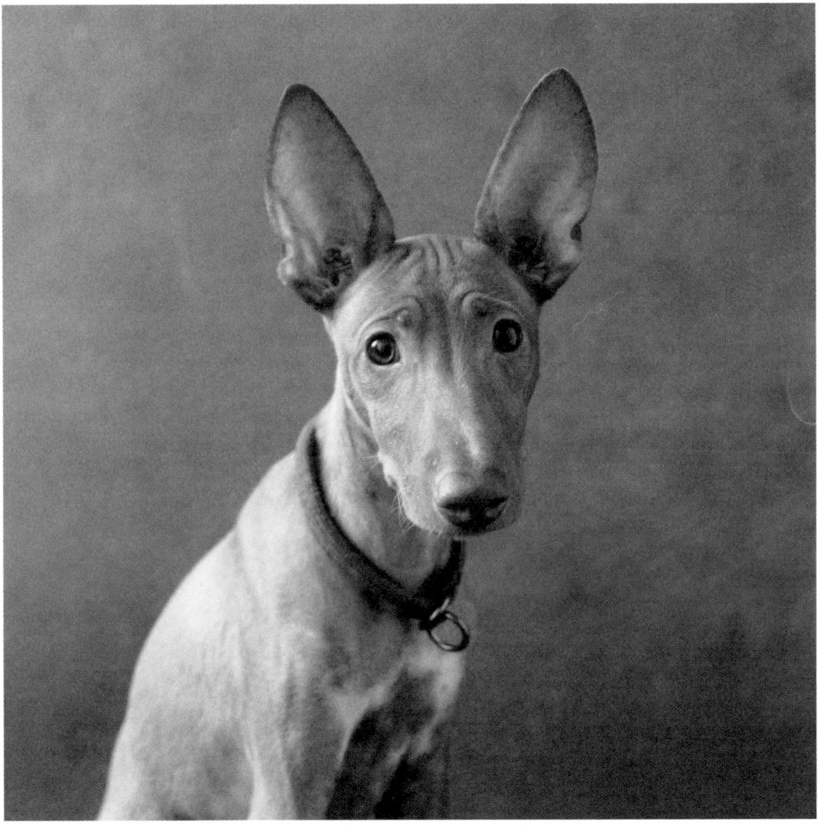

Freccia, 2008

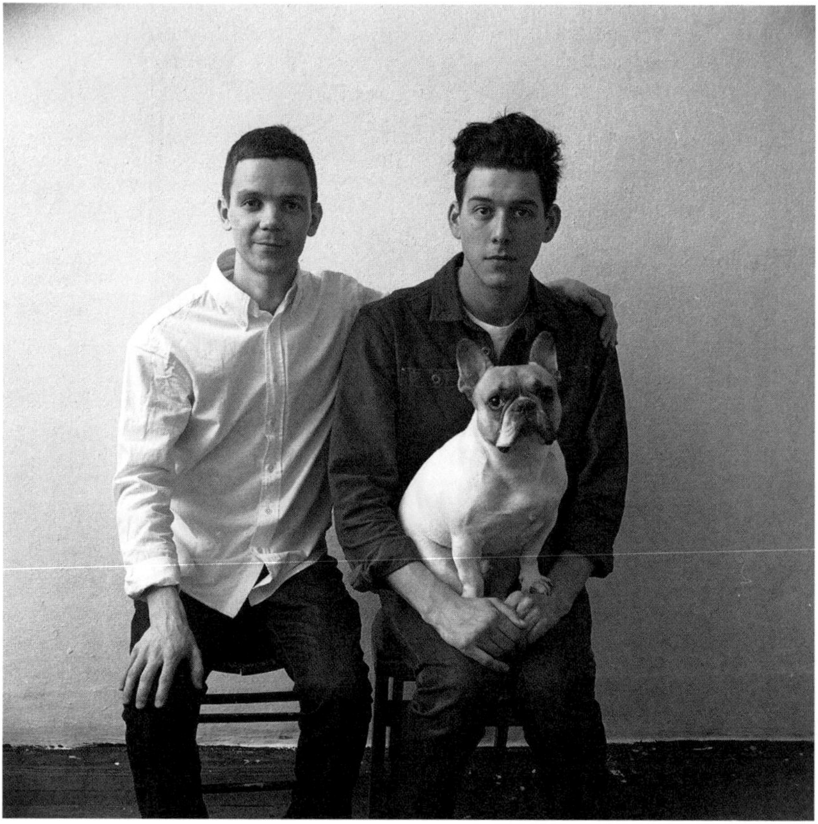

Michael, Alex and TamTam, 2014

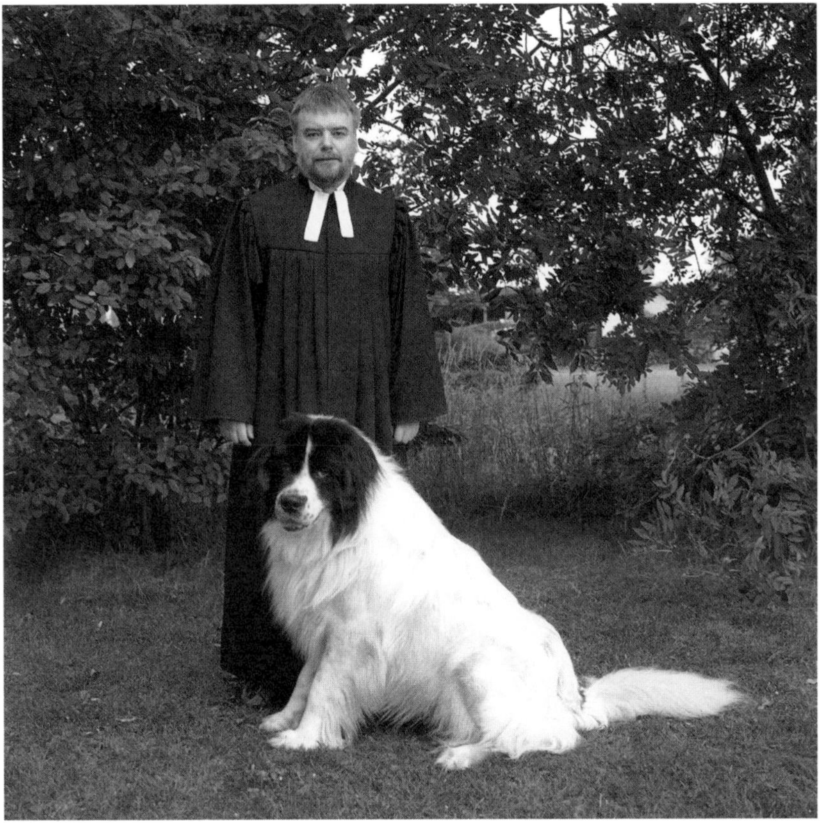

ANIMAL FARM

Daniel Naudé

Some of today's most popular dog breeds are modern concoctions: mixed breeds such as the Labradoodle, Pomsky and Chiweenie, which are loved for their cute, goofy looks or hypoallergenic coats. Other hounds have roamed the earth for centuries. The Africanis is one such breed, said to descend from the dogs of ancient Egypt.

Daniel Naudé's first encounter with an Africanis on the Karoo plains of South Africa stopped him in his tracks. A short but powerful moment of eye contact sparked a fascination with this slender, flighty creature. It set Naudé on a chase to capture similarly profound face-to-face moments with dogs roaming freely across vast, open landscapes.

His quest for the Africanis led Naudé to research the complex history of South Africa and the domestication of animals. Yet, he says, 'Nothing I have read about animals can sufficiently account for the intensity I experienced in these encounters. For me, the presence of an animal remains unfathomable, unexplained, yet incredibly potent: perhaps a threat – the presence of a predator; perhaps that of a protector.'

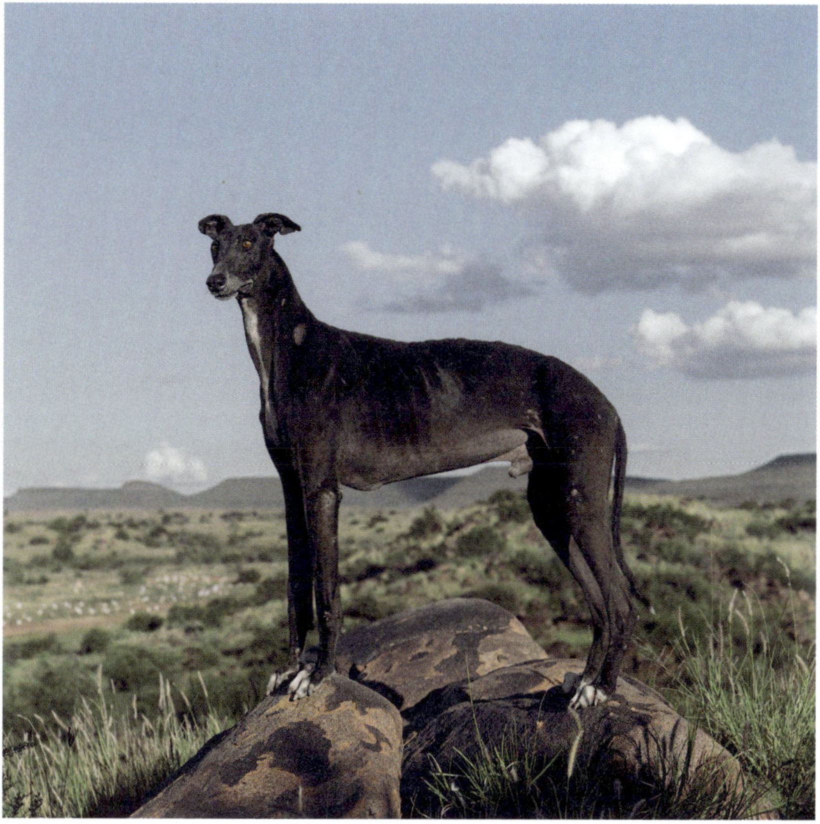

Africanis 20, 2011

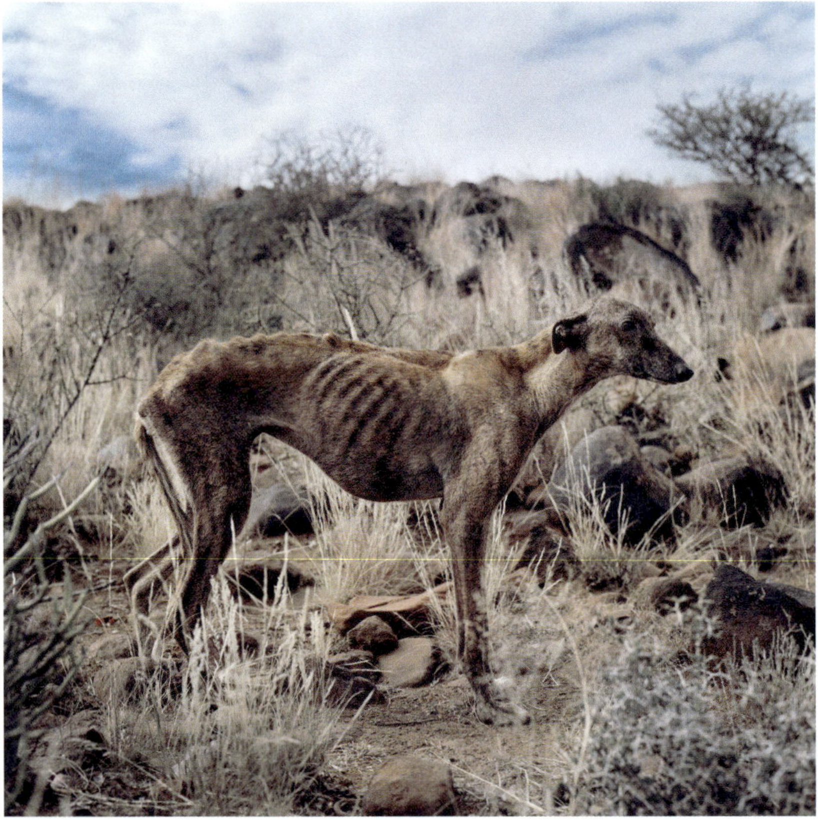

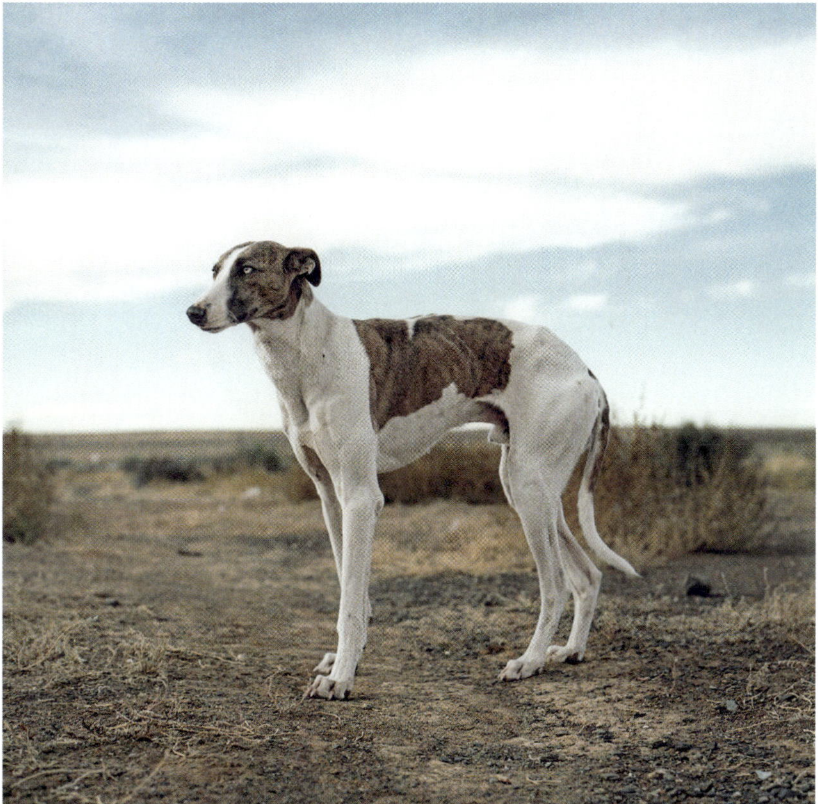

Africanis 9, 2008

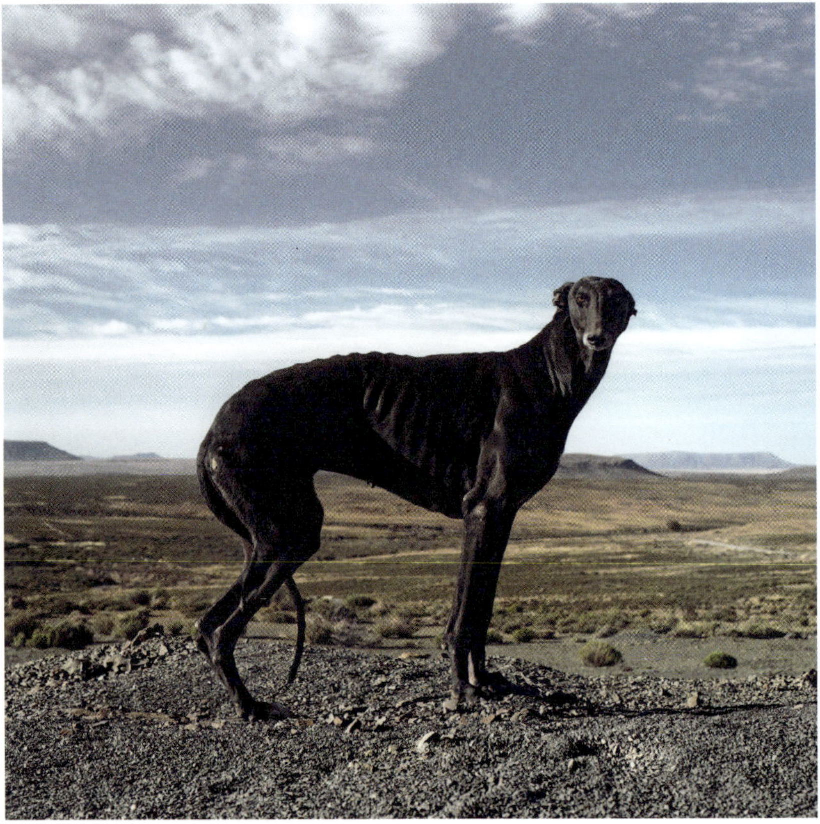

Africanis 18, 2010

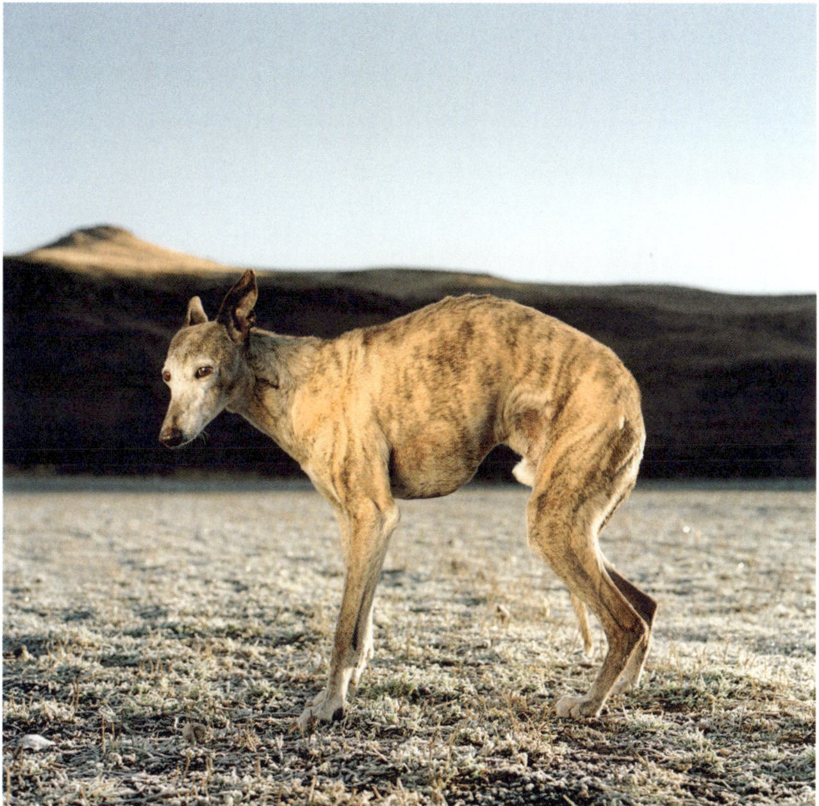

Africanis 8, 2008

RETRIEVED

Charlotte Dumas

Bretagne – the last surviving search-and-rescue dog to work at Ground Zero after the attacks of 11 September 2001 – died at the age of 16. In her final moments, the Golden Retriever from Texas was honoured with a last salute from firefighters and emergency workers. She was a dog of an extraordinary kind: not only a beloved companion, but a lifesaver in the most devastating of conditions.

For her poignant photo series, *Retrieved*, published in 2011, Charlotte Dumas tracked down 15 surviving dogs from among the nearly 100 deployed in the aftermath of 9/11. The images she had seen of them at work during the rescue operations had stayed with her for years. Amid immense loss and destruction, they had given her a small but powerful glimmer of hope.

Wanting to pay tribute to these brave and remarkable animals, Dumas travelled across the United States to photograph those that remained in their homes. Aged and weathered after lives of service, the dogs appear solemn and pensive. Having earned their rest, the eyes of these retired superheroes still speak volumes.

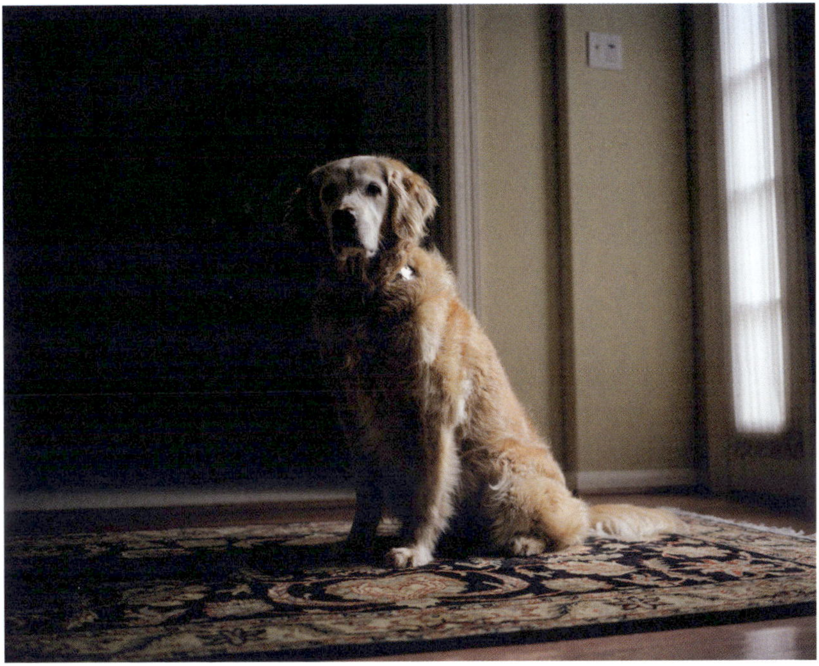

Bretagne, Cypress TX, 2011

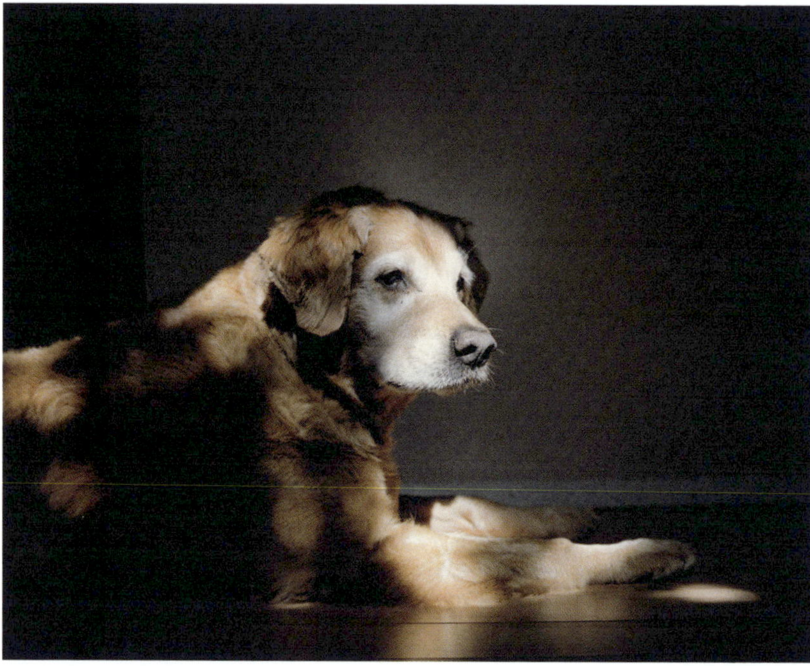

Orion, Vacaville CA, 2011

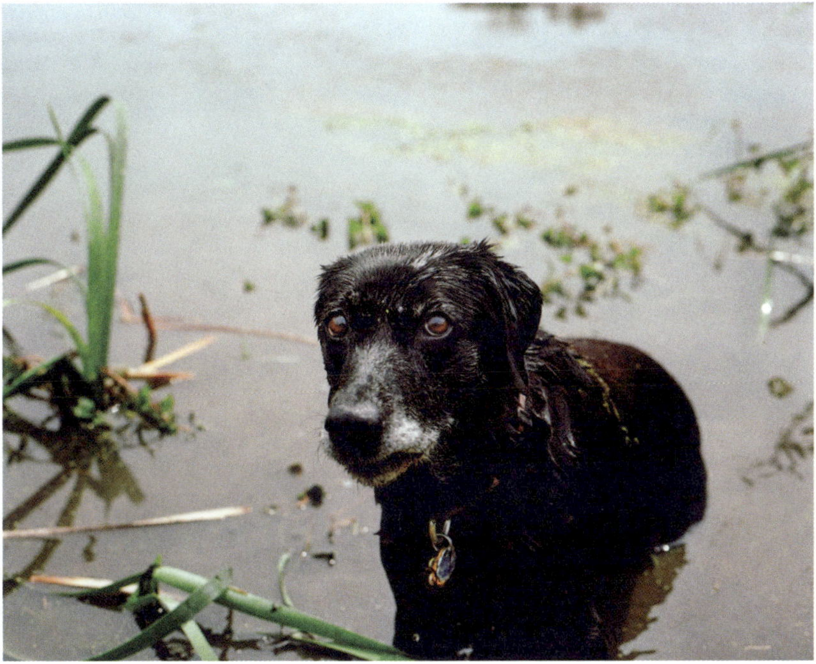

Above: *Bailey*, Franklin TN, 2011
Overleaf: *Bailey*, Franklin TN, 2011

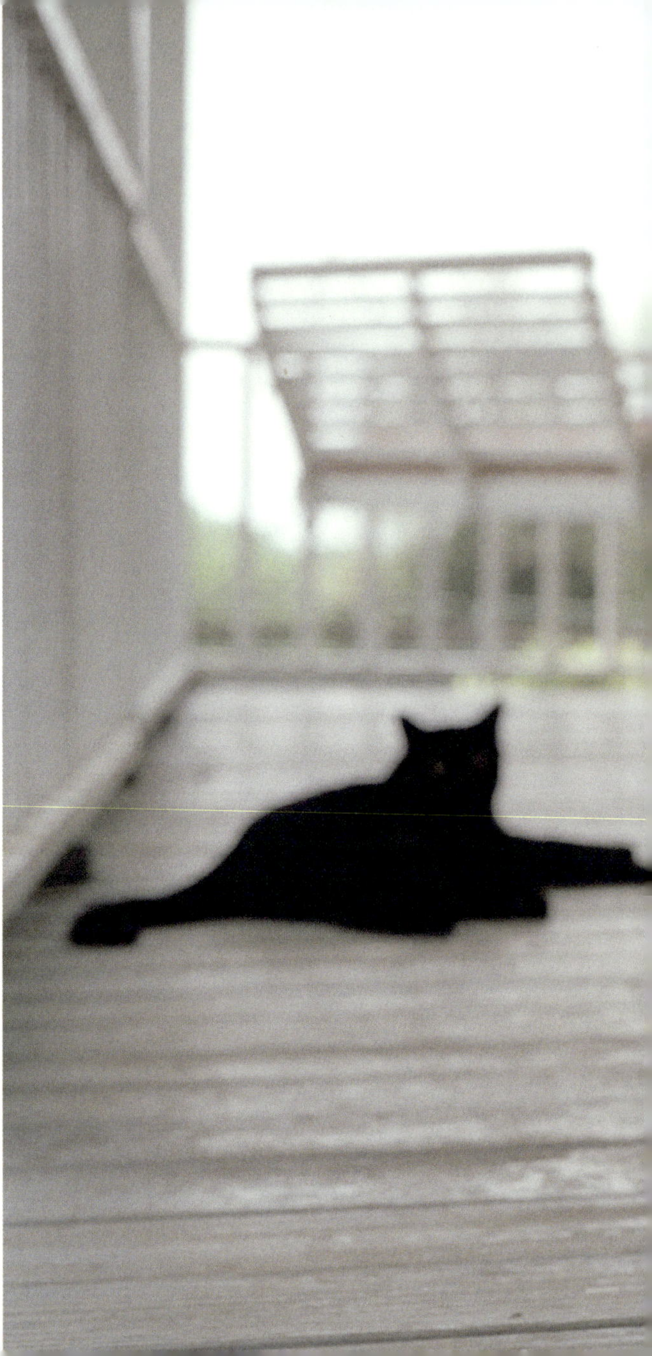

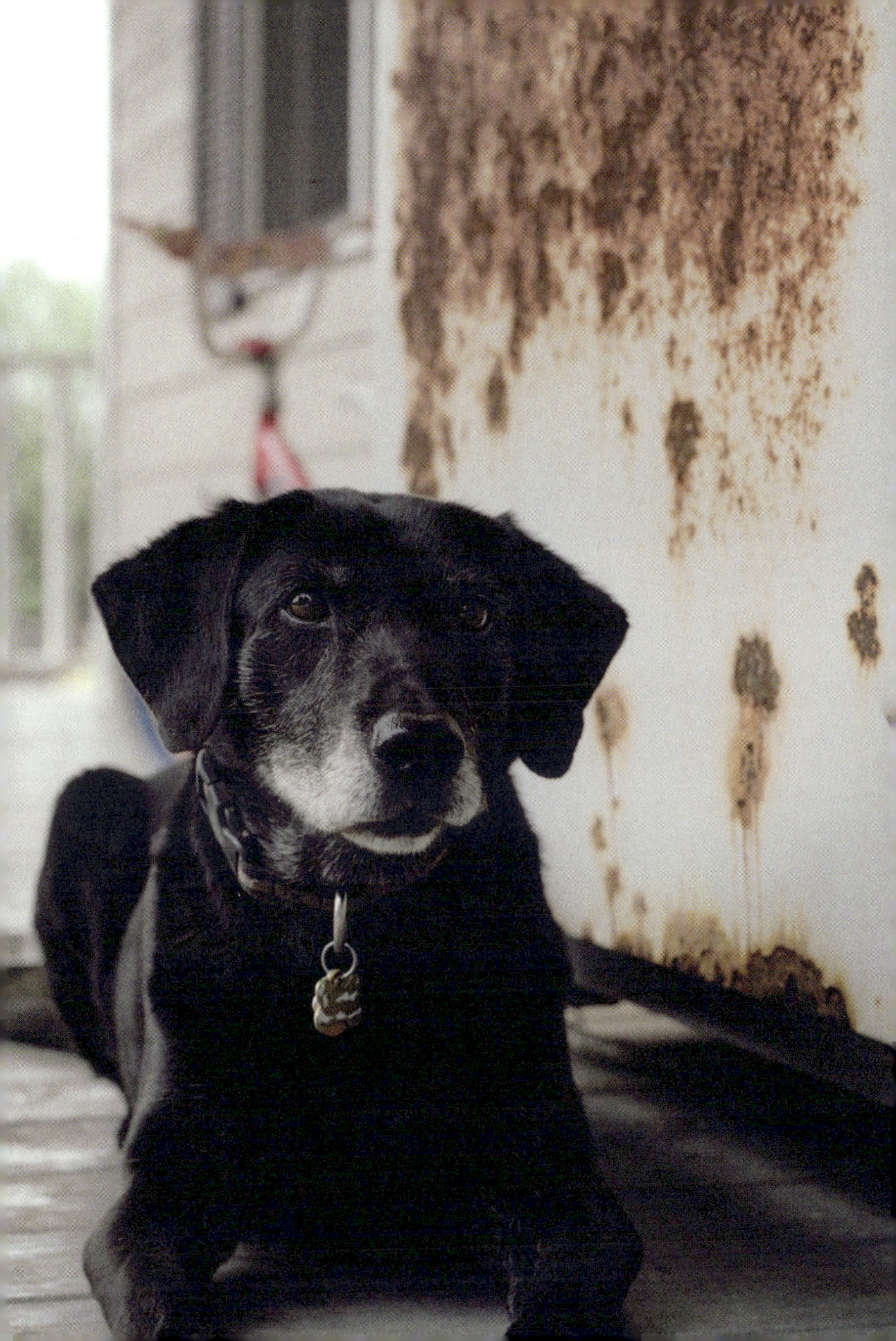

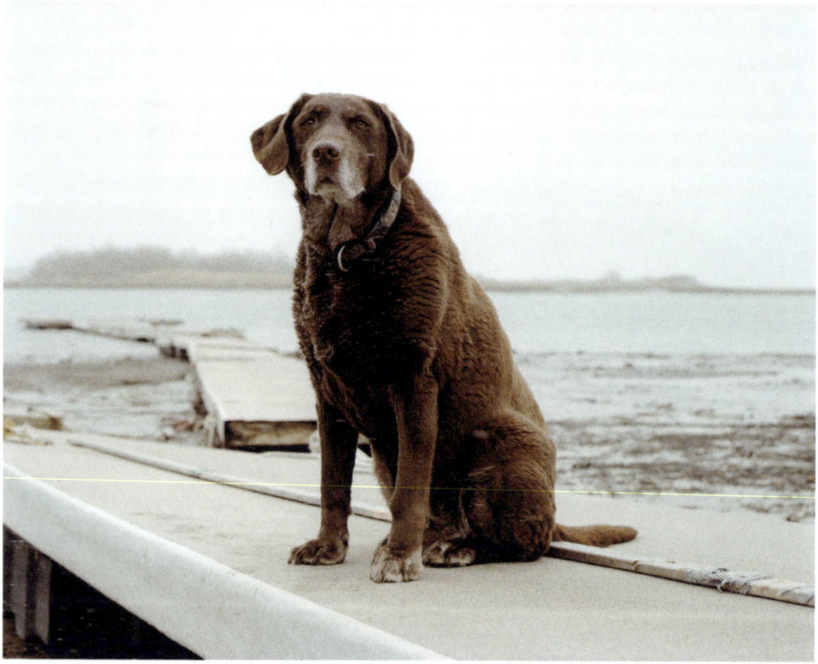

Moxie, Winthrop MA, 2011

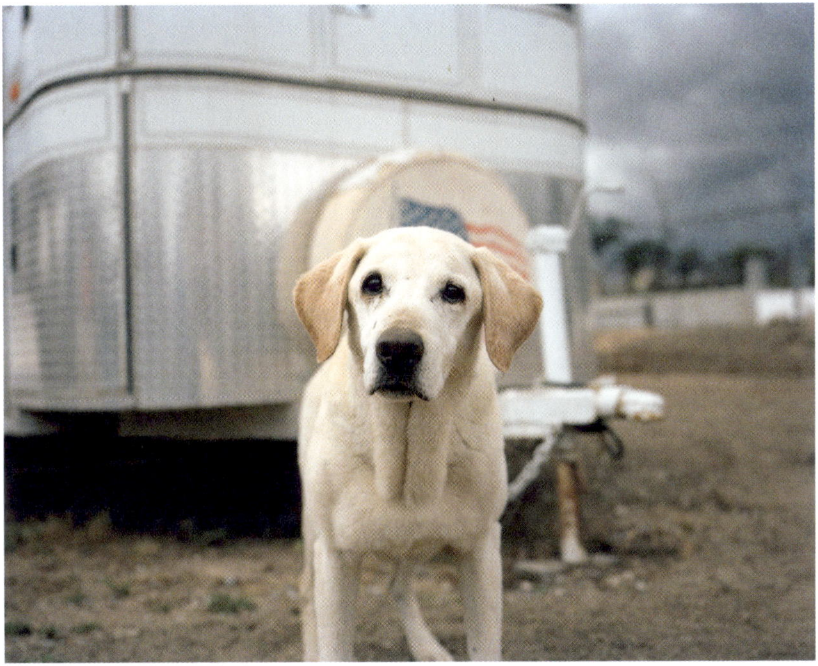

Guinness, Highland CA, 2011

GOOD DOG
Randal Ford

'Over 40,000 years ago, humans first depicted animals on cave walls. Since then, the portrayal of animals in art has remained a constant,' says photographer Randal Ford. 'As our art evolved, we began not only to depict animals but also to personify them, seeing our own emotions reflected in their expressions.'

Ford brings that instinct into the studio, turning his lens on everything from squirrels and sloths to lions, penguins and chimpanzees. His photographs tip into the hyperreal – so glossy, precise and finely detailed that they feel almost too perfect to be true, making it easy to forget that many of his sitters are untamed creatures. Yet for all their polish, the portraits never feel cold or contrived; instead, they pulse with personality and presence.

Good Dog, his book of dog portraits, arrived in 2020 at the height of the COVID-19 pandemic – a time when companionship and our relationship with the natural world took on new meaning. 'Ultimately, these portraits are meant to speak to you,' Ford emphasises. 'Whether they convey beauty, power, vulnerability or humour, my intention is to give animals the space to reveal themselves and the opportunity to connect with you.'

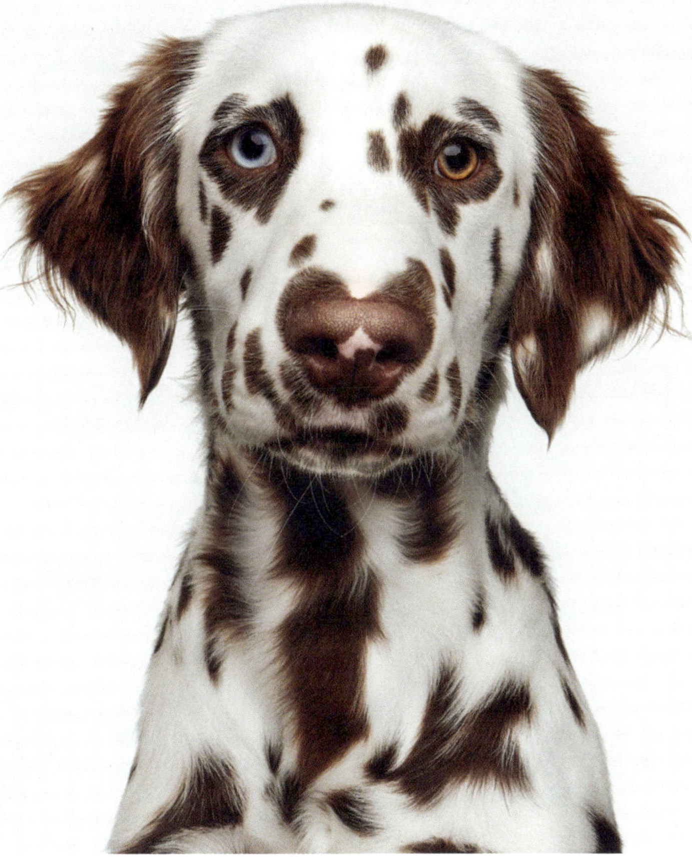

Buckley, Long-Haired Liver Dalmatian, 2020

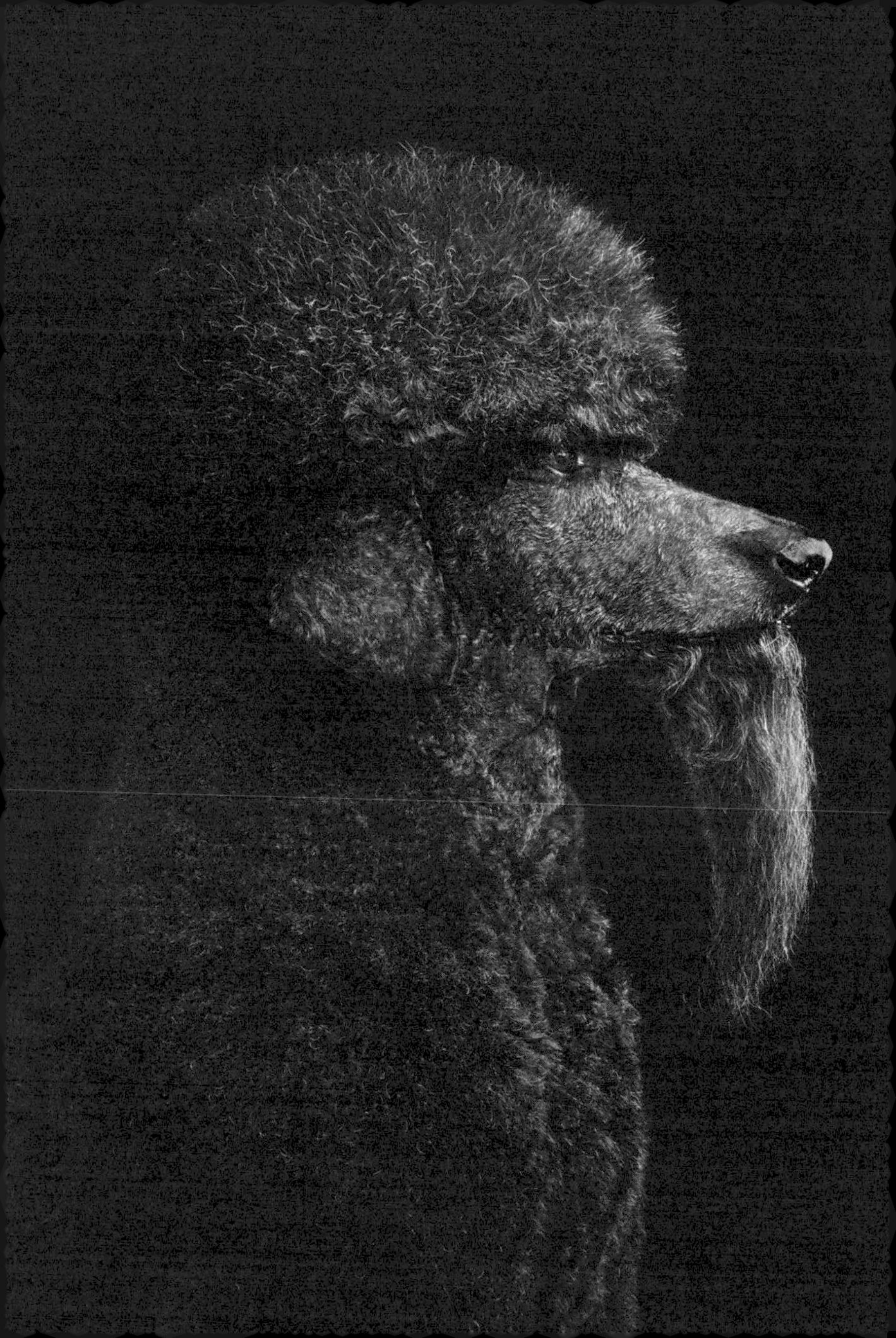

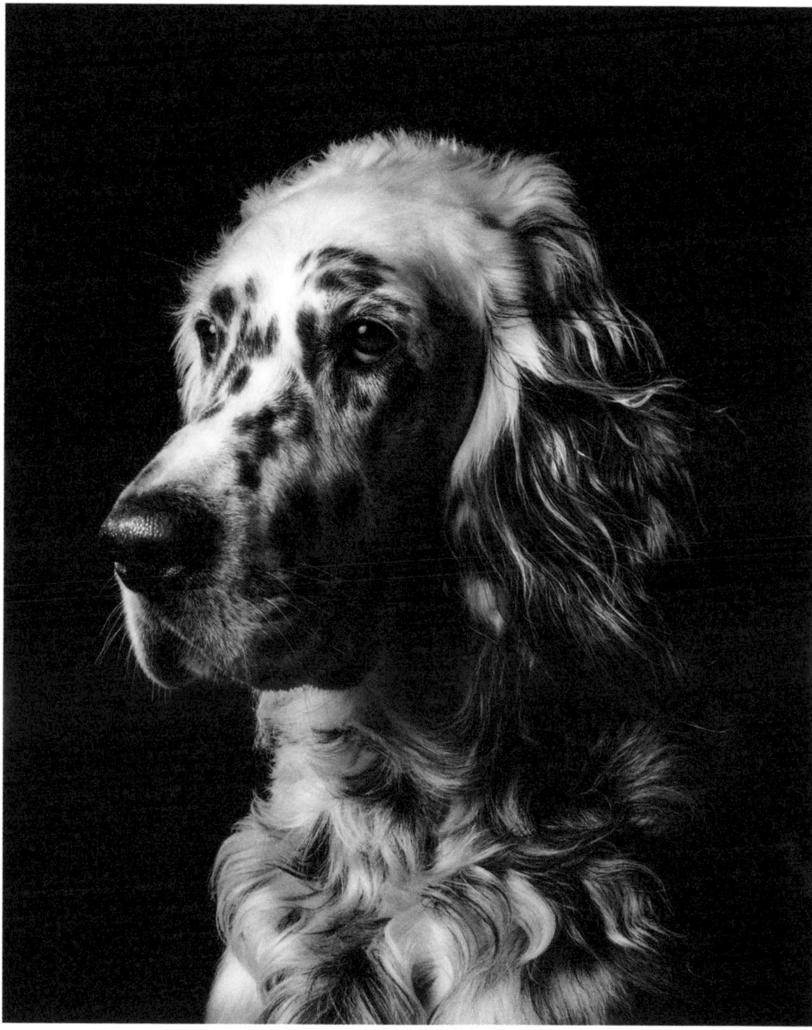

Above: *Rory,* English Setter, 2020
Opposite: *CeeLo,* Standard Poodle, 2020

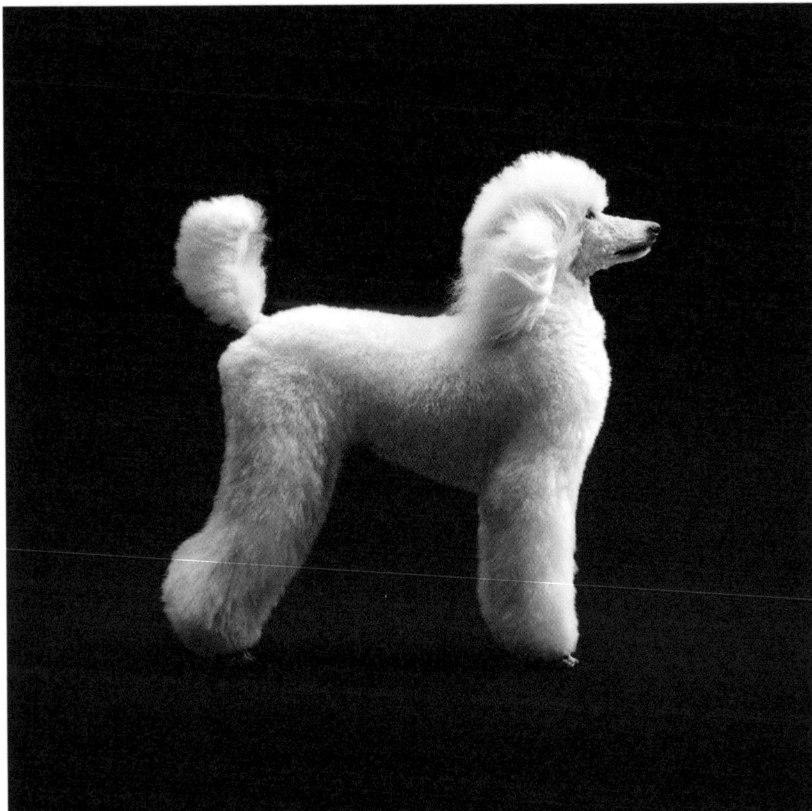

Porsche, Standard Poodle, 2020

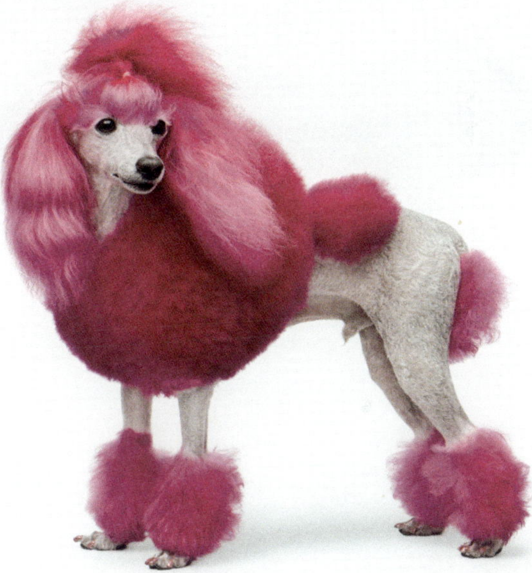

Pawpawrazzi, Toy Poodle, 2020

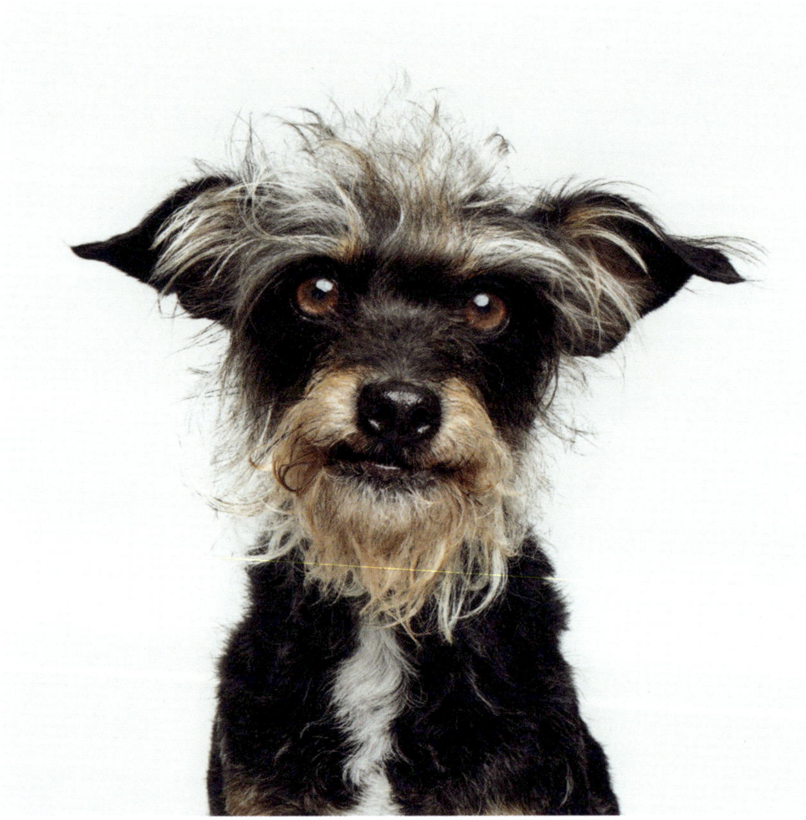

Finland, Scruff Terrier Mix, 2020

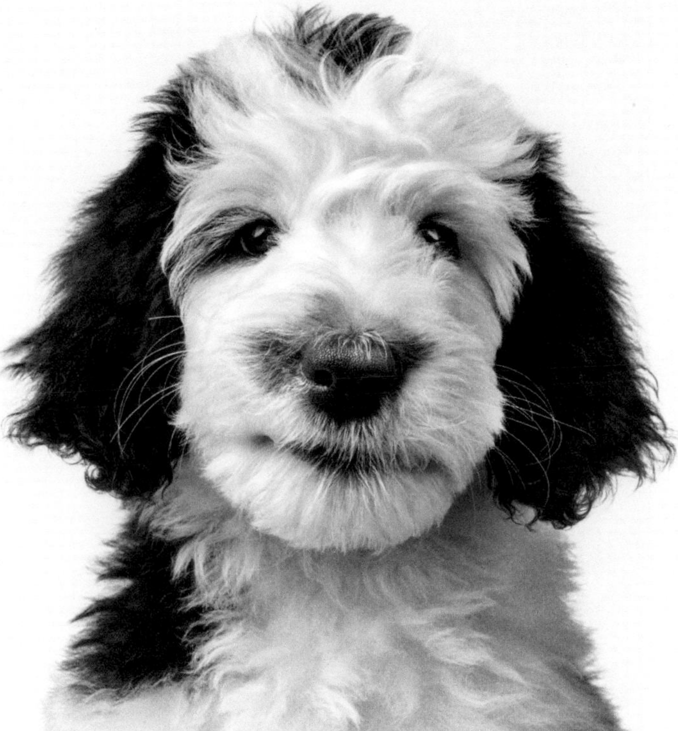

Dexi, Sheepadoodle, 2020

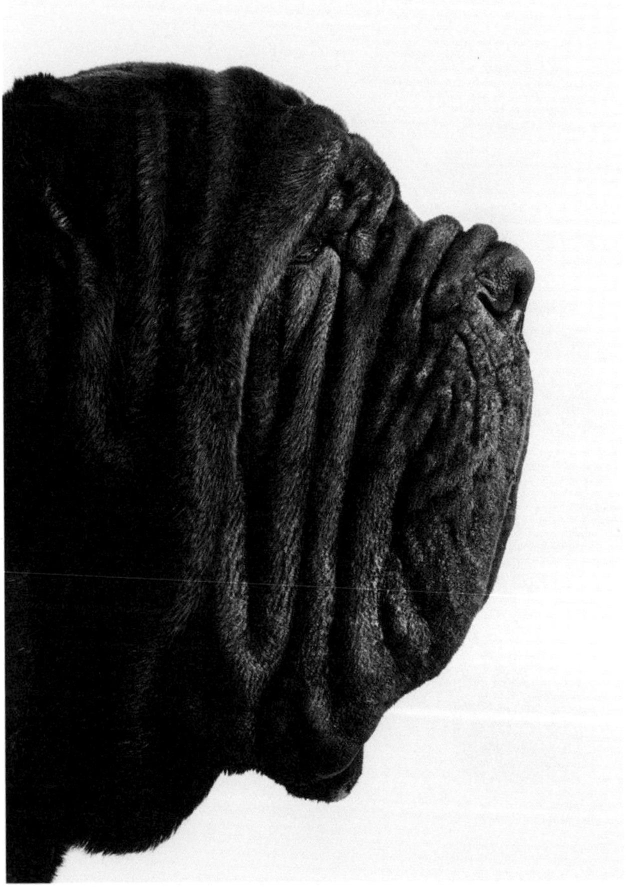

Above: *Barbaro*, Neapolitan Mastiff, 2020
Opposite: *CeeLo*, Standard Poodle, 2020

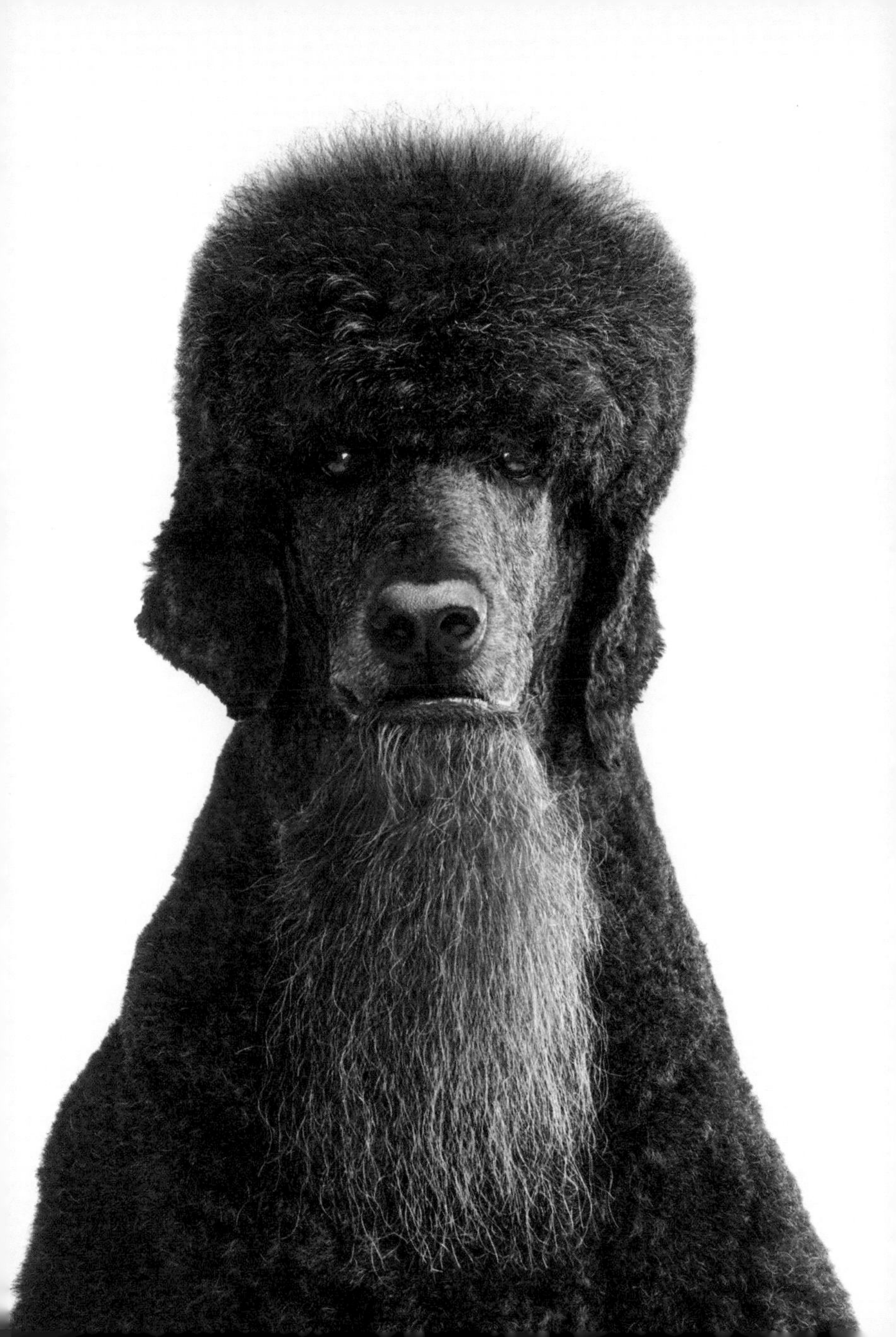

KINETIC
James Lee

'Is there anything more energetic than a dog chasing a ball across a beach?' asks San Diego-based photographer James Lee. 'You can see its boundless life-force boiling up from inside. They just GO.' In blurred black-and-white photographs that have the look of abstract paintings, Lee set out to capture that pure sensation of a dog streaking past at full speed.

He discovered the perfect setting at the mouth of the San Diego River. Where the river meets the ocean, the beach is a wide open playground where dogs can run freely off leash. Using a slow shutter speed in the late-afternoon light, the dogs Lee photographed appear on camera as whirling bursts of motion.

Over the course of a year, he threw himself into the project, shooting dogs of every shape and size mid-sprint. There's something magical about the resulting images – they are hypnotic, exhilarating and liberating. 'I want the viewer to be on the beach and share in that energy,' Lee says. 'It is joyous to watch, and to photograph.'

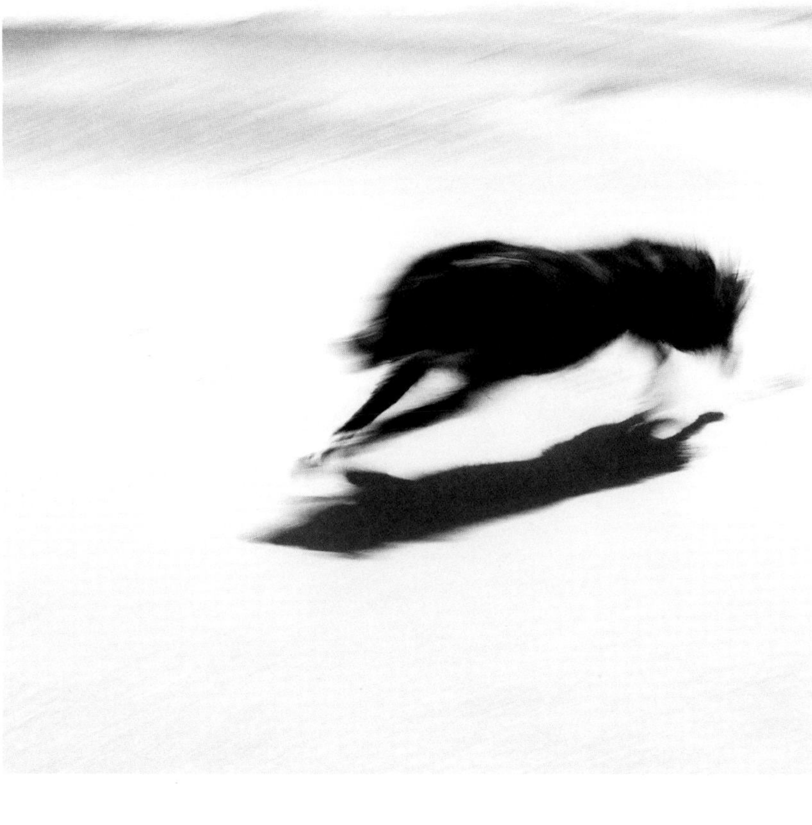

Whoosh, 2021

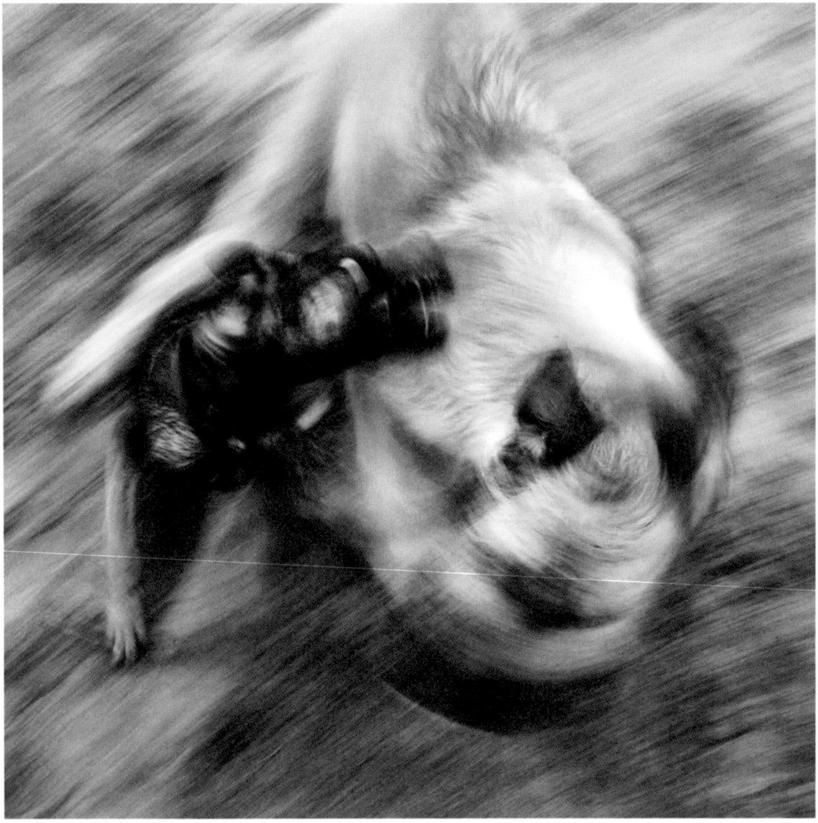

Wrestling, 2021

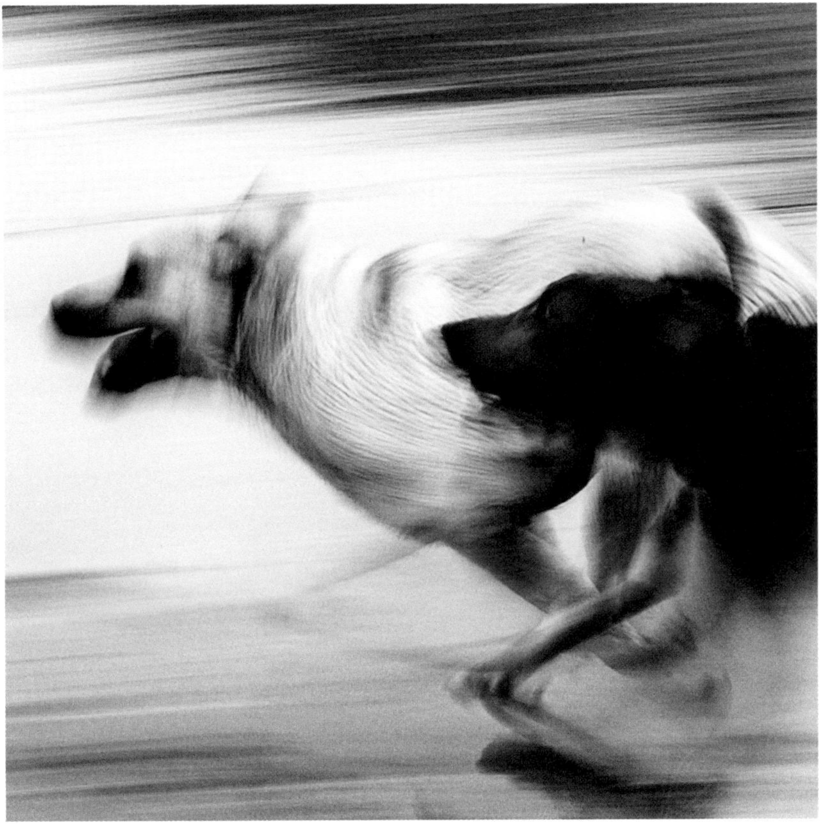

The Chase, 2021

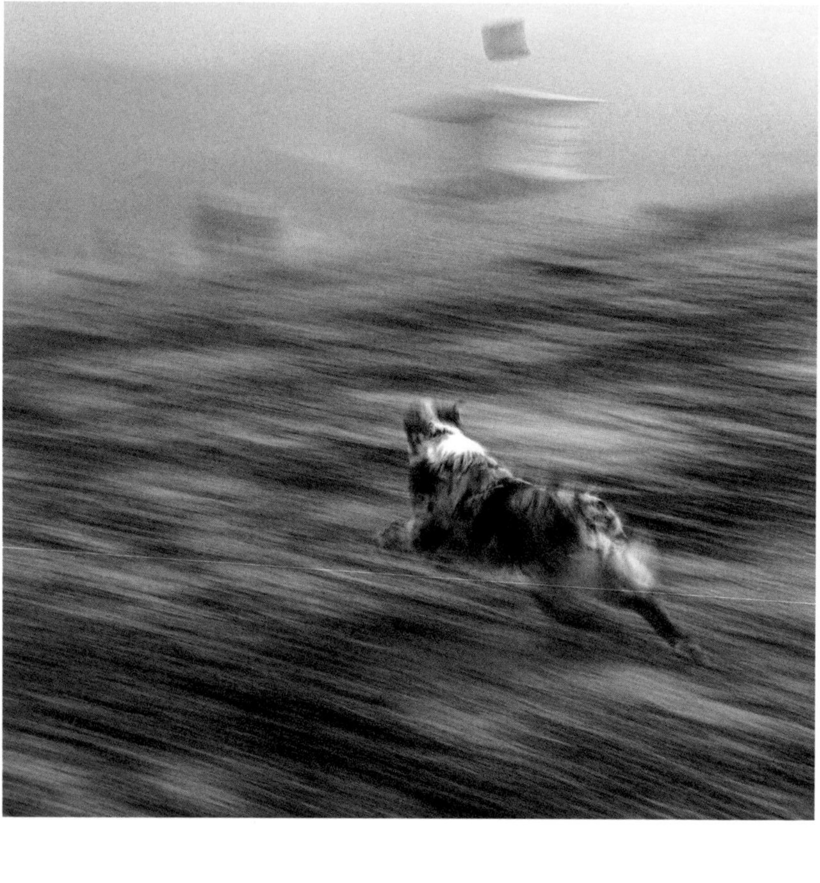

Lifeguard Tower, 2021

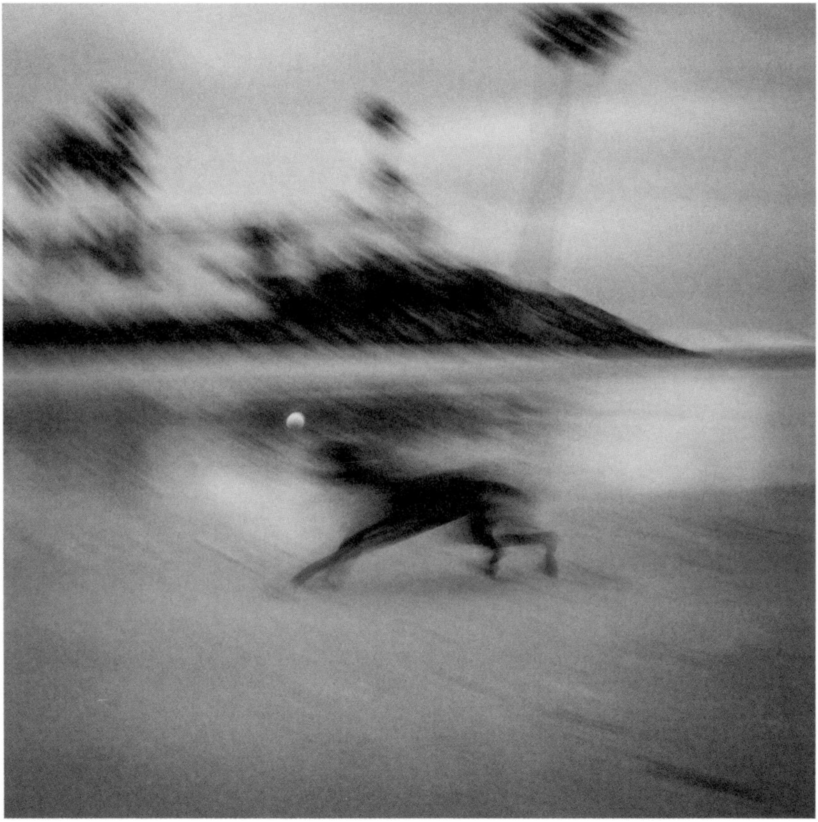

Only the Ball, 2021

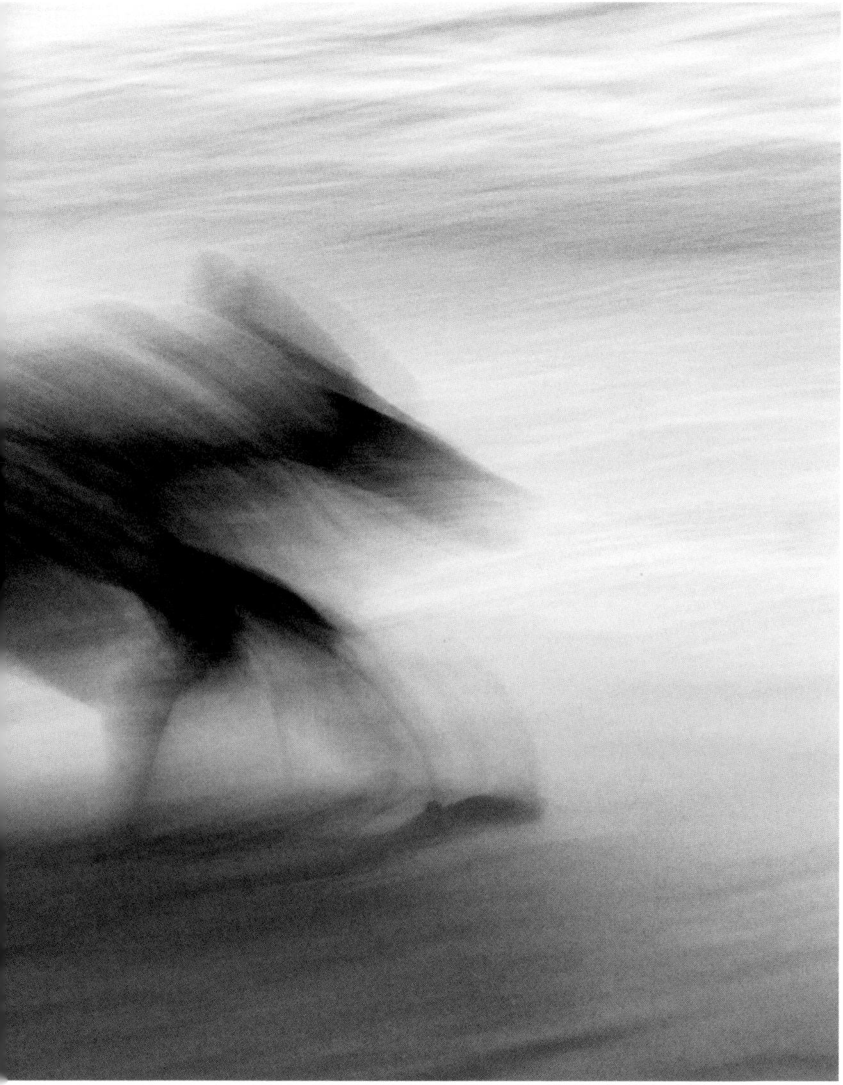

Fleeting, 2021

ALONE
Robert Bahou

Gemma and Bengal have the leading roles in Robert Bahou's cinematic film-noir photo series, *Alone*. Bahou follows their paw prints as his protagonists roam the nocturnal landscapes of their home turf. Gemma, a Canaan Dog and former Jordanian stray, was found in a shelter before being rehomed in Canada. Bengal, too, was once without a home, before being taken in by a Dutch vet.

Portrayed in pools of light and shadow, or silhouetted against illuminated city skies, the dogs command the empty streets. The stark contrasts lend the photographs a melancholy, alienating quality – as though we're glimpsing a secret world the dogs inhabit the moment our backs are turned. Their furtive presence calls to mind the urban fox: a creature close to the canine family and highly adept at evading human grasp.

It's the combination of solitude and adventure that draws Bahou to the subject – a tension that charges every frame. It is hard to tell whether these dogs are lost, stray or simply in charge of their own destiny.

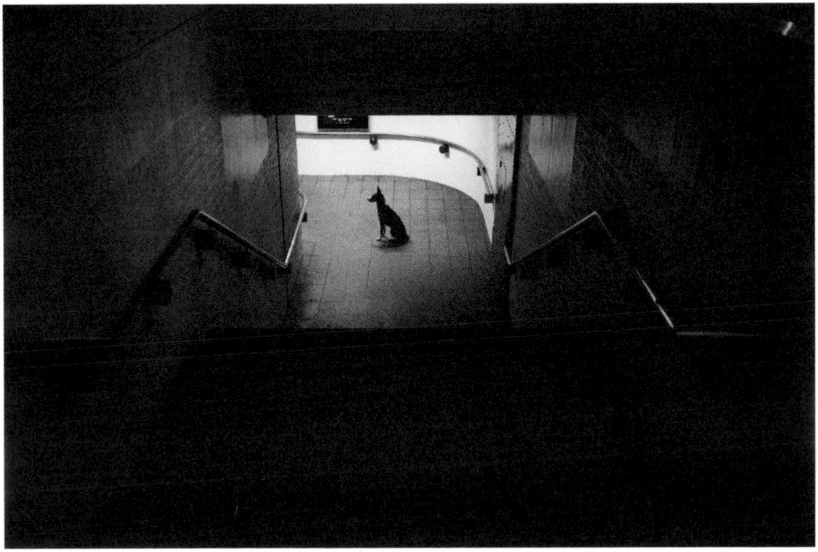

Alone, 2017

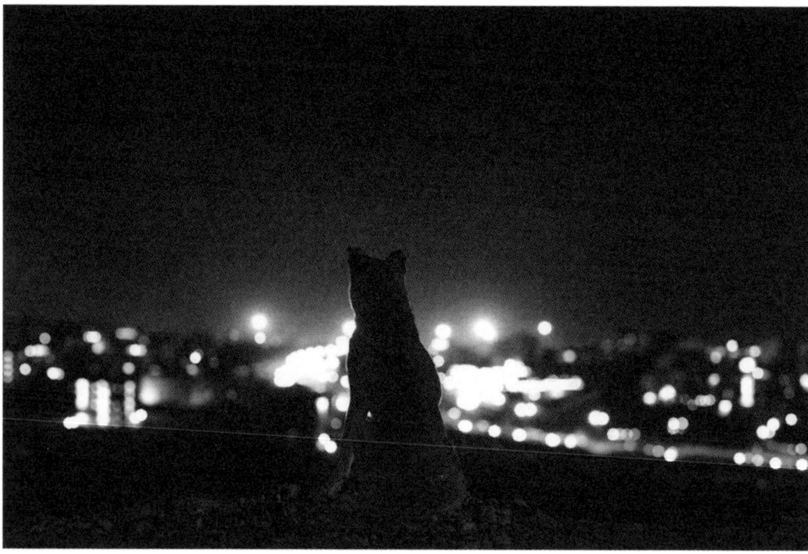

Alone, 2017

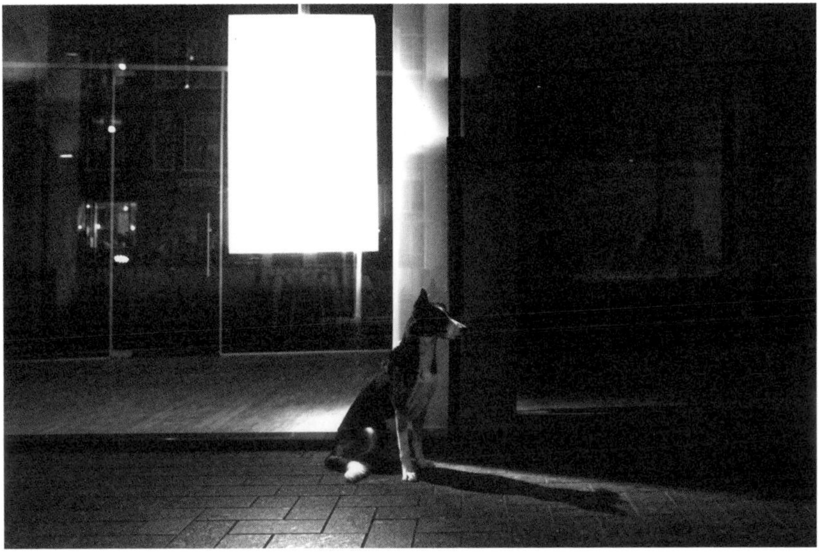

Alone, 2017

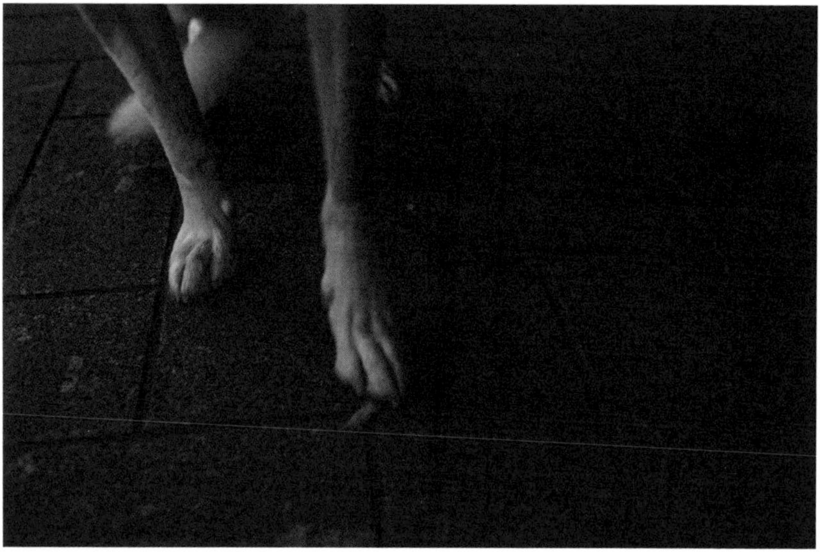

Alone, 2017

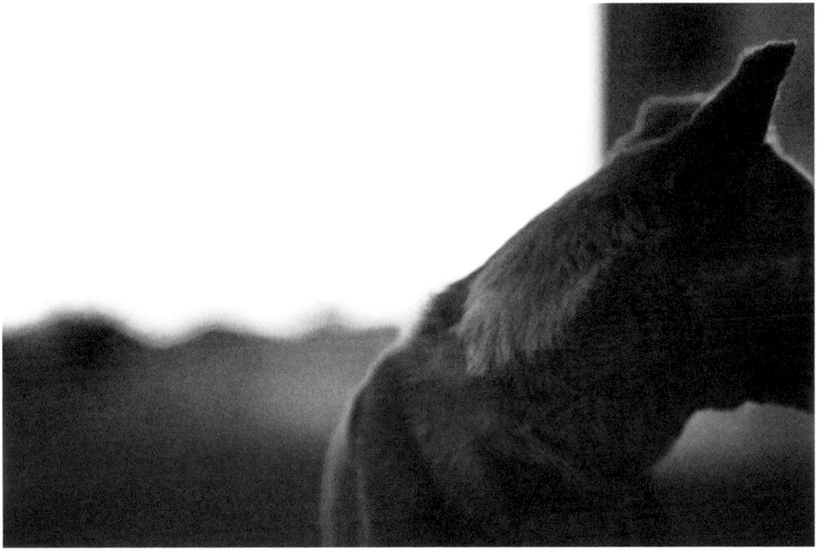

Alone, 2017

SENIOR DOGS ACROSS AMERICA

Nancy LeVine

A dog packs a lifetime into just a few short years. No wonder so many wear that wise, soulful look in their eyes. And as many owners know, their short lives make every shared moment feel all the more precious.

Photographer Nancy LeVine embarked on her project, *Senior Dogs Across America*, after watching her own companions, Lulu and Maxie, grow old. Travelling across the country, she set out to document the elder citizens of the canine world, some of them more than 20 years old. What she found was an abundance of love and devotion: dogs deeply woven into the lives of their families; their bodies quite literally imprinted on the furniture.

In LeVine's photographs, some enjoy lives of quiet leisure, dozing on soft chairs and cushioned beds. Others are still fully immersed – minding the shop, chasing cattle or standing watch. Either way, they continue to live in their present. That is what they know.

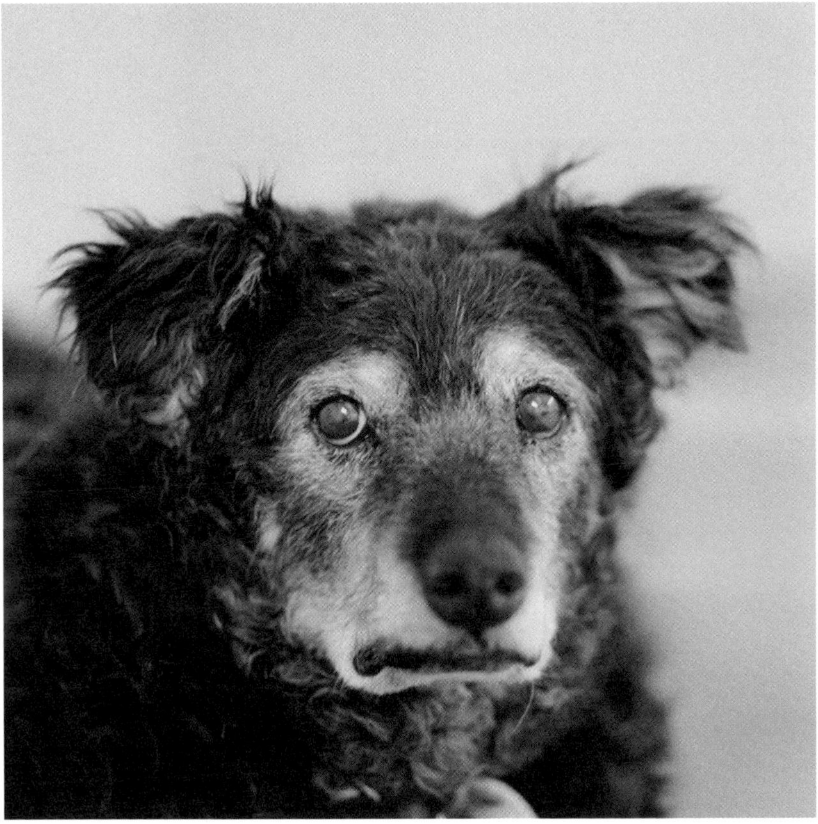

Curley, 14 years old, Kanab, Utah, Best Friends Animal Society

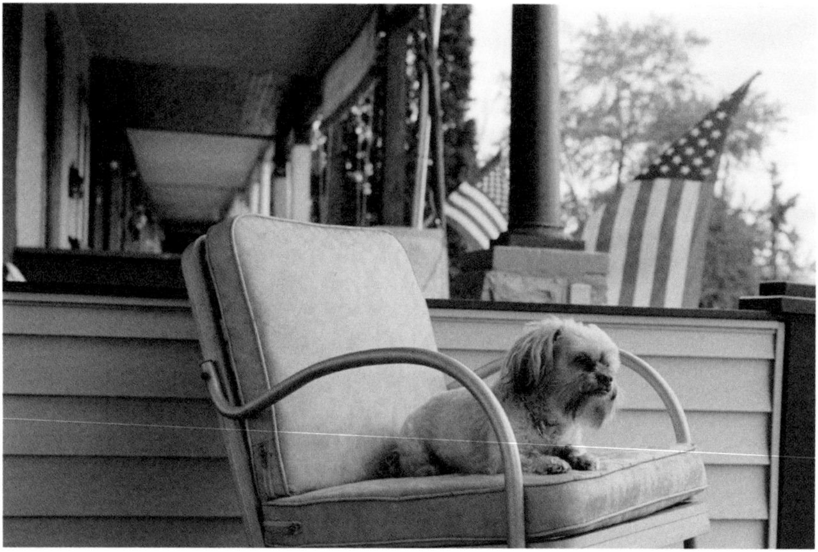

Bailey, 12 years old, Altoona, Pennsylvania

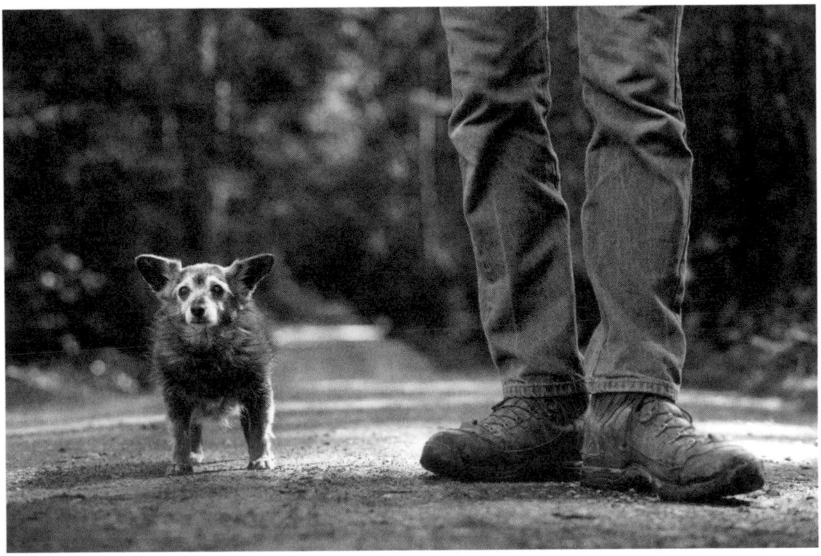

Above: *Ratzoe, 21 years old,* Vashon Island, Washington
Overleaf: *Sunshine, 14 years old,* Santa Fe, New Mexico,
Kindred Spirits Animal Sanctuary

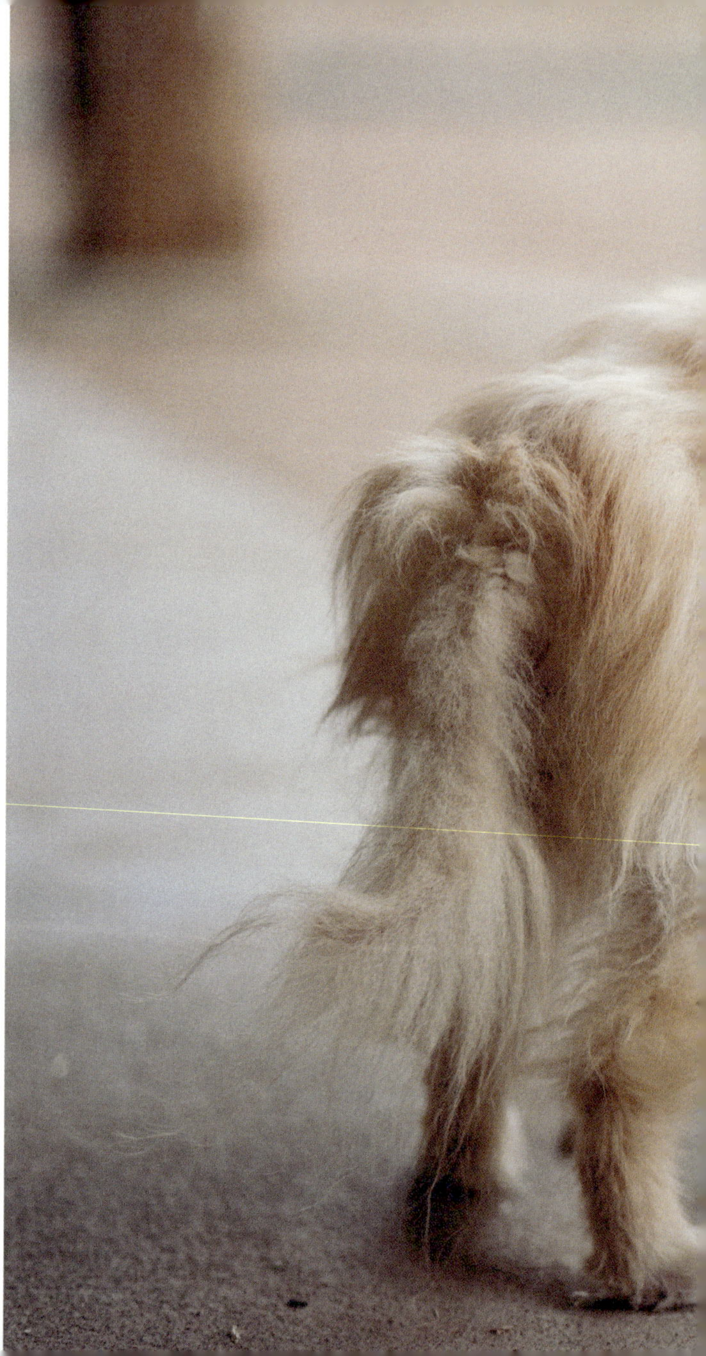

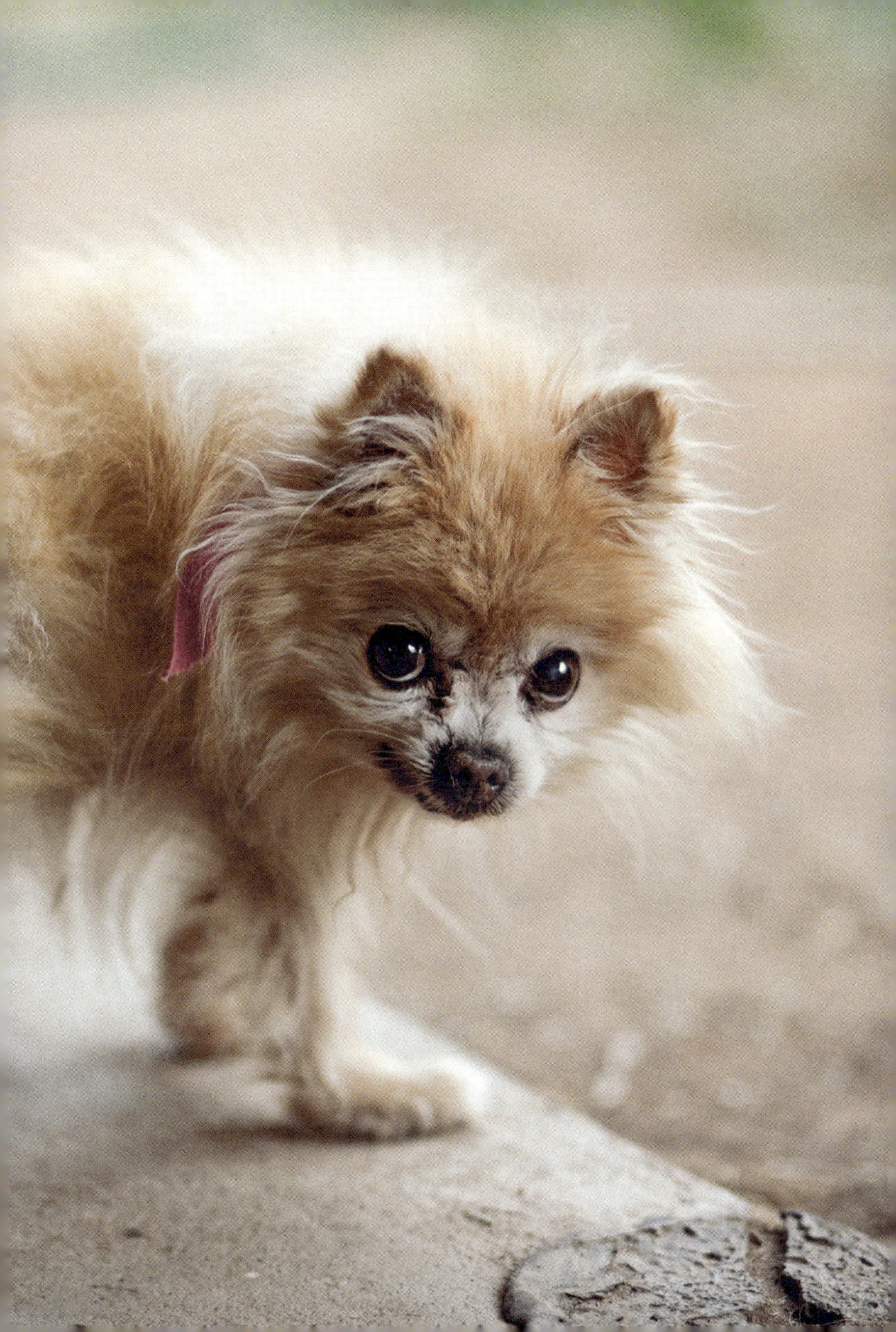

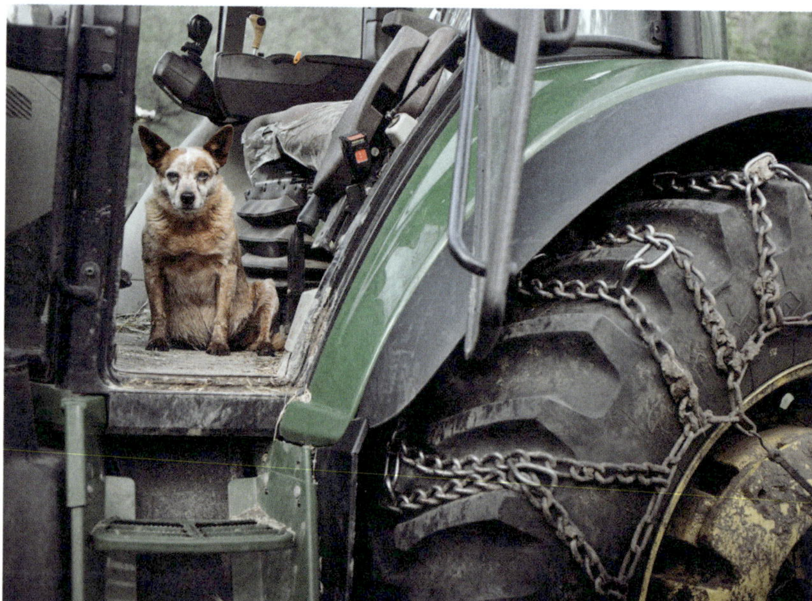

Ginger, 12.5 years old, Devils Tower, Wyoming

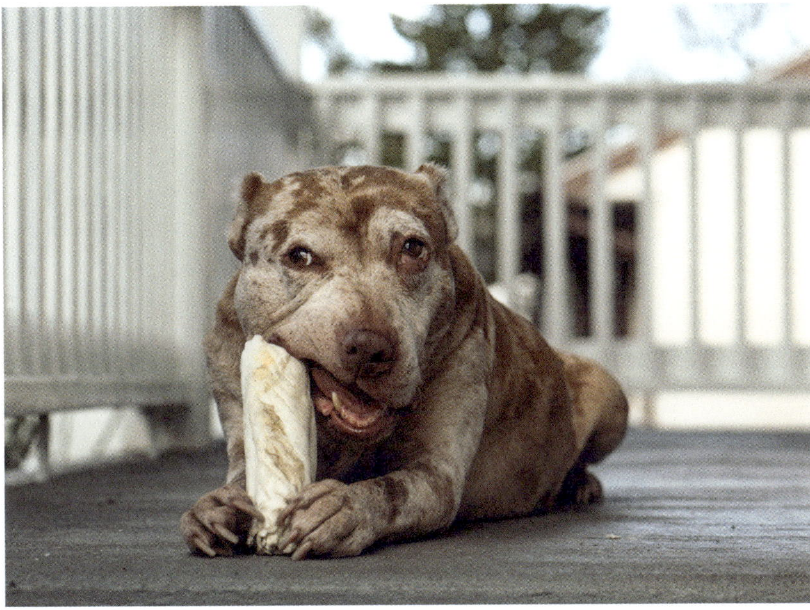

Above: *Red, 12 years old*, New Haven, Connecticut
Overleaf: *Champ, 9 years old*, Butte County, South Dakota

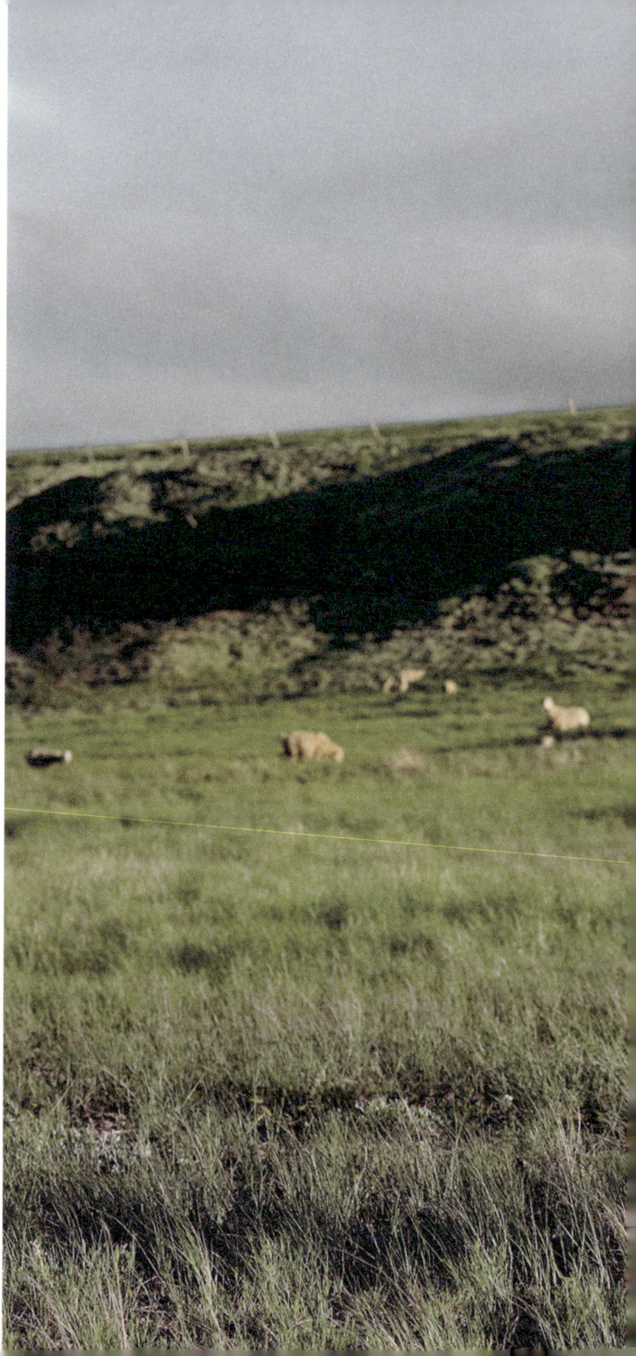

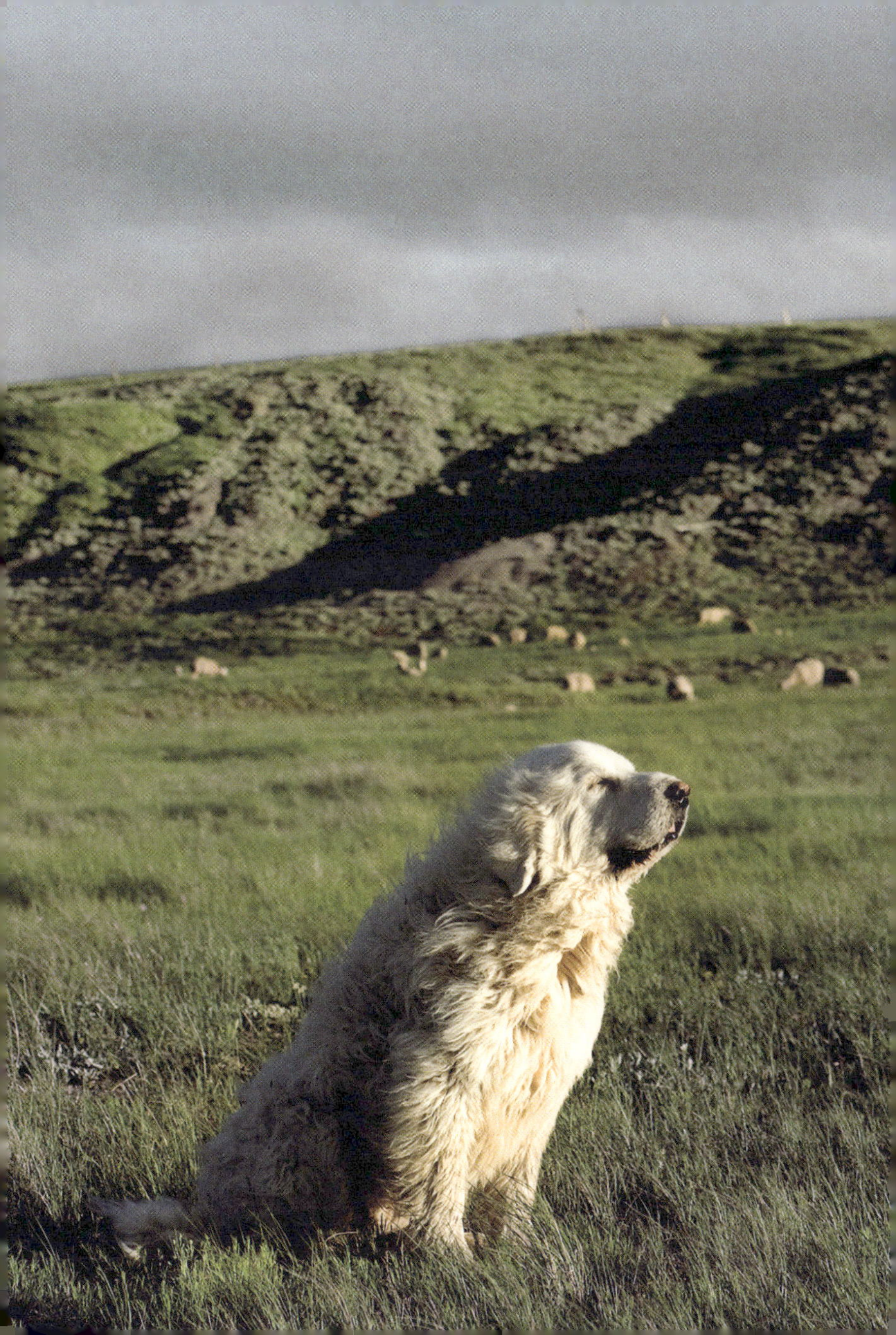

New Photography of the Dog.
First edition, first printing

Published in 2026 by Hoxton Mini Press, London

Cover image by Randal Ford
Hart, Deerhound, 2019

Text by Jilke Golbach
Editing by Kate Overy
Production design by Dom Grant
Production control by David Brimble
Proofreading by Emma Seckel
Editorial support by Emma Seckel & Olivia Kumar

Thank you to all of the individuals and institutions who have provided images and arranged permissions. While every effort has been made to trace the present copyright holders we apologise in advance for any unintentional omission or error, and would be pleased to insert the appropriate acknowledgement in any subsequent edition.

A CIP catalogue record for this book is available from the British Library.

ISBN: 978-1-917719-49-0

Printed and bound by OZGraf, Poland

Manufacturer: Hoxton Mini Press, 104 Northside Studios, 16–29 Andrews Road, London E8 4QF, UK.
www.hoxtonminipress.com
Represented by: Authorised Rep Compliance Ltd., Ground Floor, 71 Lower Baggot Street, Dublin D02 P593, Ireland.
www.arccompliance.com

Photography credits by project:
Resident Dog © Nicole England; *The Silence of Dogs in Cars* © Martin Usborne; *Dogs Gods* © Tim Flach; *Westminster Dog Show* © Cait Oppermann; *Well Heeled* © Dougie Wallace; *Hong Kong Garage Dogs* © Marcel Heijnen; *Shelter Dogs* © Traer Scott; *Where Hunting Dogs Rest* © Martin Usborne; *Dogs at Home* © Winnie Au; *The Levitators* © Ruth van Beek; *Do You Look Like Your Dog?* © Gerrard Gethings; *A Dog's Life* © Alicia Rius; *A Handbook for Dog Walkers* © Tomáš Werner; *Dogsonality* © Elke Vogelsang; *Wet Dog* © Sophie Gamand; *Shake Dogs* © Carli Davidson; *Amelia & the Animals* © Robin Schwartz; *Dogs of New York* © Dietmar Busse; *Animal Farm* © Daniel Naudé; *Retrieved* © Charlotte Dumas; *Good Dog* © Randal Ford; *Kinetic* © James Lee; *Alone* © Robert Bahou; *Senior Dogs Across America* © Nancy LeVine.

Hoxton Mini Press is an environmentally conscious publisher, committed to offsetting our carbon footprint. This book is 100 per cent carbon compensated, with offset purchased from Stand For Trees.

Every time you order from our website, we plant a tree: www.hoxtonminipress.com

FSC www.fsc.org MIX Paper | Supporting responsible forestry FSC® C163799